OPERATIONAL RISK

WILEY FINANCE SERIES

Advanced Modelling in Finance
Mary Jackson and Mike Staunton

Advance Credit Risk Analysis: Financial Approaches and Mathematical Models to Assess, Price and Manage Credit Risk
Didier Cossin and Hugues Pirotte

Dictionary of Financial Engineering
John F. Marshall

Pricing Financial Derivatives: The Finite Difference Method
Domingo A. Tavella and Curt Randall

Interest Rate Modelling
Jessica James and Nick Webber

Handbook of Hybrid Instruments: Convertible Bonds, Preferred Shares, Lyons, ELKS, DECS and Other Mandatory Convertible Notes
Izzy Nelken (ed.)

Options on Foreign Exchange, Revised Edition
David F. DeRosa

The Handbook of Equity Derivatives, Revised Edition
Jack Francis, William Toy and J. Gregg Whittaker

Volatility and Correlation in the Pricing of Equity, FX and Interest-Rate Options
Riccardo Rebonato

Risk Management and Analysis vol. 1: Measuring and Modelling Financial Risk
Carol Alexander (ed.)

Risk Management and Analysis vol. 2: New Markets and Products
Carol Alexander (ed.)

Implementing Value at Risk
Philip Best

Credit Derivatives: A Guide to Instruments and Applications
Janet Tavakoli

Implementing Derivatives Models
Les Clewlow and Chris Strickland

Interest-Rate Option Models: Understanding, Analysing and Using Models for Exotic Interest-Rate Options (second edition)
Riccardo Rebonato

OPERATIONAL RISK

Measurement and Modelling

Jack L. King

JOHN WILEY & SONS, LTD

Chichester • New York • Weinheim • Brisbane • Singapore • Toronto

Other Wiley Editorial Offices

John Wiley & Sons, Inc., 605 Third Avenue,
New York, NY 10158-0012, USA

Wiley-VCH Verlag GmbH, Pappelallee 3,
D-69469 Weinheim, Germany

John Wiley & Sons Australia, Ltd, 33 Park Road, Milton,
Queensland 4064, Australia

John Wiley & Sons (Asia) Pte Ltd, 2 Clementi Loop #02-01,
Jin Xing Distripark, Singapore 129809

John Wiley & Sons (Canada) Ltd, 22 Worcester Road,
Rexdale, Ontario M9W 1L1, Canada

British Library Cataloguing in Publication Data

A catalogue record for this book is available from the British Library

ISBN 0 471 85209 0

Typeset in 10/12pt Times by Laser Words, Madras, India
Printed and bound in Great Britain by Bookcraft (Bath) Ltd, Midsomer Norton, Somerset
This book is printed on acid-free paper responsibly manufactured from sustainable forestry,
in which at least two trees are planted for each one used for paper production.

To My Wife

Contents

Preface   xi

Acknowledgements   xiii

SECTION I—INTRODUCTION TO OPERATIONAL RISK   1

1 Introduction to Operational Risk   3

   1.1 Introduction   3
   1.2 Operational Risk Example: An Automobile Journey   4
   1.3 Defining Operational Risk   7
   1.4 Addressing Operational Risk   8
   1.5 Measuring and Modelling Operational Risk   12
   1.6 What are the Next Steps?   14
   1.7 Overview of this Book   15
   1.8 Further Reading   19

2 Historical Losses   21

   2.1 Introduction   21
   2.2 Attribution of Loss   21
   2.3 Very Large Losses   24
   2.4 Operational Risk Failures   24
   2.5 Other Losses   31
   2.6 Summary   33
   2.7 Further Reading   34

3 Regulation   35

   3.1 Introduction   35
   3.2 Background   35
   3.3 Banking Supervision   36

3.4 Corporate Governance   40
3.5 Summary   43
3.6 Further Reading   43

SECTION II—MEASURING OPERATIONAL RISK   **45**

4 A Measurement Framework for Operational Risk   **47**

4.1   Introduction   47
4.2   Framework Criteria   48
4.3   Current Framework Approaches   48
4.4   Framework Assumptions   54
4.5   Framework Definitions   57
4.6   A Framework for Measuring Operational Risk   57
4.7   Operational Risk Measures   63
4.8   How Delta–EVT™ Supports Operational Risk
      Management   64
4.9   Steps for Implementing the Framework   66
4.10 Summary   70
4.11 Further Reading   71

5 The Delta Methodology   **73**

5.1   Introduction   73
5.2   Key Concepts of the Delta Method   74
5.3   The Delta Method Implementation Steps   76
5.4   Calculating the Threshold   79
5.5   Advantages of the Delta Method   82
5.6   Detailed Examples of the Delta Method   83
5.7   Value at Risk for Operational Losses   94
5.8   Summary   94
5.9   Further Reading   95

6 The EVT Methodology   **97**

6.1   Introduction   97
6.2   Basic Concepts   97
6.3   EVT Loss Model Example for Large Operational
      Losses   105
6.4   Summary   110
6.5   Further Reading   110

SECTION III—MODELLING OPERATIONAL RISK   **111**

7   Delta–EVT™ Models for Operational Risk   **113**

    7.1   Introduction   113
    7.2   Business Model   113
    7.3   Risk Models   115
    7.4   Loss Models   120
    7.5   Scenarios   121
    7.6   Risk Measures   122
    7.7   In-Depth Example—Genoa Bank   122
    7.8   Summary   135
    7.9   Further Reading   136

8   Causal Modelling   **137**

    8.1   Introduction   137
    8.2   What is Causality?   138
    8.3   What are Causal Models?   139
    8.4   Causal Modelling Concepts   141
    8.5   Causal Relations   142
    8.6   Using Causal Models   151
    8.7   Causal Model for Settlement Risk   151
    8.8   Assessing Possible Intervention   152
    8.9   Scenario and Simulation with Causal Models   154
    8.10 Practical Issues   156
    8.11 Summary   156
    8.12 Further Reading   157

9   Causal Models for Operational Risk   **159**

    9.1   Introduction   159
    9.2   Advantages of Causal Models for Operational Risk   160
    9.3   Building a Causal Model for Operational Risk   160
    9.4   Implementing Causal Models for Operational Risk   165
    9.5   Example Calculations: Genoa Bank Example Using
          Causal Models   167
    9.6   Advanced Uses of Causal Models for Operational Risk   172
    9.7   Summary   188
    9.8   Further Reading   188

SECTION IV — MATHEMATICAL FOUNDATIONS   **189**

10   Error Propagation   **191**

        10.1   Introduction   192
        10.2   Measurement Standards   192
        10.3   Importance of Measurement Error   194
        10.4   Basic Error Model   194
        10.5   Direct Measurement   196
        10.6   Indirect Measurement   197
        10.7   Identifying Measurement Outliers   204
        10.8   Other Measurement Topics   205
        10.9   Summary   206
        10.10   Further Reading   207

11   Extreme Value Theory   **209**

        11.1   Introduction   209
        11.2   Basic Concepts   210
        11.3   Excess Loss Distribution   215
        11.4   Time-Dependent Losses   220
        11.5   EVT Applied to Internal Losses   222
        11.6   Summary   225
        11.7   Further Reading   225

12   Bayesian Methods   **227**

        12.1   Introduction   228
        12.2   What are Bayesian Methods?   228
        12.3   Key Concepts   229
        12.4   Bayes' Theorem   231
        12.5   Bayesian Networks   234
        12.6   Summary   239
        12.7   Further Reading   240

SECTION V — APPENDICES   **241**

Glossary   **243**

Bibliography   **249**

Index   **255**

Preface

Operational risk has been discussed in the financial field for some time. Unfortunately no consensus has been reached on a definition, and although regulatory rulings are pending, no clear understanding of operational risk management for financial institutions has emerged. The term operational risk has been overloaded, having been applied to performance management, financing of the firm, regulatory capital requirements, and insurance. In fact it has bordered on a Tower of Babel since the area has been expanded at times to include (among others) the vernacular of organisational behaviour, management science, quality control, capital markets, regulation, and insurance.

With this book I have tried to provide a basis for understanding operational risk by focusing on its measurement and modelling. In following others who have written on the topic of measurement, I find the words of Lord Kelvin particularly appropriate:

> In physical science the first essential step in the direction of learning any subject is to find principles of numerical reckoning and practicable methods for measuring some quality connected with it. I often say that when you can measure what you are speaking about, and express it in numbers, you know something about it; but when you cannot measure it, when you cannot express it in numbers, your knowledge is of a meagre and unsatisfactory kind; it may be the beginning of knowledge, but you have scarcely in your thoughts advanced to the state of Science, whatever the matter may be—William Thomson (Lord Kelvin) (1824–1907)

An introduction to a new field presents many challenges. On the one hand there is a need for introductory materials and practical examples so that the ideas and techniques can be applied and refined. On the other hand is the requirement to lay out a foundation theory that can serve as a guide for the many adaptations and uses that will be needed for practical applications. In trying to accomplish both I have included theoretical as well as practical material that I believe form a solid infrastructure for a theory of operational risk and its application. Beginning with the motivation for its application, I continue with a section on measurement methodology, then models and finally deeper into the theory behind it. This required using ideas from multiple disciplines, and a concerted effort to bridge the gaps between their languages and key concepts by presenting a brief background, overview and main topics of each. My goal was to make the information accessible to a wide range of people working in firms who might come into contact with the references to operational risk in one or more of the many contexts in which it appears. I have tried to pique their interest and motivate them to address the important topics that affect them. In so doing, I have given attention to introducing people who do not normally work in the disciplines to the main references and pivotal topics where possible. And I have focused on the main issues that are important to an understanding of the ideas rather than attempt to provide completeness in all areas. Some will find fault with this approach as it deprives them of the complete in-depth material on the subject, but for them I hope I have provided enough references to spend many hours of study. And I apologise to those whose field of study is covered if I over-simplified some of the methods or in general was too casual in my presentations of the theories. Unfortunately due to constraints put on such a work there are probably many more key concepts that could have been included, but in seeing the obvious shortcomings of my approach I hope you will also see the usefulness. For those who find this book an enlightening introduction to a new way of looking at the operations of a business, please appreciate that there is much more to each area that requires consideration and study, and this is only the beginning.

Acknowledgements

As with any work of a substantial nature, it could not have been completed without the help of many others. I wish to thank Carol Alexander of the University of Reading, Marcelo Cruz of UBS, and Daniel Egglehoff of Arthur Andersen for their comments and suggestions on earlier drafts. I have also benefited from comments by Mark Laycock of Deutsche Bank, Tim Kent-Phillips of Shearson-Lehman, and Thorsten Hermann of Baden-Wuerttemburgische Bank. A special thanks to Gabor Laszlo of Chase whose discussion and comments helped me solidify some of my ideas on operational risk, and whose friendship is very much valued. And thanks to John Miller who painstakingly reviewed the figures and formulas. But most important, the most special thanks to my wife, Joyce Panno, for the many hours of discussion and suggestions aimed at helping to deliver my message and for her constant love, support and understanding. Notwithstanding, the ideas expressed in this book are my own and I take sole responsibility for the content and any errors or omissions herein.

SECTION I

INTRODUCTION TO OPERATIONAL RISK

1

Introduction to Operational Risk

1.1 INTRODUCTION

Operational risk represents the next frontier in improving shareholder value by reducing the amount of risk to the earnings of the firm. Many would agree that up to now increasing the value of the firm has been approached mostly through performance management. Given the basic model for shareholder value, the value of an asset is '...the cash it can be expected to generate over time, adjusted for the riskiness over that cash stream.' (Rappaport 1998), it seems clear that value can also be added by reducing the risk associated with a firm's earnings. Although most firms now incorporate sophisticated measurement techniques such as shareholder value added to increase earnings, few have yet to implement systems designed to improve value by reducing risk. After suffering a series of large losses, financial firms pioneered risk management in the 1980's and focused on reducing the variability of earnings by managing financial risk due to interest rates, market values, and credit events. By measuring the effect of changes in their portfolio values due to changes in market values, they could implement strategies to reduce the impact on earnings from these fluctuations. However, even with such strategies in place, large swings in earnings continued to occur. Many of these were due to losses caused by breakdowns in controls and systems, and some were the result of lawsuits, natural disasters, or other external events. Consequently, there is now a growing recognition that a major source of earnings volatility is not due to financial risk. In fact, it is not related to the way a firm *finances* its business, but rather to the way a firm *operates* its business, and is called *operational* risk. Financial firms have since implemented sophisticated risk management systems for market and credit risk, and are now beginning to consider operational risk.

This book is about addressing operational risk. It has specifically been written from the perspective of operational risk in financial firms, but the ideas apply to risk management in most business environments. Many think that a book about operational risk is long overdue given the rich history of incidents such as the collapse of Barings and the movement of regulators toward recommending and requiring corporate governance practices for the management of operational risk in firms. This book aims to provide the motivation and appreciation for understanding what operational risk is, why it is important, and how to address it. It describes the problem and proposes a framework and methodology for measuring and modelling operational risk in a systematic way that provides the basis for operational risk management. The discussion of the many aspects of operational risk begins with a simple example, an automobile journey from Berlin to London. Although seemingly contrived, it provides useful insight into the key concepts of operational risk by using familiar terminology and situations. It is followed by a definition of operational risk, a discussion of how to address it, and an overview of operational risk measurement and modelling as a precursor to management. This provides the context for topics dealt with in the rest of the book. In later chapters, the definitions and approach will be discussed with much more rigour. Although the examples used in this book have been developed from the perspective of risk in financial institutions, similar situations can be found in most companies.

1.2   OPERATIONAL RISK EXAMPLE: AN AUTOMOBILE JOURNEY

Imagine you are about to make an automobile journey from Berlin to London (see Figure 1.1). You plan the trip to take place over two days and will overnight near Brussels. You calculate the distance is about 1000 km in total and you intend to travel 600 km the first day and 400 km the second day. By estimating the

Figure 1.1   Route from Berlin to London through Brussels

expected time and costs at two days and 360 Euros, you develop your plan. The trip route and table of expected time and costs are shown in Table 1.1.

So far, so good, and you make your journey. A month later you discuss the topic with a friend and review the log of your actual journey (six days and 2773 Euros) (Table 1.2) as compared with your plan. Your friend observes that the actual trip took three times longer and cost almost eight times more than was expected. You cite special circumstances and bad luck, but after going on about poor weather and speed cameras in England your friend stops you short and says:

> I often travel from Germany to England and have never experienced the nightmare you describe. In fact, you could have avoided those problems if you had done proper risk management for your travel. The automobile I drive is an advanced series that

Table 1.1 Plan for Berlin to London trip, two days and 360 Euros total cost

Day	Location	Km	Petrol (litres)	Petrol cost	Hotel nights	Hotel cost	Meals	Meals cost	Other costs
0	Berlin	–	–	–	–	–	–	–	
1	Brussels	600	30	15	1	200	2	50	
2	London	400	20	10	–	–	2	50	Ferry 35
Totals				25		200		100	Misc.35

Table 1.2 Actual for Berlin to London trip, six days and 2773 Euros

Day	Location	Km	Petrol (litres)	Petrol cost	Hotel nights	Hotel cost	Meals	Meals cost	Other
0	Berlin	–	–	–	–	–	–	–	–
1	Hanover	250	10	7.00	1	200	2	50	Blinker fine 150 Traffic delays
2	Brussels	350	17	15.00	1	200	2	50	Radiator repair 300
3	Calais	150	8	6	1	200	2	50	Lost outside Brussels
4	Dover	20	0	0	1	250	2	50	Bad weather delays Ferry 35, Wire transfer
5	Dover	0	0	0	1	250	2	50	Accident repair 800
6	London	130	7	10	–	–	2	50	Speeding fine 100
Totals				38		1050		300	Misc. cost 1385

includes monitors and controls as aids to avoiding the situations you described. For instance, my car's proximity alarm includes signals for the distance of objects from the front and rear bumpers and keeps me from having the sort of parking accident you had in Dover. And the dashboard safety monitors for blinkers and engine maintenance notify me immediately when the blinker isn't working and remind me to take my car to a qualified mechanic for periodic maintenance of belts so that my radiator stays in good condition. In addition, I have an advanced navigation computer to avoid losing my way and automatic speed control to set the speed below the limit so that I don't have to worry about speed cameras. Anyway, you wouldn't have been speeding if you hadn't lost so much time due to the other problems and bad weather. Of course you may not be able to avoid bad weather, but the advanced traction system in my automobile enables me to maintain good speeds even in the kind of poor weather you experienced. The day lost in Dover waiting for a wire transfer could also have been avoided by taking more money as a contingency fund, but with your lack of risk management and consequential unexpected costs you would need to carry a very large sum indeed. Perhaps you'd be better off next time spending money on good transportation systems that can reduce your unexpected costs and delays.

You have just read a lecture on operational risk, albeit in the realm of automobile transportation and not corporate management. The basic proposal is to consider reducing the amount of exposure you have to unexpected losses (of time and money) by improving the monitoring and control systems for the process (travelling by automobile). The essential ingredients here are the process definition (driving from Berlin to London), performance measurements (time and costs, both expected and actual), the risk factors (legal compliance, weather, navigation error, parking accident), and control systems (ABS, GPS navigation, proximity alarm, maintenance monitor, and speed control). The discussion raises a number of questions about what should be considered and how it should be evaluated. For instance, your friend does not mention alternative travelling strategies (e.g. taking the train or flying), or alternative routes that might be used to reduce the elapsed time and improve performance. This would be a more strategic discussion, and perhaps lead in another direction. Nor is there any mention of comparing the actual prices of petrol, hotel, and meals with the expected prices. Volatility of market prices is probably not discussed because it is outside your immediate control and not addressed by the solutions your friend is proposing. Although you cannot control the weather, your friend advises you to mitigate it using an advanced traction system. There is also no consideration of other risk events that might have occurred (but did not) such as automobile theft, or traffic congestion due to highway repairs. Finally, an automobile with the aforementioned control systems most likely has a substantially higher price than one without them, and many of the controls might be optionally available at an additional cost. How then does one decide which controls are worthwhile and which are 'nice to have'? Clearly, a way to frame the problem, and model and calculate a measure of operational risk is needed to make these decisions. But first, what to measure and how to measure it must be considered.

1.3 DEFINING OPERATIONAL RISK

Operational risk is concerned with adverse deviation of a firm's performance due to how the firm is *operated* as opposed to how the firm is *financed*. It is defined as *a measure of the link between a firm's business activities and the variation in its business results*. Addressing it represents a new approach to increasing the value of the firm, and complements the business management activity of creating value through increased earnings by adding the capability of increasing value by reducing the variability or *risk* of earnings. Current techniques such as Balanced Scorecard (Kaplan and Norton 1996) and Value Based Management (Knight 1997) are aimed at adding value to the firm by increasing earnings through performance improvement (Path 1, Figure 1.2). Increasing a firm's performance increases valuation because it leads to higher expectations for future cash flows, adjusted for risk. The next step, managing operational risk, is to add value by reducing the risk associated with a firm's earnings (Path 2, Figure 1.2). Reducing performance variability reduces the risk adjustment for valuation.

Operational risk focuses on the core value-adding processes in the firm and deals with the question: 'What are the causes of earnings volatility imbedded in the fundamental way the firm operates?'. Core activities are those that *cause* changes in earnings. They are linked to earnings variability by understanding

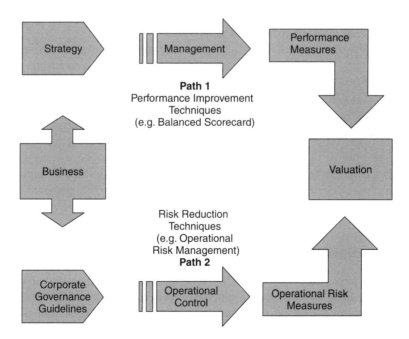

Figure 1.2 Relationship between the business and its valuation: two paths to increasing value

the causes of performance shortfalls to objectives and measuring their effect. Strategies to improve earnings that do not address the related risk may not provide the expected increase in the value of the firm because actions to increase earnings may also lead to an increase in risk. Understanding the causes of risk to earnings and their relationship to the business activity allows management of the trade-off between risk and return. If the goal is higher returns with the same or lower level of risk, then it makes sense to also manage the risks. There are many benefits to managing the risks in the operational processes, including:

1. *Avoid unexpected losses and improve operational efficiency.* Understanding the important operational risks enables management to focus on ways to reduce routine loss and improve efficiency. This also reduces the likelihood of incurring large losses and improves the quality of the operational processes.
2. *Efficient use of capital.* A business allocates capital based on expected earnings in much the same way an investor values a company. The efficient use of a firm's capital implies optimising the risk/return trade-off for capital allocation decisions within the firm.
3. *Satisfy stakeholders.* Regulators, credit agencies, and other stakeholders are increasingly interested in a firm's risk management practices. The operations of the firm are an integral part of this risk management, and a major contributor to earnings volatility that can affect the value of the firm. Risk measurement can help influence stakeholder views and improve areas that are needed to avoid stakeholder surprises.
4. *Comply with regulation.* Corporate governance recommendations and requirements view operational risk management as a board-level responsibility. The chapter on regulation describes some of the national and international guidelines and requirements for corporate governance.

Even though in a broader sense operational risk could be thought of as a measure of performance variability, the discussions in this book are generally within the context of *earnings* as the performance measure because firms often use earnings as the key measure of performance. Managers wishing to implement an operational risk measurement system based on the techniques proposed herein will also use other measures of performance.

1.4   ADDRESSING OPERATIONAL RISK

The path to addressing operational risk involves implementing corporate governance guidelines, establishing operational controls, and measuring operational risk. Corporate governance guidelines provide a set of organisational policies and objectives related to operational risk that can be used to establish the risk management process within a firm. Operational control refers to a systematic way of providing assurance on achieving desired performance objectives. Risk is

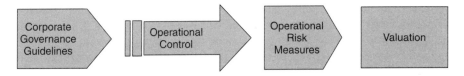

Figure 1.3   Path 2 for increasing the value of the firm through risk reduction

a measure of the random fluctuations in performance over time, and operational risk measures are the link between performance fluctuations and the business activities. Reducing operational risk leads to reduced earnings volatility and increased value of the firm. This path for increasing value is shown in Figure 1.3 and explained in the discussion that follows.

1.4.1   Corporate Governance Guidelines

Many firms are now adopting corporate governance guidelines for operational risk management. These guidelines are used to develop the organisation and procedures for addressing operational risk in the firm. They include as a first step the identification and assessment of risks to the firm's objectives. Then a monitoring and reporting system is recommended in order to provide feedback and measure the results. The tasks of identifying risks and assessing their impact are largely based on control self-assessment, an outgrowth of the internal auditing effort. The main advantage of control self-assessment is that it increases risk awareness and captures much of the existing information about risk factors in an organisation. The disadvantage is that it relies on a subjective evaluation of a series of questions about risks to try to measure the amount of risk. Much of the corporate governance guidelines and regulations for financial firms (presented in the chapter on regulation) are also based on this subjective approach of identification, assessment, and monitoring of risks. Since the beginning of such efforts (e.g. COSO 1992) operational risk losses have continued, and neither control self-assessment nor accounting audits have been effective in preventing losses associated with operational risk. One of the key reasons is that because of their lack of objectivity and timeliness, these methods cannot accurately and reliably measure operational risk (a more detailed argument is given in the measurement framework chapter). In the end, corporate guidelines are destined to be ineffective without an objective, reliable, and accurate measure of operational risk.

1.4.2   Operational Control

'Operational' implies control, and the factors that affect operational risk are often within the firm's influence or control. Business decisions require actions to implement them, and understanding the causal relation between measures and activities is essential because causation is the basis for action. In this book the emphasis is on measurement and causes because they provide a basis for risk management. The cause-and-effect relation of the measurement to a possible action or *intervention* is key to managing operational risk in a systematic and proactive way. However, since not all cause–effect relations are known, loss models that use statistical information only (e.g. no causes) are used when necessary to explain other events (i.e. whose causes are unknown). In addition, plausible scenarios that describe events and relate their consequences to the firm provide important information on potential causes and possible effects. Taken together, these three decision support techniques provide the basis for managing operational risk by creating effective measures for it. In the words of one of the eminent scholars of business, 'Whenever one analyses the way a truly effective, a truly right, decision has been reached, one finds that a great deal of work and thought went into finding the appropriate measurement' (Drucker 1967).

1.4.3 Operational Risk Measures

Measuring is a precursor to effective management, and operational risk measures are the link between performance fluctuations and the business activities. Performance measures are measures of the level of output for the key value-adding activities of the firm. Operational risk measures are measures of the amount of fluctuation in the level of the performance measures. Taken together, they represent the value of the activity and are important in helping management create sustainable, steady returns for stakeholders. They can be used to increase the value of the firm because investors use the volatility of earnings to estimate the risk or uncertainty of expected earnings.

At the firm level operational risk is an economic measure and is part of the value relation formed between risk and return. For example, given a monthly average earnings level of 13% return on equity, the variability of earnings (risk) in Firms A and B may be quite different, as shown in Table 1.3. And as shown in Figure 1.4, the fluctuations of earnings (and therefore the measure of risk) for Firm A is lower for the period. *Ceteris paribus*, this means that Firm A has a higher value than Firm B because it has achieved an identical level of return with a lower variability, or risk, over the period.

Most firms today have performance measures for both near-term and long-term operations. It then seems at first a simple matter to implement measures for operational risk. However, operational risk measures are measures of uncertainty and must reflect variances in performance measures along with their related causes. They are not simple measures because they represent an attribute for the level of uncertainty using probabilities, confidence levels, and interval measures. A level of 13% return on net assets is not an example of an operational risk measure. Rather, a measure that the earnings will not vary by more than 7% from its target

Table 1.3 Table of two risk measures for the same 13% average monthly earnings (using standard deviation as the measure)

Month	Firm A	Firm B
Jan	12.90%	11.40%
Feb	13.00%	14.10%
Mar	13.10%	13.50%
Average	13.00%	13.00%
Risk	0.1%	1.4%

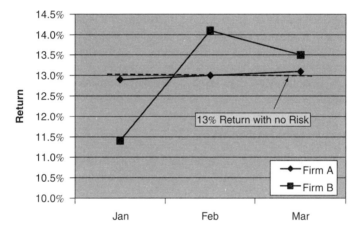

Figure 1.4 Graph of two firms with identical 13% average monthly earnings and different risks

value 95% of the time is more in line with the type of interpretation required and an example of the depth of information that operational risk measures provide. In this way operational risk measures are able to describe the variance of the performance indicators that reduce a firm's value for a given level of average performance over time. By identifying the variance and possible causes, operational risk measurement gives management the 'second-order' effects on the performance of the firm with respect to a set of risk sources (causes). With this information management can take action that not only improves performance, but also reduces the variance between target and performance in order to create more stable earnings and increase the value of the firm. In the long run, without a coherent measure of operational risk, a firm may not have enough controls and fail due to large losses, or may not be efficiently using its capital and fail due to lack of competitiveness.

1.5 MEASURING AND MODELLING OPERATIONAL RISK

Measuring and modelling operational risk effectively means measuring the fluctuations in performance and being able to predict and take action to affect them. Establishing an objective and relevant measure for operational risk is a critical step toward managing it because consistent and reliable feedback is needed for management to change behaviour. But operational risk is difficult to measure, difficult to predict, and difficult to identify causes for because of the nature of the two main sources of fluctuations. Generally, operational risk losses cannot be measured directly because high frequency, low impact losses are not adequately accounted for and low frequency, high impact losses occur so infrequently that an adequate sample is difficult to gather. A large loss due to a particular risk may occur once in several years, and a business unit that had not experienced such a large loss would have no way of measuring the risk directly. Addressing these problems requires a framework for measuring operational risk that aligns the risk measures with performance measures, a methodology that can measure the diverse sources of operational risk, and a modelling capability that allows management to both predict the level of risk and take actions for those that are controllable.

1.5.1 Measurement Framework

A measurement framework for operational risk is essential because basic definitions of operational risk, its goals, and an approach for its measurement are not yet widely established. A framework addresses these issues by providing a set of assumptions, definitions, and a methodology for measuring operational risk that each business can use to develop its specific operational risk measures based on performance measures. The relevant risk factors that explain fluctuations in the levels of performance within periods can then be identified, measured, and reported. The proposed measurement framework for operational risk starts with a business model and a set of definitions and assumptions to link operational risk measures to business performance measures. The business model defines the unit of analysis and the factors for measurement and modelling and uses the value-adding processes of the business unit as the unit of analysis for measuring operational risk. The measurement methodology provides a way of calculating the risk measure. Causal models are used to link performance fluctuations and risk factor changes. The remaining unexplained variations in performance are addressed using loss models.

1.5.2 Measurement Methodology

A methodology for operational risk must be able to measure the two sources of operational risk (variations in the process activities and rare events), and traditional measurement methods do not work well for both. On the one hand are frequent random fluctuations that are an intrinsic part of the operations that add value to the firm. And on the other hand are rare events where large fluctuations occur due to a combination of (possibly extreme) factors. The measurement methodology of the proposed operational risk framework, Delta–EVT™, provides for measurement of both sources of loss for operational risk and satisfies the framework criteria. The Delta–EVT™ methodology is a combination of two existing methods for dealing with uncertainty. The Delta methodology is introduced to deal with propagating errors in activities to fluctuations in performance. This methodology has its foundation in uncertainty measurement guidelines and practices (ISO Guide 1993). These guidelines are endorsed by the International Standards Organisation (ISO) and used by most major laboratories in the world. The Delta method works by using measures of fluctuations in the activities and the sensitivities of the outputs to the activities for the estimate of performance volatility. For the rare or extreme events, extreme value theory (EVT) is the methodology used to measure their severity and extrapolate the effect of their impact over long periods. EVT is a statistical method used in a loss model in order to estimate the impact of potentially disastrous events. It has been used for some time in the physical sciences for the safety and design of dykes, bridges, etc. and more recently has been applied to insurance (McNeil and Saladin 1997).

1.5.3 Modelling

Models are used to both predict and take action, and the proposed approach for measuring operational risk utilises both capabilities. Causal models for operational risk link the fluctuations in performance to their causes. A causal understanding is essential in order to take appropriate action to control and manage risk because causality is a basis for both action and prediction. Knowing 'what causes what' gives you an ability to intervene in order to affect your environment and control the things around you. Causation is different from correlation, or constant conjunction, in which two things are associated because they change in unison or are found together. Predictive models (such as loss models) often use correlation as a basis for prediction, but action based on associations is tentative at best. Simple cause-and-effect relations are known from experience, but more complex situations such as those buried in the processes of business operations may not be intuitively obvious from the information at hand. Loss models for operational risk are predictive. Their function is to measure the effects of losses and provide measures for risk to operations that are not linked to causes. In other words, they are needed to account for the unexplained losses and to predict them over extended periods.

Given the foregoing discussion, the connection between the risk in operations, and causality and loss can be made as follows. The impact on operations can be separated into controllable risk and uncontrollable risk. Controllable risk is defined as those risks that have assignable causes that can be influenced.

Generally, process-related risks will have assignable causes and therefore be controllable. For instance, classifying loan customers into the wrong credit categories can result in substantial differences in the default rates and loan provision requirements and is an example of a risk that is controllable because the cause is known. Uncontrollable risk is defined as those risks that do not have causal factors that can be influenced. Their impact is determined through loss models that analyse extreme values (losses), and use classification instead of causes. Ideally, extreme loss models will be used with scenarios that provide stress points for the analysis. Uncontrollable does not mean there is nothing that can be done about it. There are many mitigation strategies that can be implemented in order to reduce the effects of loss. Also uncontrollable risk may become controllable if an assignable cause can be found and corrective action is possible.

1.6   WHAT ARE THE NEXT STEPS?

This book advocates that risk should be elevated to the same level as rewards. That is, risk measures should be:

- systematically measured and modelled as a precursor to management;
- included in performance measurement systems;
- part of compensation; and
- accounted for and reported to stakeholders.

Good policies, systems, processes, and procedures for managing operational risk are based on reliable measures of operational risk. No firm would think of operating without liability and casualty insurance, but few take a systematic approach to managing the many other risks they face. History shows that any business can lose its competitive advantage and winning strategy through blunders and mishaps or by remaining complacent while profits slowly erode. Classic examples of large operational losses in financial firms include futures trading losses at Barings, copper-trading losses at Sumitomo, and long dated options losses at the former National Westminster Bank. But other famous losses such as the Bhopal plant explosion for Union Carbide, the crash of the Concorde in Paris, and a nation-wide, long-distance telephone service outage for AT&T demonstrate that operational risk is by no means confined to financial firms. These events had serious effects for the firms involved ranging from casualty loss, liability loss, reputation damage, and business impact to complete collapse and dissolution. Clearly, the consequences of operational risk can be quite severe. And even though many believe that the risk of large loss events is increasing (Perrow 1999), some businesses hold on to the belief that it cannot happen to them. Or they maintain that risk management is already part of the day-to-day operations of the firm. On the positive side, there seems to be an increased awareness of operational risk in most organisations, and several have taken steps to address it. On the negative side, such efforts are usually reactive and have not yet become a core part of the firm's operating strategy. Using the techniques presented in this book, firms can do much more to avoid future disasters by taking a systematic step toward managing the operational risks they face.

What this book proposes is that financial firms should now embrace the idea of managing operational risk in a similar way as market risk, and non-financial firms should view operational risk as the next step in performance measurement. Because operational risk is a complex problem, each firm should establish an operational risk expertise to help business managers develop effective measures for operational risk within their units and to coordinate the operational risk measurement with other parts of the organisation (such as audit and compliance). Operational risk management information systems should be established in order to make the process of operational risk measurement systematic and efficient. At the same time, a review of operational risk measures should become a routine part of performance review for all businesses. Finally, the end result should be incorporation of operational risk measurement into management compensation schemes in the same manner as performance, and into accounting and reporting documentation for stakeholders.

1.7 OVERVIEW OF THIS BOOK

Operational Risk provides a motivation, framework, methodology, and theory for understanding the amount of risk in the activities of a firm. Using an operational risk measure, a firm can create long-term sustainable value by reducing its operational risk while at the same time improving performance. Understanding the link between risk valuation, analysis of some famous operational losses, and a review of regulations provides the motivation for addressing operational risk. A set of definitions and assumptions for dealing with the measurement of operational risk objectively and linking it to performance establishes a measurement framework. The measurement methodology provides a way of calculating the risk measures, using models to link the calculations to the business in a way most useful for the firm. And finally, nothing is so useful as a good theory, and the theoretical foundations ensure that the methodologies for operational risk are generally applicable and stable over time. The main ideas of the book are summarised below.

- Firms can increase their value by reducing the operational risk associated with performance.
- Operational risk is an inherent part of the way a firm conducts its business and is closely linked to performance.
- Making good decisions about operational risk requires an objective, relevant measure for it.
- Operational risk results in fluctuations in performance that can generally be classified as frequent, low level fluctuations or large jumps in performance that occur rarely.

- Measurement of operational risk requires a combined methodology such as the proposed Delta–EVT™ because traditional techniques do not deal well with both types of fluctuations.
- Causality is the key to understanding what part of operational risk can be controlled and what cannot, and provides the basis for management action.

This book is organised into five sections. Section I introduces the concepts and provides background on the history and regulations related to operational risk. The primary purpose is to promote operational risk awareness and provide motivation for why operational risk needs to be addressed systematically. This is a good three-chapter exposure to the issues of operational risk that can be appreciated by management as well as quantitative experts. Section II is the architecture for realising operational risk management in a systematic way. Anchored around a comprehensive framework and proposed new measurement methodology called Delta–EVT™, it also includes a chapter on each of the two analytical techniques that comprise Delta–EVT™ in which the formulas and procedures for calculating operational risk measures are provided. This is the core of the book, written specifically as a recipe for analysts, risk managers, and others who are involved in the day-to-day application of measuring, modelling, and managing their firm's operational risk. Section III deals with operational risk modelling and the importance of causal models to the process of calculating relevant operational risk measures. Delta–EVT™ models for operational risk are built for a fictitious Genoa Bank to demonstrate how to build basic risk factor models, loss models, and generate scenarios. The next chapter on causal models describes the technique of building causal models, and the third chapter shows how to implement the Delta–EVT™ methodology using causal models and the Genoa Bank example. Section IV is an in-depth treatment of the mathematics for measuring and modelling operational risk, and includes a chapter each on error propagation, extreme value theory, and Bayesian methods. The purpose is to provide an introduction to the theory behind the framework and methodology. The intended audience is technical experts who want to modify, tailor, or expand upon the techniques, and who have an appropriate background and interest in the fundamentals. Section V is a complete bibliographical listing of the material in support of writing this book, and suggestions for further reading are included at the end of each chapter.

Chapter 2 (Historical Losses) begins by introducing some loss categorisation schemes to help identify and address breakdowns in operational systems and controls. Then some of the more famous historical loss incidents are presented. Each is categorised and assessed in order to provide a background for problem definition and motivation for addressing operational risk. Historical losses are used as a way of motivating firms to reduce vulnerability to large losses through sufficient operational control systems, and to appreciate that in many cases large losses originate from smaller ones.

Chapter 3 (Regulation) reviews the regulations relating to operational risk in corporations as well as in banking. It shows how regulation has been a key factor in banking, and in recent years to the corporate world as well. In most cases regulation has followed disaster, so this chapter begins with a chronological outline relating the environment to the resulting regulation. Then banking supervision and corporate governance in general are discussed and details on some important individual regulations are given. Finally, the current regulatory approach is summarised.

Chapter 4 (Measurement Framework) begins Section II of the book. It addresses one of the fundamental problems with operational risk, namely a lack of relevant measurement information on which to base decisions. The core of this book is a framework for measuring and modelling operational risk that sets out the basic definitions and assumptions that are needed to gain agreement, promote discussion, and create productive approaches in order to move things forward. In this chapter the criteria for an operational risk framework and several existing and proposed approaches to it are reviewed. Then a framework for measuring and modelling operational risk and a new measurement methodology called Delta–EVT^{TM} are introduced and discussed, followed by an outline of how Delta–EVT^{TM} both satisfies the criteria of an operational framework and provides a means for realising the benefits of operational risk management. Then the basic steps for implementing the framework are outlined. The chapter concludes with a brief summary of the main points and discussion of alternative methodologies.

Chapter 5 (The Delta Methodology) contains an in-depth discussion of the Delta methodology for measurement of operational risk. The Delta methodology is the calculation technique for determining the value of the assignable losses in the firm. Delta uses the techniques of classic error analysis to measure the wide spectrum of losses occurring in financial operational processes due to errors and omissions. This chapter is mathematically oriented, and begins with a discussion of the key concepts of the Delta method, followed by an outline and explanation of the steps for implementation as a measure for operational risk. Then some advantages of using the Delta method are described, along with its limitations. Finally, detailed examples of Delta calculations for the three financial processes of investment, lending, and service are presented, and the chapter concludes with a summary of the main points.

Chapter 6 (The EVT Methodology) describes extreme value theory and its application to financial loss events. Loss models are an important element of operational risk measurement, and EVT is the technique used to determine losses due to control breakdowns and external events (not included in the Delta method). The chapter begins with a brief description of the general form for loss models and an example to model historical losses. Next, extreme value theory (EVT) and the method of peaks over thresholds (POT) are discussed. Then a detailed example of calculating operational risk for excess losses is presented. Finally, some thoughts on data and validation for loss models are offered, along with a summary of the main points.

Chapter 7 (Delta–EVT™ Models for Operational Risk) begins Section III of the book. The application of the Delta–EVT™ methodology to operational risk requires the development of a specific set of business models, risk factor models, loss models, plausible scenarios, and risk measures for the firm. This chapter presents a skeletal set of these components, and begins with a business model template and identification of the related value-adding processes and activities. Then models for measuring the operational risk associated with the business model are developed based on the Delta method. Next, techniques for building loss models are presented along with some ideas for generating large loss event data from scenarios. Finally, operational risk measures are briefly discussed and then calculated in an example based on a fictitious firm called Genoa Bank.

Chapter 8 (Causal Modelling) describes the notion of causal modelling. Based on Bayesian decision theory, it is a technique wherein *causality* (real-world relationships) instead of associations (co-relation of states) is used as the basis for building operational risk measurement systems. This chapter covers the basic ideas of causal modelling, and includes an example from the Bayesian chapter to help connect the key concepts. Then a more formal definition of the basic causal relation is motivated by a simple sprinkler example. Next the main ideas behind building and using causal models are described using a famous example from statistics known as Simpson's paradox. The chapter concludes with examples of applications of causal models to operational risk in finance and a brief description of their use.

Chapter 9 (Causal Models for Operational Risk) is about building causal models to implement the proposed measurement framework for operational risk. Although operational risk measures can be calculated without causal models by using the proposed Delta–EVT™ methodology, causal models provide many advantages and are well suited to the measurement and analysis of operational risk. In this chapter the advantages of causal models for operational risk are summarised (such as their applicability to both performance and risk measurement). Next, the steps for building a causal model for operational risk are presented, followed by an in-depth example for the fictitious Genoa Bank to underscore the benefits and show some sample calculations. Then, for the more experienced practitioner, advanced uses of causal models for operational risk are discussed and examples presented. The chapter concludes with a brief summary.

Chapter 10 (Error Propagation) begins Section IV of the book, and is the first of three chapters on the mathematics behind the methodology. It is a common misconception for the layperson to think of errors as mistakes, but here 'error' is the term used for *uncertainty in measurements* and not necessarily mistakes. This important distinction lays the foundation for a discussion of the basic concepts of measurements, the sources of uncertainty, and the theory of error propagation. The chapter begins with an overview of measurement standards and the organisations that sponsor and promote their use, and a discussion of the importance of measurement error and its effect. Next, basic concepts of error modelling are explained, followed by discussions of direct and indirect measurement and the need for error propagation. Then the use of error models to establish intervals for measures and for classifying blunders is presented. Finally, the art of getting good measures requires dialogue with business managers to capture the characteristics of measures and criteria for evaluating them, and the chapter closes with some thoughts on other measurement topics that support this objective.

Chapter 11 (Extreme Value Theory) is the second of three chapters in the mathematics section. Extreme value theory (EVT) coupled with the Delta method was introduced earlier in the book as the cornerstone of a new operational risk methodology. The theory is well developed for physical processes and presents a viable alternative to traditional loss models for rare events and control breakdowns associated with operational risk. The application of the Delta method to finance is not new, but the application of EVT to finance is relatively recent (mostly insurance) and for that reason this chapter has been devoted to it. The chapter begins with an overview of the basic concepts behind EVT and examples of its use as an important tool for reliability and failure analysis of many physical systems. It continues with an analogous problem regarding the stock market crash of 1987 which leads into a discussion of excess loss and threshold. Next, discussions of time-dependent losses in the context of a classic insurance actuarial model and the follow-on application of EVT to internal losses for financial institutions are presented. The chapter concludes with a brief summary.

Chapter 12 (Bayesian Methods) concludes the mathematics section and completes the book. It provides a brief introduction to Bayesian decision theory, which is important to operational risk analysis because it addresses the problem of how to make decisions under uncertainty, and important to operational risk measurement because Bayesian networks form the basis for causal models. Key concepts are defined and the use of Bayesian networks as a tool for decision support is discussed. The chapter begins with an explanation of Bayesian methods and continues with a discussion of some of the key concepts. Next, Bayes' Theorem is introduced and two short examples are provided to reinforce the main concepts and illustrate the techniques. This is followed by an in-depth discussion of Bayesian networks, the basis on which causal models are built. Then a simple Bayesian network for one of the earlier examples is built and discussed to demonstrate the technique.

1.8 FURTHER READING

There are several good descriptions of value-based management beginning with Porter (1985) and Rappaport (1998) for the basics, and Olve, Roy and Wetter

(1999) and Knight (1997) for more application-oriented work. Drucker (1967) is still timeless in his description of the need for measurement to change behaviour. Books abound on the subject of risk and generally fall into one of two categories: tales of catastrophes such as Neumann (1995) and Perrow (1999), and descriptions of financial disasters, e.g. Gapper and Denton (1996) and Jorion (1997).

2

Historical Losses

2.1 INTRODUCTION

One of the principal ways operational risk management can contribute to more stable earnings is to help avoid large losses due to breakdowns in systems and controls. Looking back in time, many of the largest losses incurred by investment banks have been due to operational risk. They were not caused by a market movement or credit event, but rather were the result of failures of the bank to sufficiently monitor, control, and manage the risk associated with the operational processes. In this chapter some of the more famous historical loss incidents from which very large losses have resulted are categorised and quantified in order to provide a background for problem definition and motivation for addressing operational risk. But first, three categorisation schemes (accounting, human factors, and value-based) are outlined along with an argument that the accounting approach is necessary for loss attribution because it is well defined and comprehensive and the value-based scheme is a good supplement and reinforcement of internal assessment practices through which the causes of errors can be identified. Then the historical losses are described and evaluated using the accounting and value-based categorisations to demonstrate how the schemes can be applied and also to discuss the example losses. Next several other important but not-so-famous losses that have resulted in insurance claims are presented. These are included because they demonstrate how external losses in the context of operational risk can constitute a significant amount for many financial institutions. Finally, a summary and some observations are offered.

2.2 ATTRIBUTION OF LOSS

In order to take action to prevent or mitigate similar losses in the future, losses must be attributed to a cause. There are many ways to categorise loss according to their source. The categories depend on whether one thinks of the cause of a problem as numerate, behavioural, or analytical. Numerate schemes are based on counting attributes of the events. Behavioural schemes focus on people and their actions. Analytical approaches look for causes of the events. Three common loss categorisation schemes are accounting, human factors, and value-based.

2.2.1 Accounting Categorisation of Loss

The accounting scheme has its roots in the basic double-entry accounting system and includes the categories of valuation, reconciliation, compliance, and timeliness. Each of these accounting categories is described below.

1. *Valuation Risk*: Error in the amount of the transaction (wrong amount). Banking transactions today are marked to the market and use a contract accounting method where the revenues from a transaction often depend on the terms of the contract and a set of market values. Models for calculating the value of a contract based on its terms and relevant market values are subject to revision and interpretation. Since they may not represent the 'true' value of the contract, there may be losses associated with 're-valuation'.
2. *Reconciliation Risk*: Error in the account entry (wrong account). Since there are literally millions of accounts in a large financial operation the prospect of crediting or debiting the wrong account must be considered. As with all errors, if this is not recoverable, it results in a loss.
3. *Compliance Risk*: Error in the procedure used to process the transaction (wrong procedure). For instance, the contracts for financial services are subject to a number of rules and regulations, both internal and external, that govern the procedures used to originate and manage the contract. Lack of compliance with these regulations can subject the firm to losses such as fines and dispute settlements.
4. *Timeliness Risk*: Delay in processing the information (wrong time). Money has an intrinsic time value and delay in processing transactions can result in losses. The most common is a cost of carry, but market volatility can create larger losses due to delays in contract processing.

Because this categorisation system essentially ensures the integrity of the accounting books, it is comprehensive and can be 'objectively' administered. A limitation is that it assumes that all capabilities meet requirements, so system failures and lack of capacity are not well represented. Also it probably does not go far enough in identifying the causes of errors and may need to be supplemented for use by operations management in order to be actionable.

2.2.2 Human Factors Categorisation of Loss

Another way of categorising loss is due to the people in the organisation, and a human factors scheme for loss categorisation might include:

- Management oversight error
- Management fraud
- Employee activity error
- Employee fraud.

Management oversight and execution of transactions by employees are subject to errors and deliberate fraudulent activity. These are simple sub-categories, but the difficulty is in deciding between them when loss occurs.

For example, a system error could either be attributed to the software programmer who wrote the code or the manager who was responsible for testing it. In short, the human factors scheme by nature lacks an effective relationship for control, seldom leads to correctable actions, and has a high degree of subjectivity. For these and other reasons, this loss categorisation method will not be considered further.

2.2.3   Value-based Categorisation of Loss

A third but not so commonly used categorisation is based on the value hierarchy of the firm. The value hierarchy contains the core competencies and capabilities that the firm's management considers essential for adding value. Weightings would be attributed to several areas in the firm's value hierarchy so that the cause of the loss is spread over these areas. Assuming a simple value hierarchy for control includes people, technology, process, and business specific capability at the top level, a percentage of the loss based on the values expressed for each one would be attributed to each area (and sub-areas). For instance, if the values of the firm reflected a basic belief that people are always ultimately responsible, and the people area includes the value statement: 'People are ultimately responsible for the accuracy of all transactions', then this categorisation scheme might end up similar to the human factors categorisation described above. However, normally there would be several sub-categories, such as training, turnover, and compensation, in the human factors area to which the loss could be attributed. Thus, instead of simply an employee activity error, a portion of the loss would be attributed to employee training, turnover, or compensation scheme. In each, a set of questions relating to 'best practice' for that sub-category could be used to score the loss. The questions are answered relative to the specific loss (incident) as opposed to the general condition as might be done in a standard control self-assessment. For example, using the categories shown in Figure 2.1, a loss percentage would be attributed to each category and sub-category for each incident under consideration based on the values of the firm.

The advantage of the value hierarchy for attribution of loss is that it can also be used to perform general control self-assessment for the entire organisation. In this manner, the regular reviews of control through self-assessment are reinforced and calibrated with specific incident reviews of large losses. But it must be noted that the value-based categorisation reflects the values of the firm, and is

Figure 2.1   Value-based control hierarchy for loss categorisation

by definition subjective and firm specific. Thus, it cannot be the basis for an objective evaluation by stakeholders outside the firm, but it can be an effective supplement to other less-subjective approaches such as the accounting scheme.

2.3   VERY LARGE LOSSES

Looking back in time, many of the largest losses incurred by investment banks have been due to operational risk. There are several reported cases of individual traders in banks losing over one billion US dollars (USD) through lack of proper operational risk management. These more famous losses include Yasuo Hamanaka of Sumitomo (2.6 billion), Nick Leeson of Barings Bank (1.4 billion), Toshihide Iguchi of Daiwa in New York (1.1 billion), and Yukihusu Fujita of Shell in Japan (1.1 billion). Runners up include Howard Rubin (377 million) and Joseph Jett of Kidder Peabody (350 million). These cases are well known and have resulted in business failures due to the losses, along with market repercussions. Understanding how to avoid these kinds of losses and being able to quantify a capital charge for them is essential in maintaining the financial solvency of an institution. Getting the right definition and approach is also important because operational risk includes more frequent, smaller losses such as those due to settlement failure, portfolio errors, and model errors. Examples and discussions of smaller losses due to operational risk are provided later in the chapter, but first we discuss some of the famous operational risk failures.

2.4   OPERATIONAL RISK FAILURES

The famous losses of Sumitomo, Barings PLC, Deutsche Morgen Grenfell, NatWest Markets, Bank of New York, and Banque Paribas among others provide a rich background for the operational risk loss attribution discussion. A brief description of each loss is quoted from the original source, and then evaluated using the accounting and value-based categorisations to demonstrate how the loss attribution scheme can be applied and also to discuss the example losses. The reader should note that the information presented here is public knowledge (references are given), and no implication of any kind is intended toward these institutions or the people working in them. Rather, these particular examples were chosen because they represent a broad range of loss types and provide a rich platform on which to continue the discussion of operational risk.

2.4.1 Sumitomo

Source: Jim Kharouf. *Futures*. Financial Communications Co. August 1996 (Reproduced with permission)

> The disclosure of the $2.6 billion copper trading related loss at Sumitomo Corporation has been the most surprising event both in the commodity market and in the financial markets in 1996. The size of the loss surpasses similar debacles at Daiwa Bank Ltd, Barings PLC, and Orange County in the past two years (see the 1996 Yearbook and Chapter 2 for more on Orange County, Barings PLC, and Daiwa Bank Ltd).
>
> The president of Sumitomo said the loss was incurred secretly over a ten-year period by its trader, Yasuo Hamanaka, through unauthorised trades. Sumitomo also indicated that the trades involved highly risky derivative instruments.
>
> Yasuo Hamanaka is a name most in the copper business knew before June 13, when his employer, Sumitomo Corp., publicly blamed him for single handedly losing $1.8 billion trading copper. Hamanaka, king of the copper market for the past 10 years, now makes losses from Codelco's alleged rogue trader Juan Pablo Davila look like a petty miscalculation. Davila is in a Santiago prison facing charges that as Codelco's chief trader he lost $200 million in an alleged scheme whereby he diverted business to various dealers for kickbacks. Davila says he lost the money on a computer error.

Categorisation (Table 2.1)

Table 2.1 Sumitomo loss categorisation

Scheme	Sumitomo categorisation			
Accounting:	Valuation	Reconciliation	Compliance	Timeliness
Value-based:	Staff 70%	Technology 20%	Process 5%	Environment 5%

Discussion

Relying on staff values creates a vulnerability to human errors and fraud. Even good control systems can fail miserably when fraud or forgery is involved. Accurate reconciliation systems resist forgery and could report limit violations even though they had been 'authorised'. Exceptions and special circumstances do occur, but a proper reconciliation system should report limit violations whether or not they have been 'authorised'. In this way the system maintains a sanity check by assuming the default of compliance and limit management and overages are the exceptions that must be substantiated.

2.4.2   Barings

One of the most celebrated losses was the bankruptcy of Barings. It has been written about in official public documents, the press, popular books, and by Nick Leeson himself in his book *Rogue Trader* (a film bearing the same name has also been made). Yet surprisingly little factual information is available to provide an insight into the workings of the bank, and what the specific monitoring and control systems failures were that allowed him to amass over 1 billion USD in losses over a period of a few years. One of the most cogent observations was made by Stephen Fay in *The Collapse of Barings* (Fay 1996, p. 268):

> Ignorance was what allowed Leeson to play his game for thirty-two months. Had Barings purchased a system that enabled the settlements department in London to reconcile trades made in any part of the world with clients' orders from any part of the world, instead of relying on branch offices like Singapore for the information, Leeson's fraudulent use of the 88888 account would have been exposed within months, if not weeks. Such a system, known as BRAINS, would have cost about £10 million. Barings did give it the go-ahead, but too late—in January 1995. Consider the savings that would have been made if BRAINS had been in use earlier.

Categorisation (Table 2.2)

Table 2.2   Barings loss categorisation

Scheme	Barings categorisation			
Accounting:	Valuation	Reconciliation	Compliance	Timeliness
Value-based:	Staff 45%	Technology 45%	Process 5%	Environment 5%

Discussion

Proper accounting requires reconciliation at key control points in the process. For most banks this includes reconciling trades on the exchange with trades in the back office, and reconciling client orders with trades made. In addition, house accounts are compared with limits. If this simple accounting had been applied to Barings, the lack of reconciliation might have been discovered due to the 88888 account, even though Nick Leeson was in charge of both the trade and the back office, because the numbers would not have added up. As well, client confirmations and trades would have fallen out of balance, and the house account might have shown that Leeson took proprietary positions that far exceeded his trading limits. As with the example above, again we see a value-based incident report that attributes the failure to staff. For a company relying on technology, there would be much higher weightings on technology and process and less on staff.

2.4.3 Deutsche Morgan Grenfell and Jardine Fleming

Fines are seemingly more common as regulators resort to punitive action when banks are found not to be in compliance with regulation. Some of the recent incidents include:

Source: *Electronic Telegraph*. 17 April, 1997 (Reproduced with permission)

> A RECORD fine of £2m, plus an order to pay costs of more than £1m, was imposed on Morgan Grenfell Unit Trust Managers by City regulators yesterday. About 90,000 investors in three of Morgan's unit trusts which were incorrectly priced for more than a year will receive compensation of £200m within the next few weeks. A spokesman for Deutsche Bank, which owns Morgan, said the total cost of the 'Peter Young affair' was likely to exceed £400m.

Source: *Asia Week*. 27 September, 1996 (Reproduced with permission)

> JARDINE FLEMING STARTED THE investor worries. Last month, British and Hong Kong regulators said JF star manager Colin Armstrong had taken advantage of lax controls at Asia's largest fund-management company to enrich himself at investors' expense. Days later, American giant Fidelity, Asia's second-largest fund manager, had a brush with notoriety. Financial adviser Tony Taylor, a former Fidelity agent in Ireland, went missing, leaving $2.2 million in client money unaccounted for... JF has set up a $19.3-million package, one of the biggest payouts in fund-management history, for investors in the three funds the SFC says were disadvantaged... JF group chairman Alan Smith says the company's focus in hindsight, was 'too much upon investment performance and not enough upon compliance.'

Categorisation (Table 2.3)

Table 2.3 Morgan Grenfell & Jardine Fleming loss categorisation

Scheme	Morgan Grenfell & Jardine Fleming categorisation			
Accounting:	Valuation	Reconciliation	Compliance	Timeliness
Value-based:	Staff 50%	Technology 20%	Process 25%	Environment 5%

Discussion

It is easy to see the subjectivity problems for loss attribution in the value-based scheme by stakeholders outside the firm. Taking advantage of 'lax controls' is indeed a human action, but depending on the values of the corporation arguments can be made for and against the above categorisation distribution. One observation is that the reporting of these incidents tends to be sensationalised with an emphasis on the individual. Also, firms do usually try to manage the information made available to the press.

2.4.4   National Westminster

Source: *New York Times*. Friday, 27 June, 1997 (Reprinted with permission of The Associated Press)

SCANDAL AT LONDON BANK PROMPTS SIX EXECUTIVES TO QUIT

A former trader at National Westminster Bank PLC of London covered up losses totalling £77 million ($129 million) for two years, an inquiry reported yesterday, and the bank said six senior executives had quit.

Source: NatWest Group Web Page. June 26 1997
http://www.natwestgroup.com/pr_nwenq.html

NatWest Announces Findings of Independent Inquiry into Losses at NatWest Markets

NatWest Group announced today (26 June 1997) the results of the investigation into the losses that occurred at NatWest Markets in the London interest rate options business. The initial findings of the independent review, carried out by Linklaters & Paines and Coopers & Lybrand, were announced on 13 March 1997.

The full report of the independent investigation has confirmed the net charge against pre-tax profits of £77 million, as originally announced on 13 March. It also found that the losses were confined to the London interest rate options business. There is no evidence of any loss to clients or personal gain as a result of collusion with third parties. For legal reasons and reasons of commercial confidentiality it is inappropriate to publish the report.

It has been sent to the Bank of England and the SFA. The SFO has also been fully briefed. Following the report six people have already left, or agreed to leave, NatWest Markets. A number of other people are subject to internal disciplinary measures.

The losses and mis-pricing in the London interest rate options business went undiscovered because of deliberate concealment and weaknesses in the operations and internal controls in this area. Improvements were already being made to the controls over a period of time, and it was as a result of these that the losses were detected at the end of February 1997.

The Main Findings of the Report

- The original losses were incurred in interest rate swaptions and options books, mainly Deutsche Mark and Sterling, and were the result of poor trading and adverse market movements.
- These losses were concealed by deliberately mis-pricing and over-valuing options contracts. The volatilities input into pricing models for long-dated, out-of-the-money swaptions were falsely adjusted to increase the value of the books.
- There were also unauthorised transfers of value between options books that were made deliberately to conceal losses and to transfer false profits.
- The independent price-checking regime for the interest rate options area did not have sufficiently robust procedures for procuring external quotations and checking the pricing of options.

Categorisation (Table 2.4)

Table 2.4   NatWest loss categorisation

Scheme		NatWest Categorisation		
Accounting:	Valuation	Reconciliation	Compliance	Timeliness
Value-based:	Staff 70%	Technology 20%	Process 5%	Environment 5%

Discussion

The conclusion of deliberate mis-pricing makes a strong case for attributing most of this loss to the staff sub-category. The Group of Thirty (1993) recommends independent verification of market values for contracts (*Derivatives: Practices and Principles*). Using a valuation server, the independent valuation is compared with the front office price. The differences are reported and tracked statistically for significance and bias. Using this technique, mis-pricing can be detected more quickly and corrective action taken before large losses are incurred.

2.4.5   Bank of New York

Source: *Wall Street Journal.* Monday, 25 November, 1985

A Computer Snafu Snarls the Handling of Treasury Issues by Phillip L. Zweig and Allanna Sullivan Staff reporters of the Wall Street Journal NEW YORK—

A computer malfunction at Bank of New York brought the Treasury bond market's deliveries and payments systems to a near-standstill for almost 28 hours Thursday and Friday. Although bond prices weren't affected, metal traders bid up the price of platinum futures Friday in the belief that a financial crisis had struck the Treasury bond market. However, Bank of New York's problems appeared to be more electronic than financial. The foul-up temporarily prevented the bank, the nation's largest clearer of government securities, from delivering securities to buyers and making payments to sellers—a service it performs for scores of securities dealers and other banks. The malfunction was cleared up at 12:30 p.m. EST Friday, and an hour later the bank resumed delivery of securities. But Thursday the bank, a unit of Bank of New York Co., had to borrow a record $20 billion from the Federal Reserve Bank of New York so it could pay for securities received. The borrowing is said to be the largest discount window borrowing ever from the Federal Reserve System. Bank of New York repaid the loan Friday, Martha Dinnerstein, a senior vice president, said. Although Bank of New York incurred an estimated $4 million interest expense on the borrowing, the bank said any impact on its net income 'will not be material.' For the first nine months this year, earnings totaled $96.7 million. Bank of New York stock closed Friday at $45.125, off 25 cents from the Thursday, as 16,500 shares changed hands in composite trading on the New York Stock Exchange. Bank of New York said that it had paid for the cost of carrying the securities so its customers wouldn't lose any interest. Bank of New York's inability to accept payments temporarily left other banks with $20 billion on their hands. This diminished the need of many banks to borrow from others in the federal funds market. Banks use the market for federal funds, which are reserves that banks lend each other, for short-term funding of certain operations. The cash glut caused the federal funds rate to plummet to 5.5% from 8.375% early Thursday. The electronic snafu is by far the largest of computer problems that periodically have bedevilled the capital markets.

Categorisation (Table 2.5)

Table 2.5 Categorisation of loss for Bank of New York

Scheme	Bank of New York categorisation			
Accounting:	Valuation	Reconciliation	Compliance	Timeliness
Value-based:	Staff 10%	Technology 80%	Process 10%	Environment 0%

Discussion

System failures can be modelled to calculate loss under scenarios that include the failure or limited availability over a specific time period. In this manner, a bank can decide if the loss of a critical system is adequately covered by the backup (or alternative) process. Executives must be aware of the potential loss due to failures in order to cost justify duplicate systems, backups, higher reliability alternative systems, and other failure-avoidance and recovery strategies for systems, people, and processes.

2.4.6 Banque Paribas

One of the more subtle losses to banks is the increased cost of borrowing associated with a lowered rating by one or more of the large ratings agencies. Standard & Poor's advises the following:

> To meet the demands of members and the trading community at large, exchanges and clearing houses must have exceptional computer systems and back office capabilities. Each day they must process a multitude of transactions and track trading activities for compliance purposes. An exchange's or clearing house's reputation hinges on its ability to compare, clear, and settle both sides of a trade accurately and on a timely basis (Bank Ratings Criteria, Standard & Poor's, 1995).

Obviously this also applies to investment banking and firms that focus almost entirely on it. It also applies to other credit rating agencies, as Banque Paribas discovered.

Source: *Two-Ten Communications*. New York, 4 April, 1996

Banque Paribas's short-term bank rating for structured transactions is lowered to 'F-1' from 'F-1+' by Fitch.

This action follows a review in the wake of the bank's 1995 loss of FFR 2.9 billion (US$580 million). The downgrade largely reflects falling core profitability and risk management controls, which have not kept pace with the bank's broad-based investment banking profile. With assets of FFR 980 billion (US$196 billion) as of year-end 1995, Banque Paribas remains one of the largest financial institutions in France with significant business domestically and abroad.

Categorisation (Table 2.6)

Table 2.6   Bank Paribas loss categorisation

Scheme	Banque Paribas categorisation			
Accounting:	Valuation	Reconciliation	Compliance	Timeliness
Value-based:	Staff 20%	Technology 20%	Process 55%	Environment 5%

Discussion

Clearly operational management is a key ingredient for any bank, and it is especially important to exchanges and clearing houses. Specifically a bank should ensure that it has adequate organisational structure, compliance handbook, procedures for clearing, and disaster recovery/contingency plans available for the rating agencies.

2.5   OTHER LOSSES

In addition to publicised losses of very large value, there are numerous other losses due to operational risk depending on which definition of operational risk is assumed. Interest claims due to late settlement are a regular occurrence and usually small, but some back office errors can result in wrong positions being traded, and changes in the value of the instrument to be delivered due to sudden market movements can dwarf any potential interest claim. Payment errors and reconciliation breaks are also common, as are fraudulent applications and payments in retail banking.

Although such losses may not be widely publicised, they nevertheless constitute a significant amount for many financial institutions. Other sources of losses are also available, such as insurance claims. The following table is an example of large losses occurring in the banking industry that have resulted in insurance claims. It represents about 8.5 billion USD in losses over 10 years.

Table 2.7 Example of large losses

ID	Date	Amount ('000)		Business	Category
1	4/4/88	$	60 000	Commercial	Fraud
2	8/16/88	$	2100	Retail	Fraud
3	9/1/88	$	20 000	Corporate	Fraud
4	4/3/89	$	45 000	Capital Markets	Fraud
5	7/25/89	$	37 500	Commercial	Fraud
6	6/22/90	$	30 000	Brokerage	Competence
7	2/20/91	$	3830	Retail Brokerage	Competence
8	3/22/91	$	15 000	Asset Management	Competence
9	7/26/91	$	45 000	Retail Brokerage	Fraud
10	2/5/92	$	30 000	Corporate	Competence
11	3/27/92	$	8000	Fund Management	Competence
12	3/27/92	$	18 600	Brokerage	Fraud
13	7/27/92	$	163 000	Corporate	Fraud
14	2/18/94	$	1200	Brokerage	Fraud
15	3/31/94	$	100 000	Underwriting	Fraud
16	4/15/94	$	221 000	Corporate	Fraud
17	5/2/94	$	430 000	Brokerage	Fraud
18	8/25/94	$	72 000	Fund Management	Fraud
19	10/10/94	$	20 000	Corporate	Fraud
20	12/19/94	$	390 000	Underwriting	Competence
21	6/20/95	$	80 000	Asset Management	Fraud
22	2/10/92	$	77 500	Underwriting	Fraud
23	9/16/92	$	42 000	Brokerage	Fraud
24	10/7/92	$	7000	Brokerage	Fraud
25	2/26/93	$	2000	Retail Brokerage	Fraud
26	3/4/93	$	91 000	Retail Brokerage	Fraud
27	7/15/93	$	371 000	Retail Brokerage	Fraud
28	8/18/93	$	55 000	Retail Banking	Fraud
29	10/14/93	$	33 000	Fund Management	Fraud
30	10/19/93	$	30 000	Corporate	Competence
31	10/21/93	$	10 000	Fund Management	Competence
32	6/19/95	$	750	Underwriting	Competence
33	8/10/95	$	1400	Brokerage	Fraud
34	8/15/95	$	1350	Brokerage	Fraud
35	10/9/95	$	5500	Retail Banking	Fraud
36	10/27/95	$	24 000	Brokerage	Fraud
37	11/19/98	$	100 000	Capital Markets	Process
38	1/1/93	$	157 000	Capital Markets	Process
39	1/1/94			Capital Markets	Process
40	6/2/88	$	105 000	Commercial	Process
41	3/30/90	$	56 000	Brokerage	Process
42	4/11/90	$	370 500	Retail Brokerage	Process
43	9/26/90	$	800	Retail Brokerage	Process
44	10/22/90	$	1250	Retail Brokerage	Process
45	2/18/91	$	507	Retail Banking	Process
46	9/30/91	$	1500	Commercial	Process
47	12/9/91	$	41 100	Underwriting	Process
48	2/3/92	$	100	Commercial	Process
49	4/2/92	$	137 000	Brokerage	Process
50	10/19/93	$	30 000	Corporate	Process
51	5-Nov	$	6000	Retail Brokerage	Process
52	12/1/93	$	30 000	Retail Brokerage	Process
53	1/5/94	$	25 000	Fund Management	Process

Table 2.7   (Continued)

ID	Date	Amount ('000)		Business	Category
54	1/5/94	$	32 000	Brokerage	Process
55	7/19/94	$	30 000	Retail Brokerage	Process
56	8/22/94	$	28 000	Underwriting	Process
57	9/13/94	$	63 000	Corporate	Process
58	11/1/94	$	14 000	Retail Brokerage	Process
59	1/6/95	$	3640	Capital Markets	Process
60	1/31/95	$	1000	Corporate	Process
61	2/8/95	$	3200	Capital Markets	Process
62	2/14/95	$	1000	Capital Markets	Process
63	3/2/95	$	7000	Capital Markets	Process
64	3/2/95	$	7000	Capital Markets	Process
65	7/28/95	$	200 000	Retail Brokerage	Process
66	9/7/95	$	2500	Underwriting	Process
67	12/9/95	$	30 000	Capital Markets	Process
68	1/1/96	$	1000	Retail Brokerage	Strategy
69	3/1/95	$	6900	Unknown	Strategy
70	10/1/90	$	27 400	Banking	Strategy
71	1/1/97	$	2700	Capital Markets	Strategy
72	11/19/98	$	123 000	Capital Markets	Systems
73		$	50 000	Capital Markets	Systems
74	11/1/96	$	176 100	Firm	Strategy
75	4/1/92	$	157 000	Firm	Strategy
76	5/1/92	$	124 000	Firm	Strategy
77	12/1/93	$	107 300	Firm	Strategy
78	1/1/93	$	105 000	Firm	Strategy
79	10/1/94	$	89 500	Firm	Strategy
80	1/1/97	$	81 500	Firm	Strategy
81	7/1/91	$	66 000	Firm	Strategy
82	6/1/95	$	50 000	Firm	Strategy
83	3/1/93	$	45 000	Firm	Strategy
84	1/1/99	$	1540	Capital Markets	Systems
85	11/19/98	$	200 000	Capital Markets	Systems
86	11/19/98	$	350 000	Capital Markets	Systems
87	3/30/92	$	995	Capital Markets	Systems
88	11/19/98	$	126 000	Capital Markets	Systems
89	11/19/98	$	2 600 000	Capital Markets	Systems

2.6   SUMMARY

With the increase in complexity and volumes of transactions, financial institutions have become even more vulnerable to large losses. Most large losses occur over long periods of several months or even several years. Since very small mistakes can lead to very large losses, financial institutions need special approaches to controls that, although based on them, must necessarily differ from traditional quality control concepts due to the increased requirements for very low failure rates for the process. The elimination of small errors should also have obvious 'side-effects' such as reducing small losses.

This chapter introduced some loss categorisation schemes as background for problem definition and motivation for addressing operational risk. Some examples of famous and very large losses were used to demonstrate both how the categorisation scheme could be applied and to facilitate the discussion. Other important but not-so-famous losses were also presented because they demonstrate how losses, even in the narrow definition of operational risk, can constitute a significant amount for many financial institutions. Failures to monitor, control, and manage the risk associated with the operational process can affect earnings in a big way. The modern-day bank-robber is much more likely to use a computer and to be from within the bank. Banks must have sufficient control systems to avoid these kinds of losses, or at least an effective way to detect them quickly so as to minimise their severity. A few main points to keep in mind include the following:

- History shows that risk associated with the operational process can produce bank-breaking losses.
- Loss attribution schemes help identify and address breakdowns in operational systems and controls.
- Sufficient operational control systems reduce vulnerability to large losses.
- Large losses originate from smaller ones.

2.7 FURTHER READING

General financial newspapers and journals regularly carry articles about operational risk. There are also some journals and newsletters that focus on risk, including *Risk Magazine* and *Operational Risk Manager*.

3

Regulation

3.1 INTRODUCTION

Regulation has been a key factor in banking activities and its management, and in recent years some have spilled over into the corporate world. In addition to regulation, several disastrous events such as terrorism, environmental catastrophes, and widespread technology failures have influenced the way firms view operational risk. In this chapter the regulations relating to operational risk in banking as well as in corporations are reviewed. Banking regulation documents have to do with the supervision of financial institutions. Corporate governance regulations deal with the responsibility of directors of a corporation to understand the risks of the firm in a general way. In most cases regulation has followed disaster, so this chapter begins with a chronological outline relating the environment to the resulting regulation. Then banking supervision and corporate governance in general are discussed and more details on some important individual regulations are given. Finally, the current regulatory approach is summarised.

3.2 BACKGROUND

In 1974 the Herstatt Bank in Germany failed leaving 628 million USD in unpaid foreign exchange settlements and to this day settlement risk is sometimes referred to as 'Herstatt risk'. In the 1980s banking regulation was reformed and many banks failed due to inadequate controls and poor management. In the United States the 'Savings and Loan Disaster' resulted in the failure of several hundred banks and led to new banking regulation (CAMEL). In the early 1990s shady dealings in the financial markets and a series of highly publicised frauds resulted in new corporate governance regulations in the United States (COSO 1992), Canada (CICA 1995), the United Kingdom (ICAEW 1999), Germany (KonTraG 1998), and Australia (AS 4360 1999). Throughout the late 1980s and early 1990s a series of large losses due to derivatives were widely publicised and led to a revision of the Basle Accord for international banks trading these new products. The Group of Thirty study *Derivatives: Practices and Principles* (1993) contained recommendations regarding operational risk management practices for derivatives users where operational risk is defined as 'Uncertainty related to losses resulting from inadequate systems or controls, human error, or management'. Also in the early 1990's a series of bombings in financial districts caused a major push to provide contingency planning for banking operations. The late 1990's saw the introduction of wider definitions of operational risk to include legal actions taken in the United States and Australia that resulted in several multi-million dollar settlements due to discrimination. In this time-period events in the environment expanded the focus for operational risk from settlement to corporate governance, to derivative mishandling, to contingency planning, and legal risk.

3.3 BANKING SUPERVISION

There have been three regulatory documents from the Bank for International Settlement (BIS) in Basle dealing with operational risk (BIS 1998a, 1998b, 1999). They are the *Framework for the Evaluation of Internal Control Systems* (January 1998), *Operational Risk Management* (September 1998), and *A New Capital Adequacy Framework* (June 1999). The first document contains a description of internal control systems and their evaluation by banking supervisors. The second is a survey document on operational risk that includes a description of current practices and attitudes toward operational risk management. The third is a consultative paper on revising the 1989 Basle Accord that includes references to operational risk and the suggestion that banks may be required to set aside capital for it as they do for market and credit risk. In addition to the BIS the European Union has published a consultative document, entitled *A Review of Regulatory Capital Requirements for EU Credit Institutions and Investment Firms Consultation Document* (November 1999), that includes a proposal for operational risk. Each of these documents is considered in turn along with their implications for operational risk.

3.3.1 *Framework for the Evaluation of Internal Control Systems* (Basle, January 1998)

The most important document relating to operational risk to date is the *Framework for the Evaluation of Internal Control Systems* (January 1998). In this document the cogent observation is made that 'Several recent cases demonstrate that lax internal controls can lead to significant losses for banks'. It goes on to identify five basic types of control breakdowns as follows:

1. Lack of adequate management oversight and accountability, and failure to develop a strong control culture within the bank;
2. Inadequate assessment of the risk of certain banking activities, whether on or off balance sheet;

3. The absence or failure of key control activities, such as segregation of duties, approvals, verifications, reconciliations, and reviews of operating performance;
4. Inadequate communication of information between levels of management within the bank, especially in the upward communication of problems;
5. Inadequate or ineffective audit programs and other monitoring activities.

Next, the objectives of the internal control system for a bank are categorised as follows:

1. efficiency and effectiveness of operations (operational objectives);
2. reliability and completeness of financial and management information (information objectives); and
3. compliance with applicable laws and regulations (compliance objectives).

And finally, a mandate for bank supervisors is given.

Principle 14: Supervisors should require that all banks, regardless of size, have an effective system of internal controls that is consistent with the nature, complexity, and risk of their on- and off-balance-sheet activities and that responds to changes in the bank's environment and conditions. In those instances where supervisors determine that a bank's internal control system is not adequate (for example, does not cover all of the principles contained in this document), they should take action against the bank to ensure that the internal control system is improved immediately.

The key parts of the document have to do with how the supervisor carries out these responsibilities. In fact, the proposals are to:

- use the information from the internal audit department;
- conduct a control self-assessment;
- use the information from external audits; and
- perform an on-site examination including a review of the business process and a reasonable level of transaction testing in order to obtain an independent verification of the bank's own internal control processes.

In most large banks, the on-site examination will probably need to be performed. In so doing, the document prescribes the following for the goals of the examination:

- the adequacy of, and adherence to, internal policies, procedures and limits;
- the accuracy and completeness of management reports and financial records; and
- the reliability (i.e., whether it functions as management intends) of specific controls identified as key to the internal control element being assessed.

These guidelines seem right on, but the question remains as to what level of assurance can be achieved in practice with an on-site examination. Consider a medium sized investment banking operation with a few thousand transactions per day. For a reasonable confidence level the sample size should be about 20%. This means 1000 transactions might need to be checked per day. Using a risk-based auditing approach this figure might be reduced to as low as 100 transactions per day. However, this still is a daunting task for regulators without some very special tools to assist them. In today's environment, such tools are not yet widely available.

3.3.2 *Operational Risk Management* (Basle, September 1998)

A working group from Basle interviewed 30 banks regarding operational risk and produced this document to summarise their findings. They concluded that virtually all banks assign the responsibility for operational risk to the business unit line manager and that the objective is to provide the proper incentives for these managers for good operational management by using one of the following approaches:

- allocating capital for operational risk;
- including operational risk management in the performance evaluation process; or
- reporting operational risk details of losses and corrective actions directly to the bank's top management.

The report also describes the difficulties banks are having in accomplishing this task of incorporating operational risk management into the business and providing the proper incentives for it.

3.3.3 *A New Capital Adequacy Framework* (Basle, June 1999)

This consultative paper was issued for comments in March 2000 and deals primarily with revisions to credit risk capital requirements. However, it does make reference to operational risk and the widely-held belief that the intention is to require banks to hold capital for operational risk provided the difficulties described above can be resolved to the satisfaction of Basle to include in the final *Capital Adequacy Framework*. This intention is clearly stated as follows:

> The existing Accord specifies explicit capital charges only for credit and market risks (in the trading book). Other risks, including interest rate risk in the banking book and operational risk, are also an important feature of banking. The Committee therefore proposes to develop a capital charge for interest rate risk in the banking book for banks where interest rate risk is significantly above average, and is proposing to develop capital charges for other risks, principally operational risk.

A capital charge for operational risk may be the required impetus needed to marshal enough resources to overcome the difficulties described by the banking survey on operational risk. However, it is likely that the calculation formula would be necessarily simple in order to be applicable to all banks. If so, there is a good chance it may produce a pejorative effect and may even lead to a decrease in the level of operational risk innovation.

3.3.4 A Review of Regulatory Capital Requirements for EU Credit Institutions and Investment Firms Consultation Document (November 1999)

This consultative document focuses on credit risk, but gives consideration to operational risk under the area of 'other risks'. The committee puts forth that '. . .other risks will be defined as all risks that are neither credit risk, market risks nor interest rate risk (arising from the banking book). This broad definition of "other risks" will encompass (but will not be confined to) operational risk, legal risk and reputational risk.' The paper goes on to suggest a strong qualitative assessment process for operational risk that focuses on the risk culture, contingency plans, and control systems. It also recognises risk mitigation as part of the overall risk management process. Perhaps the most controversial part of the document refers to a formula for setting a capital charge for operational risk as a 'linear function of size and income (i.e. $K = \alpha A + \beta I$), and of possible other indicators for other risks'. The paper would also provide for adjustment of the capital charge by the supervisors based on a set of criteria in order to provide incentives to develop sound risk management controls. After briefly discussing alternatives, the Commission document concludes with:

> 60. The Commission services propose **the 'top-down' approach based on reasonable proxies for other risks as the standard methodology for setting the minimum capital requirement applicable to other risks in EU countries** (emphasis in original). This approach has the main advantages of being both simple and universally applicable:
>
> - The capital charge will be easy to calculate, since it is based on aggregates already available from either supervisory reports or public documents. The 'regulatory burden' would thus be limited;
> - This approach is applicable to all categories of credit institutions and investment firms, with no distinction between listed and unlisted companies.

The document goes on to request comments on the merits and drawbacks of the different approaches that could be used for capital adequacy. However, it appears that the Commission is committed to a simple approach, and any effective modelling technique is likely not to be simple. The assumption is that potential losses due to breakdowns in controls and systems are related to the firm's assets and income. This simple linear relation may be difficult to substantiate because of the many complex relationships in a bank's financial reporting structure.

3.4   CORPORATE GOVERNANCE

In addition to the banking supervisory regulation, several corporate governance regulations and proposals have been forthcoming from governments, exchanges, institutes, and committees. They are intended to introduce good risk management into the corporate sector after the fashion of the *Basle Framework for Internal Control* document. Some documents (ICAEW 1999) claim the need for risk disclosure and transparency as a requirement for proper capital market pricing, but most take an audit control attitude. A survey of these is provided in this section, along with a brief discussion of their implications.

3.4.1   US COSO (1992)

In September 1992 the Committee of Sponsoring Organisations of the Treadway Commission produced the *Internal Control—Integrated Framework* document that includes a set of evaluation tools and a discussion of the requirements for good internal control. The document is based on the work from the National Commission on Fraudulent Financial Reporting (Treadway Commission) in the late 1980s. The stated objectives of internal control are:

- Effectiveness and efficiency of operations.
- Reliability of financial reporting.
- Compliance with applicable laws and regulations.

The components needed are described in the categories of control environment, risk assessment, control activities, information and communication, and monitoring. The tools include more specific areas in each of the categories that need to be addressed (e.g. risk assessment and adequacy of mechanisms to identify risk arising from external sources (supply, technology, etc.)).

3.4.2   Canadian COCO (1995)

In November 1995 the Canadian Institute of Chartered Accountants published its *Guidance on Control*. It adopts the COSO definition for internal control objectives; however, it goes on to describe its component categories of purpose, commitment, capability, and monitoring and learning. This categorisation is probably a reflection of the more general management trend of using a balanced set of financial and non-financial performance indicators for corporations. It also provides a set of criteria and sample assessment questions such as (under Commitment): 'Are our principles of integrity and ethical values shared and practised?'. The primary difference from COSO is that COCO recognises the objectives of the organisation as both a goal and a measure for the degree of effectiveness.

3.4.3 UK Combined Code (Turnbull Report) (1999)

The London Stock Exchange sponsored a committee to make recommendations on corporate governance (Cadbury Committee) and subsequently combined its report with work by the Greenbury Committee on directors' roles and responsibilities to produce the *Combined Code*. (A committee chaired by Nigel Turnbull carried out this work.) The resulting document is very similar to the COSO document from the United States, but it is mandatory for companies listed on the London Stock Exchange. The stated motivation is that a full disclosure of risks as they relate to company objectives will establish a better basis for pricing capital for the firm. The Institute for Chartered Accountants of England and Wales (ICAEW) has produced several documents relating to the combined code and its implementation. The primary guidance is one of how to identify risks, determine their source, evaluate them, and take appropriate action. Companies implementing Turnbull would start by:

- identifying the risks inherent in the company's strategy as well as ranking and sourcing them;
- selecting the appropriate risk management approaches and transferring or avoiding those risks that the business is not competent to manage or prepared to manage;
- implementing controls to manage the remaining risks;
- monitoring the effectiveness of the company's risk management approaches and controls; and
- making improvements before starting on the whole process again and reconfirming that the company is addressing the right risks (ICAEW 1999).

The company would go on to disclose those risks and actions that were appropriate for an annual report.

3.4.4 German KonTraG (1998)

On 1 May 1998 the law for control and transparence in companies went into effect in Germany (*Gesetz zur Kontrolle und Transparenz im Unternehmensbereich*). Known as *KonTraG*, it requires German firms to undertake a risk management system in order to identify, assess, and communicate risks to the firm. Specifically the boards of publicly traded firms are required to develop a risk monitoring system, assess the risks, and communicate and report them. Auditors of publicly traded firms must report on:

- Identification of risks that may threaten the performance of the firm.
- The assessment of the potential impact of these risks.
- The development of a risk identification, monitoring and early warning system.

These measures must be in effect for the company reports ending after 31 December 1998. The following three paragraphs are taken from the *Gesetz zur Kontrolle und Transparenz im Unternehmensbereich* (*KonTraG*) and are the original reference for the three points made above.

(2) *Die Beurteilung des Prüfungsergebnisses soll allgemeinverständlich und problemorientiert unter Berücksichtigung des Umstandes erfolgen, daß die gesetzlichen Vertreter den Abschluß zu verantworten haben. Auf Risiken, die den Fortbestand des Unternehmens gefährden, ist gesondert einzugehen.*

Der Lagebericht und der Konzernlagebericht sind darauf zu prüfen, ob der Lagebericht mit dem Jahresabschluß und der Konzernlagebericht mit dem Konzernabschluß sowie mit den bei der Prüfung gewonnenen Erkenntnissen des Abschlußprüfers in Einklang stehen und ob der Lagebericht insgesamt eine zutreffende Vorstellung von der Lage des Unternehmens und der Konzernlagebericht insgesamt eine zutreffende Vorstellung von der Lage des Konzerns vermittelt. Dabei ist auch zu prüfen, ob die Risiken der künftigen Entwicklung zutreffend dargestellt sind.

"(2) Der Vorstand hat geeignete Maßnahmen zu treffen, insbesondere ein Überwachungssystem einzurichten, damit den Fortbestand der Gesellschaft gefährdende Entwicklungen früh erkannt werden."

Although vague in implementation specifics, KonTraG would seem to be on a par with the UK Turnbull requirement that listed firms implement a risk management system and disclose that they have undertaken a risk identification, assessment, and monitoring activity and to some extent disclose what material risks are present.

3.4.5 Australian AS 4360 (1999)

The Joint Standards Australia/Standards New Zealand Committee OB/7 on risk management was published in April 1999 as a revision to the AS/NZS 4360 of 1995. This document is narrower than the others and simply provides guidelines for a classical risk management process, including the following steps:

1. Establish Context
2. Risk Identification
3. Risk Analysis
4. Risk Evaluation
5. Risk Mitigation

It also encourages the communication of risks and appropriate monitoring. Several examples are included, but the document falls short of providing a descriptive framework for good risk management. This basic approach was originated in engineering safety assessment (e.g. nuclear plants) and has been augmented with analytical methodologies such as fault tree analysis and probabilistic safety assessment. The general approach can be made much more rigorous through the use of a coherent methodology and analytical tools (King 1996).

3.5 SUMMARY

This chapter is a review of current banking and corporate governance regulations and the implications to operational risk. In general, the regulatory environment has attempted to provide a sound governance guideline for corporations and capital adequacy for banks. The role of the market in promoting competition for corporations has adopted the governance guidelines used in banking and is promoting them as a means of improving shareholder value through better capital pricing in the markets. (In several countries credit ratings provide the incentive for capital structure by supplying information to the credit markets for pricing.) This impetus for regulation of operational risk was also evident in the previous chapter on historical losses, where some of the more famous loss incidents were presented and discussed as a motivation for addressing operational risk in financial institutions. Unfortunately, governance regulation has not been effective at preventing operational risk losses, possibly due to the lack of a clear measure for operational risk. According to some views '. . .an efficient governance of banks requires (I) accurate measures of its solvency and of the nature of its activities . . .' (Dewatripont and Tirole 1993).

The message through regulations is clear that firms must:

- Improve efficiency and effectiveness of operations to remain competitive;
- Improve the level of corporate governance to maintain trust with the stakeholders;
- Retain a level of capital cushion that can carry it through potential losses due to volatility in its earnings stream; and
- Implement a system of controls that provides assurance that the above objectives are met.

3.6 FURTHER READING

Original documents are available from the organisations such as the Bank for International Settlements, the Group of Thirty, and the European Union. National accounting organisations (e.g. ICAEW, AIPA, CICA) are a good source of corporate governance information. Many of these documents are also available in electronic form on the web at the organisation's own web site.

SECTION II
MEASURING OPERATIONAL RISK

4

A Measurement Framework for Operational Risk

4.1 INTRODUCTION

A framework creates the needed environment for managing operational risk in a systematic way. Operational risk is concerned with the risk to the firm's performance due to how the firm is *operated* as opposed to how the firm is *financed*. Operating managers are faced with adverse deviations from expected performance and the related consequences in the normal course of their management duties. As such, operational risk is very familiar to them. However, many firms do not address operational risk in a systematic way. Instead, they deal with issues as they occur (often after a catastrophic event) and base their decisions on general impressions of situations and events. This can result in inconsistent performance and earnings 'surprises' for the firm's stakeholders. Recent efforts to manage operational risk have struggled with a lack of objective and relevant measurement information to use for decision-making. This has led to discussions about what to measure and how to measure it. In fact, the basic definitions of operational risk have been debated, along with the goals for its measurement. A framework addresses these issues by providing a set of assumptions, definitions, and methodology for measuring operational risk.

This chapter begins by putting forth criteria for a framework, and reviewing and evaluating several existing approaches to operational risk within that context. Then a framework for measuring and modelling operational risk is introduced, which combines a basic business model with a new measurement methodology called Delta–EVT™. A discussion of the two analytical techniques that comprise Delta–EVT™ and the approach for combining them is provided. Connected with this is a listing and description of the available output measures, followed by an outline of how Delta–EVT™ both satisfies the criteria of an operational framework and provides a means for realising the benefits of operational risk management. Then, the five basic steps for implementing the framework are outlined within the context of finance. The chapter concludes with a brief summary.

4.2 FRAMEWORK CRITERIA

Based on ideas from nuclear safety (e.g. Cacciabue and Papazoglou 1996) that have been adopted and adapted in financial audit and corporate governance (e.g. COSO 1992), an effective framework provides the ability to:

- identify important risks to the firm;
- classify risks as controllable and uncontrollable;
- identify causes for controllable risks;
- assign uncontrollable risks to mitigation categories; and
- provide measured feedback on changes in risks and relate them to management actions.

The objective of operational risk management is to decide which risks are important to the firm, and then to accept, control, or mitigate them in accordance with the risk strategy of the firm. A framework enables management to identify risks, classify them, and take appropriate actions, and supports management by providing the architecture and requirements for the systems and processes needed to measure and model operational risk. Good operational risk measures provide consistent information for managing, financing, and regulating the firm. It is not unreasonable to assume that management will *choose* to exercise control over operational risk to the extent possible, and to accept or mitigate those risks that are not controllable. However, in order to identify important risks a measurement capability is needed that can provide relative measures for a wide range of earnings changes. Therefore, a framework for effective management of operational risk must provide a measure that has a defined relationship to a risk factor that can be assigned as controllable or uncontrollable. This enables management to determine an appropriate intervention for controllable risks by focusing on their causes, and to mitigate the effects of uncontrollable risks through financial measures or contingency plans. Additionally, the measure must be related to actions taken or planned so that feedback for decision support is provided.

4.3 CURRENT FRAMEWORK APPROACHES

Currently, there are several existing and proposed approaches to an operational risk framework aimed at meeting the above criteria. Four of the more noted ones are:

1. Control self-assessment
2. Process analysis

3. Loss categorisation
4. Performance analysis.

Each framework is briefly discussed and compared with the criteria, and a general set of conclusions is presented.

1. *Control self-assessment.* One of the most popular approaches to establishing a framework for operational risk uses the technique of control self-assessment. In this approach a questionnaire or series of workshops is used to identify important risks to the firm by asking the responsible parties within the firm to subjectively assess various parts of the organisation and its characteristics. Control self-assessment is generally endorsed by auditors and has been promoted by regulators as the main tool for complying with corporate governance guidelines. It has been implemented in some form by many financial firms. An example of a control self-assessment framework showing the major categories included is given in Figure 4.1.

In the control self-assessment framework, the categories correspond generally to departments or functions within the organisation. For each category, specific questions are answered to gain insight into the associated risks and their severity. The type of questions that might be included are shown in the example for control self-assessment in the operations area (Figure 4.2).

Scoring is typically a sum of the rank order value for the question (Likert scale), but the main benefit is identification of high-risk areas and the follow-up actions to reduce risks. Control self-assessments rely primarily on subjective information gathered infrequently (usually yearly). These shortcomings (as well as many problems with bias) make them difficult to use for control adjustment, management performance review, or allocation of capital. Control self-assessment is most effective at identifying important risks to the firm, but generally has difficulty satisfying the other criteria.

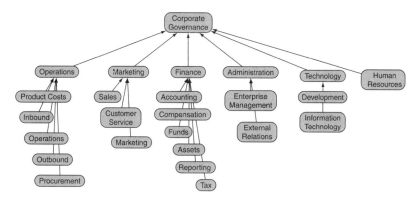

Figure 4.1   Example of control self-assessment framework for identifying and classifying risks

Control Self-Assessment

<u>Area</u>: Operations

<u>Activity</u>: Managing and Scheduling Operations

1. Does the company use standard documents to prepare and communicate sales forecasts?
      Always ☐   Mostly ☐   Usually ☐   Sometimes ☐   Never ☐

2. Are production schedules approved?
      Always ☐   Mostly ☐   Usually ☐   Sometimes ☐   Never ☐

3. Are incidences of insufficient or excessive raw materials inventory monitored and reported?
      Always ☐   Mostly ☐   Usually ☐   Sometimes ☐   Never ☐

Figure 4.2   Example questions for control self-assessment in the operations area

2. *Process analysis.* A second approach used to identify and quantify operational risk is process analysis. In this method, the operational processes of the firm are analysed at a task level in order to determine the possible risk of errors in the procedures, their execution, and in the associated controls for the process. Detailed diagrams of process tasks and controls are used to compile a list of key control points and related risks in the process. The procedures serve as guidelines for performance of the tasks and controls in the process. An example of a process diagram is shown in Figure 4.3.

Process analysis is most useful when re-engineering a process or revising its controls. It provides an overview and design for writing the associated procedures. Since it is a very detailed description of a complex process, it results in a lot of bulk for a large organisation (hundreds of diagrams with tens of tasks and controls in each). This level of detailed documentation is difficult to maintain and use effectively for risk management. Process analysis lacks good measures for quantitative feedback, and normally relies on subjective evaluation such as audit scores. It can identify, classify, and determine causes of risks associated with the processes, but it says little about risks outside the process and fails to provide objective and relevant measurement feedback for management.

3. *Loss categorisation.* A third approach to risk management is loss categorisation. In this approach, operational losses are entered into a database along with an explanation of the loss and an attribution to a category of losses. To begin a loss database, a data model for losses is needed, and there are several available (e.g. BBA 2000). Detailed analysis is required to ensure the categories can be used for risk measurement (i.e. the categories must constitute a mutually exclusive and exhaustive set of classifications for risk if the analysis is to result in a coherent measure). Ideally the categories would be organised so that all losses fit

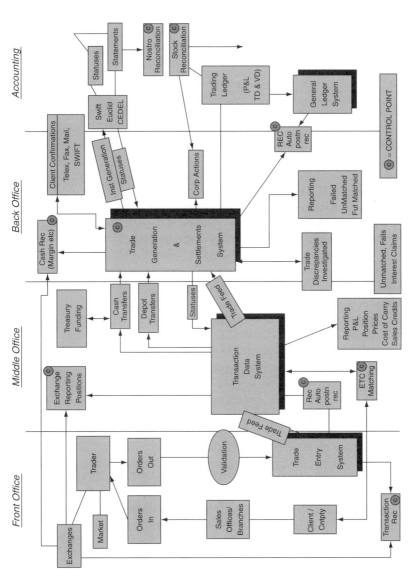

Figure 4.3 Sample process diagram for investment banking operations

Table 4.1 Example of a data model for loss categorisation

Operational risk loss categorisation (top level)
1. People
2. Physical
3. Technology
4. Process
5. External

into one and only one category and can be aggregated. However, it is often the case that categories overlap and that some losses do not fit well into any of the defined categories. An example of a data model for loss categorisation is given in Table 4.1.

It is easy to see that these categories will likely lead to overlap of losses. For instance, a common loss event such as a settlement or reconciliation consists of a person making a mistake in input that was not detected by the controlling software program and results in a loss for the process. The loss could be recorded in 'People' due to the input error, 'Technology' due to the poor control of the input, or 'Process' due to the lack of additional checks and controls to prevent loss from such a mistake. This type of overlap between categories will be pervasive in such systems. Refining the categories to a more detailed level is to invite more complex overlap within the categories and between the detail levels of categories. For instance, 'legal' could appear as a sub-category under virtually any of the higher categories in English law jurisdictions. Overlap between categories can result in 'double counting' and make allocation of risk measurement difficult at best. Many external loss databases lack the transparency needed for a complete analysis, and it is likely they suffer the same overlap problem. Without a standard (such as GAAP) to account for losses, a loss database must be used with care. Loss categorisation can provide an objective measure of feedback (the loss amount), but can only identify losses that have occurred and has difficulty with assigning them and determining causes for the reasons given.

4. *Performance analysis.* A fourth approach to developing an operational risk framework is through performance analysis. In this approach the performance measures of the businesses are used to develop associated risk measures. The reasoning is that if the performance measures reflect the cause-and-effect relation between the business activities and the earnings of the firm, then a measure of volatility for the performance measure will reflect the cause-and-effect relation between the business activities and the risk of earnings. Performance models for the firm such as the Value Chain (Porter 1985) and the Balanced Scorecard (Kaplan and Norton 1996) offer a generally accepted approach to measuring the performance of the firm through causal-based measures. The Value Chain analysis identifies the key value-adding processes in the firm (Model 1, Figure 4.4), and

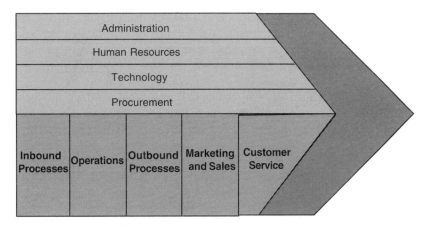

Figure 4.4 Model 1: Value-adding processes of the firm based on Porter's (1985) Value Chain showing support (top) and delivery (bottom)

Table 4.2 Model 2: Top level categories for performance measures for Balanced Scorecard (Kaplan and Norton 1996), reproduced by permission . . .

Balanced Scorecard measurement categories:

- Financial
- Customer
- Internal
- Learning and Growth

---

the Balanced Scorecard (Model 2, Table 4.2) offers the measurement categories (shown for the top level only).

These two models are used in a large number of firms and have proven successful in a variety of business types. Their use for risk measurement would provide consistency between performance and risk. However, they are focused on levels for performance drivers that create gains, not variability of risk factors that can cause losses. And because they are meant to be used collectively and not aggregated they also suffer the same problem of overlapping categories as loss models. In practice the current performance measures in financial firms may not be sufficient and this approach would require a review of performance measurement within the firm before the risk measurement could begin. For firms whose goal is risk-adjusted performance measures, the risk measurement problem is part of performance measurement. Although performance measurement is a proven method for measurement and control, it is difficult to use it as an approach for identifying risks to the firm because of the focus on gains.

In general, the following conclusion can be drawn. Although all the afore-mentioned approaches to an operational risk framework have their proponents and are useful in specific applications, none of them is able to provide an objective, relevant measure for operational risk that fulfils the criteria stated earlier. Specifically, the control self-assessment approach lacks objectivity and timeliness needed for management feedback. Process analysis does not consider uncontrollable risks, and loss categorisation does not adequately identify causes in order to provide decision support. Performance analysis begs the question by assuming that a comprehensive framework already exists, and setting the focus on levels of gains from performance drivers instead of variability from risk factors. What is needed is a framework for measuring operational risk that includes a methodology that addresses both controllable and uncontrollable risk, provides an objective measure, and links the controllable risk to causes that can serve as a basis for management intervention. Such a framework is introduced and described in the following sections, beginning with a set of basic assumptions that can be adopted as a common standard followed by definitions used in the framework description.

4.4   FRAMEWORK ASSUMPTIONS

The operational risk measurement framework introduced in this chapter is based on the following six assumptions:

Assumption 1. *Operational risk management benefits all stakeholders.*

There is general agreement in firms that operational risk management is, in principle, a good thing. The debates usually focus on the approach. However, some of the basic assumptions regarding the benefits of an effective opera-tional risk management approach should be stated. In the context of financial institutions, the following benefits are expected from effective operational risk management:

1. The individual firm's earnings are more stable, thereby increasing the value of the firm for shareholders and giving management more control over earnings volatility and performance in order to achieve the firm's goals and remain competitive.
2. The financial system is safer and less prone to severe disruption, (benefiting world economies) and depositors have more assurance that their funds remain available over very long periods (fewer institutions fail).
3. Regulators are able to spend more time on qualitative improvement of finan-cial operations (instead of capital adequacy).

Assumption 2. *In order to manage operational risk properly, a measurement system is needed that causally links operations of the firm to earnings volatility.*

Behaviour must be adjusted using specific actions that are designed to manage operational risk in order to achieve the potential benefits. Measurement is essential in developing the tools and techniques to control operational risk because it provides the feedback for determining the effectiveness of actions that are taken. Inaccurate or irrelevant measures can invoke perverse behaviour and reduce the potential benefits of operational risk management. Simple economic measures for risk that are based on assets or costs do not satisfy this requirement since the goal of risk management is not to reduce cost, but to reduce risk (i.e. earnings volatility). Although costs or assets might vary along with earnings for some firms during some periods, it may be difficult to establish a causal link between costs or assets and earnings volatility. In order to gain commitment and affect operational risk, the firm's management must have a clear understanding and evidence of the link between activities and risk measures.

Assumption 3. *An operational risk measure must be able to reflect the variability of earnings as a result of losses due to errors and omissions and control breakdowns or rare events, reflecting the two categories of (a) high frequency, low impact events that are expected and cause operating losses and (b) low frequency, high impact events that occur unexpectedly and cause extraordinary or excess losses.*

One of the difficulties posed by operational risk is the two-dimensional aspect of losses. Firms are familiar with the high frequency losses and may be able, in general, to take action to reduce them. But properly accounting for a large volume of small losses is difficult, so good loss information is generally unavailable. Low frequency, high impact losses come from control breakdowns or external events that are mostly uncontrollable for the management of the firm, and thus it is difficult for management to accept responsibility for them. Even if this problem is addressed, the rare events occur so infrequently that good loss information is also generally unavailable. Much effort has gone into trying to understand rare events and predict them, while ignoring the high frequency–low impact losses as being too small to worry about or having already been included in performance targets. Herein lies a more subtle argument regarding operational risk management: Why try to deal with something that is either too small to worry about or so infrequent as to be unpredictable?

Assumption 4. *The amount of control in a firm is reflected in the combination of controllable loss resulting from errors and omissions (generally high frequency–low impact events) and the uncontrollable loss resulting from exceptions, control breakdowns and rare events (generally low frequency–high impact events).*

This assumption implies that there is a 'normal' amount of operating loss, and that these losses are predictable and controllable. In addition, there are also excess losses over which management has little or no control. However, large impact rare events will arguably occur more often if management has implemented fewer effective controls in the firm. The categorisation of operating loss and excess loss refers to the firm's predictions for errors and omissions and control break-downs, respectively. On the one hand management might argue that they do not intend to eliminate but rather control the losses so that there is a predictable amount of loss included in the cost of doing business and reflected in perfor-mance targets. On the other hand large losses are often the result of a very large sample of very small error rates or combinations of errors. This implies that accepting a larger amount of 'normal' loss will result in a greater chance of 'rare' events.

Assumption 5. *Operating losses are the result of causal factors in the activi-ties of the value-adding processes and must be predicted using a technique that incorporates these factors into the model.*

The causes of operating losses are errors and omissions in the activities associated with value-adding processes. These losses can be predicted based on error prop-agation techniques using the Delta method where the uncertainty in the relevant factors is propagated to earnings using sensitivities. This approach is based on expected variance, the foundation of portfolio theory (Elton and Gruber 1991), and provides a basis for determining the effects of management intervention. Since operating losses have a relatively high frequency, a factor-based technique such as the Delta method is easily applied and provides good estimates.

Assumption 6. *Excess losses result from rare events or control breakdowns and are not related to causal factors for the activities of the value-adding processes. They must be analysed using an approach that combines actual internal events, external events, and near misses into plausible scenarios of extreme events.*

Large losses resulting from rare events occur infrequently (hence the term 'rare') and building models from such sparse data is difficult using traditional ap-proaches. It may also be difficult to establish relevance for known events because of changes in the environment that have occurred since the event and differences between operations for external events. Finally, the integrity of a large loss event will be questionable due to lack of disclosure, basis for attribution, and differ-ences in semantics for details such as the amount of loss, date of loss, and causes of the loss. For these reasons, information about large loss events should be used to develop clear, informative scenarios that are relevant to the firm and well understood. Given a set of plausible scenarios and their associated losses, extreme value theory (EVT) can be used to generate a probability distribution for large losses that is needed for risk measurement. EVT is well established in engineering (Castillo 1988) and has been applied to insurance (Embrechts *et al.* 1997). Since this technique deals only with the tails of distributions, it is well suited to excess loss.

4.5   FRAMEWORK DEFINITIONS

In addition, a set of basic definitions for operational risk must also exist. The definitions for the proposed operational risk measurement framework are as follows:

- *Business unit*: A unit in a firm that produces a profit and loss statement or other clear measure of performance.
- *Earnings*: A financial measure of profitability for the firm. Typical measures are net profit, profit before tax, return on equity, return on net assets, and shareholder value added.
- *Causal factor*: A factor whose value impacts earnings. A change in the causal factor will cause a change in earnings.
- *Performance driver*: A causal factor that creates a change in earnings for a change in the factor.
- *Risk factor*: A causal factor that creates a change in earnings for a change in the factor and has random uncertainty associated with it.
- *Value-adding process*: Building blocks by which a firm creates a product valuable to its customers.
- *Loss*: A negative change in earnings, or generally an adverse deviation in performance.
- *Assignable loss*: A loss that can be explained by a risk factor for a process.
- *Unassignable loss*: A loss that cannot be explained by a risk factor.
- *Controllable loss*: A loss caused by a risk factor that management has decided can be addressed.
- *Uncontrollable loss*: Either an unassignable loss or an assignable loss that management has decided will not be addressed.
- *Errors and omissions*: Deviations from standards, procedures, or planned activities.
- *Control breakdowns*: Failure of a control to be effective in limiting loss although it covers the event.
- *Loss models*: Models based on loss data. Loss models normally separate the frequency and severity of loss events and analyse each statistically (although not necessarily).
- *Causal models*: Models based on causal factors. Causal models use the relation between the factor and earnings to estimate values for earnings from values for the factors.

4.6   A FRAMEWORK FOR MEASURING OPERATIONAL RISK

A proposed framework for measuring operational risk is now introduced. The framework uses a business model and a measurement methodology to measure operational risk. The business model defines the unit of analysis and the factors for measurement and modelling. The measurement methodology provides a way of calculating the risk measures. Models link the calculations to the business in a way most useful for the firm. The proposed framework for measuring operational risk is shown in Figure 4.5, and explained in the discussion that follows. The dashed arrows represent the path for traditional earnings performance measurement that focuses on performance drivers and gains in earnings, which is not the focus of this book. Bold arrows show the path for operational risk that will be discussed, including risk factors, losses, and earnings volatility.

4.6.1   Business Model

The business model for the operational risk measurement framework uses the value-adding processes of the business unit as the unit of analysis for measuring operational risk, as shown in Figure 4.6. A firm is made up of business units that have value-adding processes. Value-adding processes are defined as the building blocks by which a firm creates a product valuable to its customers. An activity in the value-adding process employs purchased inputs, human resources, capital, and some form of technology to perform its function (Porter 1985). Since a business unit has profit and loss reporting (by definition), its value-adding processes are the key components that make up the profit and loss for the business unit. For each value-adding process an earnings figure is available which is based on the causal factors for the business. Causal factors are defined as factors whose values impact earnings. They are made up of performance drivers and risk factors. The path for traditional earnings performance measurement focuses on the performance drivers, or those factors that create gains in earnings, and the interest is in the level of earnings. But operational risk measurement deals with risk factors that result in losses for the value-adding processes, and measures the variability of earnings due to these losses. This point is so fundamental to the idea of measuring operational risk that it is stated again:

Operational risk measurement uses risk factors, which are those causal factors that create losses with a random uncertainty, to measure the variability of earnings.

This justifies the use of a business model for operational risk that focuses only on the risk factors that create losses for the value-adding processes of the business unit.

Assignable and Unassignable Loss

The business model as described above is a good start for measuring operational risk but not all losses can be tied to risk factors so the model needs to be expanded. As noted earlier, one of the difficulties posed by operational risk is the two-dimensional aspect of losses. Some losses such as control breakdowns and rare events are difficult to attribute to any change in a factor related to the value-adding process. Therefore, losses for a value-adding process are broken

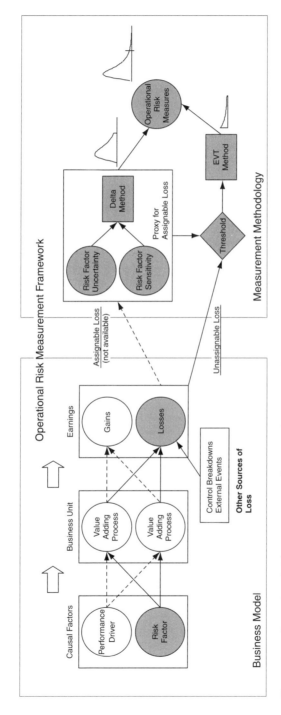

Figure 4.5 Operational risk measurement framework consists of a business model and a measurement methodology

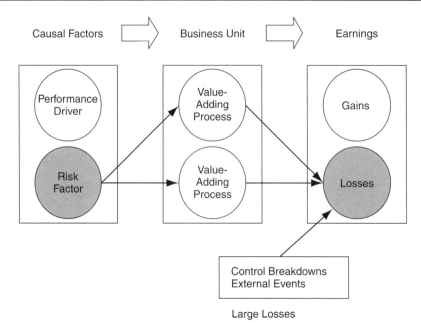

Figure 4.6   Business model for the operational risk measurement framework

down into two components—assignable and unassignable loss. Assignable loss is linked to a risk factor and a change in the risk factor is what causes the loss. An unassignable loss cannot be tied to a risk factor, either because the cause is unknown, or because it is due to an external event. It is the result of an external or uncontrollable event that affects the earnings of the value-adding process, but is not part of the causal model for it. Control breakdowns and rare events are examples of events that can create unassignable losses. Assignable losses due to risk factors are related to earnings by an earnings function. An earnings function is used because losses within a business unit are not generally accounted for in a systematic way that would allow their direct assignment to risk factors. This is noted in the operational risk measurement framework by the dashed arrow labelled 'Assignable Loss (not available)' linking losses to the measurement methodology (see Figure 4.7). (The earnings function will be described in more detail in later chapters, but for now it is enough to know that an earnings function is used to describe how the change in earnings depends on changes in the risk factor.) Unassignable losses cannot be explained by a change in a risk factor, so they do not have an earnings function. This important but subtle distinction is reflected in the business model by the addition of sources of loss not explainable by causal factors. This is shown in the lower right corner of Figure 4.6 and labelled 'Large Losses'.

4.6.2 Measurement Methodology

The measurement methodology of the operational risk framework provides a way of calculating the measures of risk for the factors defined through the business unit analysis. The measurement methodology proposed is called Delta–EVT™. Delta–EVT™ provides for measurement of both sources of loss for operational risk and satisfies the framework criteria. Delta–EVT™ involves the use of two familiar analytical techniques (the Delta method and extreme value theory), and the calculation of a threshold. Delta–EVT™ is a new approach that uses the Delta method to estimate losses from risk factors in the processes (assignable), and EVT for large losses due to control breakdowns and external events (unassignable). Threshold is used to separate losses to be analysed using the Delta method from those to be analysed using EVT. The methodology is shown in Figure 4.7.

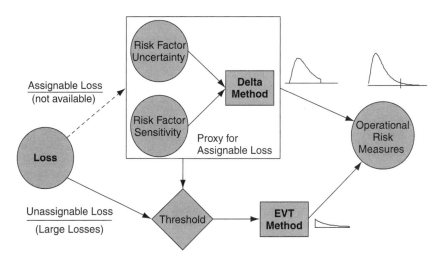

Figure 4.7 Delta–EVT™ uses risk factors as proxy for assignable loss in the Delta method and filters all losses through a threshold for applying EVT

Delta Method for Assignable Losses

In Delta–EVT™ the Delta method is used to set the maximum loss threshold that determines the classification of 'large losses' to be modelled using EVT. The Delta method uses factors that lead to loss and their sensitivities to generate loss distributions in the business unit. Losses within a business unit are not generally accounted for in a systematic way that would allow their direct assignment to risk factors. Since there are a large number of small losses, many firms simply aggregate operational losses in general accounts along with other entries. They may be included as a cost of doing business or simply buried in the profit and loss accounting. Without a loss figure that can be linked to risk factors, a direct measurement of operational risk due to assignable loss is not possible from existing business information. The Delta measurement method solves this problem. In this way, the analysis proceeds without the need to accumulate large volumes of loss information. Since the losses are generally high frequency, Delta models are able to do a good job of estimation.

EVT Method for Unassignable Losses

In Delta–EVT™, EVT is used to deal with the tails of the loss distributions and to set the minimum loss threshold that defines a minimum large loss. EVT includes a parametric model that, given a series of large losses, can be used to predict the occurrence of losses that have not yet happened (i.e. outside the data range). Low frequency, high impact losses are usually unassignable because they are due to rare events or control breakdowns that, although well described, occur infrequently and seldom repeat. This makes it difficult to measure them directly and regard them as relevant measures for decision-making using traditional techniques. A large loss due to a particular risk may occur once in several years, and a business unit that had not experienced such a large loss would have no way of measuring the risk. The EVT measurement model is used to address this problem. By coupling the historical losses and scenarios into a large loss model using EVT, the appropriate risk measurement can be estimated.

Thresholds

Threshold is used to separate losses to be analysed using Delta from those to be analysed using EVT. Generally speaking, Delta deals with small losses, EVT deals with large losses, and the threshold is the transition point from small loss to large loss. However, to make sure that all losses are covered and that there are no overlapping calculations, care must be taken to set the threshold properly. Losses assigned to risk factors using the Delta method are assumed to have random error properties and Delta is used to estimate the central tendency of this uncertainty. But losses far from the mean are not well described by Delta, and 'blunders' or rare events are not included in the loss distribution it generates. This means that some large losses, such as control breakdowns, may be assignable, but since they are usually larger than the threshold they are analysed using EVT. The maximum loss estimated by the Delta method is defined as its threshold. In a similar way EVT deals with the extreme values of loss, and its method only considers loss amounts above a minimum level defined as its threshold. Its application relies on using a set of losses that excludes 'normal' or 'expected' events. Ideally, the minimum loss estimated by EVT is the maximum loss from Delta. Setting the Delta maximum loss threshold and the EVT minimum threshold to compatible values gives the Delta–EVT™ method a threshold to use for combining the two loss distributions.

Why Delta–EVT™?

The Delta method for errors and a loss model using EVT is proposed for several reasons. First, error models using Delta are well understood and can capture the key operational risk in processes immediately using existing information on errors and performance. This provides a proactive and responsive link to the business management of the firm. Second, EVT provides a method of augmenting the Delta error models to include rare events and external shocks resulting in large losses that are characteristic of events in a firm's operations like control breakdowns and external events. Third, the two methods are complementary since Delta estimates the central tendency of the loss distribution and EVT deals with the tails of the distribution. EVT is needed for Delta in order to deal with the rare events and control breakdowns that create losses at the extremes of the Delta distributions. And Delta is needed for the EVT approach in order to set the threshold that determines the classification of 'large losses' to be modelled using EVT. Fourth, the Delta method for process measurement is an ISO (International Standards Organisation) standard and in use by virtually all major Western laboratories and government scientific bodies to measure uncertainty. EVT models for large losses are a well-known technique for analysing physical processes and accepted by many government agencies for determining maxima related to safety and health. In short, the combination of Delta with EVT is based on accepted standards and provides the needed coverage for operational risk losses that may be high frequency and low impact, or low frequency and high impact, and helps to separate these losses into controllable and uncontrollable causes.

4.7 OPERATIONAL RISK MEASURES

The results of calculations using Delta–EVT™ are operational risk measures for the business unit. The risk measures are statistics from the two loss distributions, namely operating loss and excess loss, which are combined using a specific threshold. The measures from the operating loss distribution are the basis for improving operational efficiency and avoiding loss in the business unit. The measures from the excess loss distributions are the basis for decisions on financing and regulating. Taken together, the proposed approach provides a systematic way based on consistent measures for managing, financing, and regulating the firm. Definitions for the operational risk measures and related statistics are introduced below.

- *Threshold*: The value of loss in the loss distribution that separates assignable losses (those that are less than the threshold) and unassignable losses modelled using EVT that are greater than the threshold.

- *Coverage Factor*: Multiples of the standard deviation used to determine the confidence level (assuming a normal distribution).
- *Operating Loss*: A loss from a business unit below a given threshold. This loss is part of the operating loss distribution.
- *Excess Loss*. A loss above a given threshold. This loss is part of the excess loss distribution.
- *Operating Loss Distribution*: The distribution of losses estimated for a value-adding process using the Delta method (assignable loss).
- *Excess Loss Distribution*: The distribution of losses above a threshold calculated using the EVT method (unassignable loss).
- *Overall Loss Distribution*: The combination of operating loss and excess loss distributions using a compatible threshold.
- *Maximum Operating Loss*: The value of operating loss from the operating loss distribution at a specific confidence level (e.g. 95%).
- *Maximum Excess Loss*: The value of excess loss from the maximum loss distribution at a specific confidence level (e.g. 95%).
- *Value at Risk*: The cumulative value of the operating losses at a specific confidence level (e.g. 95%) and for a specific period (e.g. one year).
- *Excess Value at Risk*: The cumulative value of the excess losses at a specific confidence level (e.g. 95%) and for a specific period (e.g. one year).

These risk measures can be used to develop a comprehensive financing and performance compensation strategy. For instance, business units could be required to set aside a provision for operating loss and capital for excess loss using amounts based on value at risk and excess value at risk. Sample loss data can also be recorded for operating and excess losses and compared with the estimates for maximum operating loss and maximum excess loss in a back testing exercise.

4.8   HOW DELTA–EVT™ SUPPORTS OPERATIONAL RISK MANAGEMENT

4.8.1   Meeting the Framework Criteria

As presented in the introduction to this chapter, an effective framework for measuring operational risk provides the ability to:

- identify important risks to the firm;
- classify risks as controllable and uncontrollable;
- identify the causes of controllable risks;
- assign uncontrollable risks to mitigation categories; and
- provide measured feedback on changes in risks and relate them to management actions.

The analysis of value-adding processes using the business model and the development of a model of large losses through historical analysis and scenarios help management to identify risks that are important to the firm. Clearly defined scenarios and value-adding processes enable management to assess whether the factor can be influenced or not, and identify potential causes. Risks that have causal factors that can be influenced and should be controlled are classified as controllable. The remaining assignable and unassignable risks can be allocated to mitigation categories using the causal factor for assignable and 'external' for the unassignable. Assignable loss provides several measures suitable for management feedback such as maximum operating loss and value at risk. Unassignable loss provides an overall financial measure for long-term strategic planning.

4.8.2 Realising the Benefits of Managing Operational Risk

As presented in Chapter 1 of this book, the benefits to managing operational risk include:

- Avoid unexpected losses
- Improve operational efficiency
- Allocate capital to business lines
- Calculate economic capital
- Satisfy stakeholders.

A framework that meets the criteria should also support the goals of operational risk management and help to realise its benefits. The proposed measurement framework supports the benefits of operational risk in the following manner:

- *Avoid unexpected loss.* The unexpected loss due to control breakdowns and rare events is measured using the EVT portion of the new Delta–EVT™ methodology in the proposed measurement framework. The framework provides a categorisation of losses and a threshold for qualifying as a control breakdown or rare event. This large loss scenario database can then be used to develop risk transfer and mitigation strategies for the uncontrollable loss.
- *Allocate capital to business lines.* Business can be allocated capital based on their operating and excess loss measures. The business unit is able to control its operating losses and thereby influence the capital allocated and mitigate (at least to some extent) the unexpected loss amount. This is analogous to the current situation of cost allocation, where controllable costs are a large part of the operation, but uncontrollable costs (e.g. overhead allocation) are also part of the business unit's burden.
- *Calculate economic capital.* Economic capital requirements can be based on the sum of the two losses measured from the Delta–EVT™ method: operating loss and excess loss. Portions of the two losses can be covered using the profit and loss for the period, provisioning, or capital, according to the

financing strategy of the firm. In the absence of good loss information, the Delta-measured losses can be factored to get an estimate for economic capital (similar to regulatory capital for market risk).

- *Improve operational efficiency.* The loss due to errors and omissions in the processes is measured as expected loss using the Delta portion of the Delta–EVT™ methodology. The framework provides an indication of the causes of the loss and its key indicators. These causes and key indicators can then be examined by management so that actions can be developed and implemented in order to reduce loss and improve efficiency.
- *Satisfy stakeholders.* Regulators and other stakeholders have implied that they are interested in promoting good operating management practice among firms and responsible financing to cover large losses using a generally accepted methodology. The Delta–EVT™ method provides a transparent model for operating management practice and its verification using losses, and both techniques are based on accepted standards (see Chapter 6 on EVT and Chapter 10 on Error Propagation for further information and references).

4.9   STEPS FOR IMPLEMENTING THE FRAMEWORK

Given the foregoing assumptions, definitions, and measurement methodology, the five basic steps for implementing the framework for measuring operational risk are:

1. Establish the business model with value-adding processes and activities, and any available (historical) large losses.
2. Determine the risk factors for the major activities in the value-adding processes and their relation to earnings (the earnings function).
3. Estimate operational losses using uncertainty of the risk factors propagated to the risk in earnings (Delta method).
4. Set the threshold of operating losses from the processes using the risk factor uncertainties and operating losses from the Delta method, and filter the large losses using the threshold.
5. Create a set of excess losses greater than the threshold using plausible scenarios based on actual historical losses, external events, and near misses and model them using extreme value theory (EVT).

Figure 4.8 shows the flow of the five basic steps. A discussion of each step within the context of finance follows.

4.9.1   Step 1: Establish the Business Model with Value-adding Processes and Activities

The goal is to provide for the measurement of the two components of operational risk (controllable and uncontrollable) in the firm and develop the corresponding

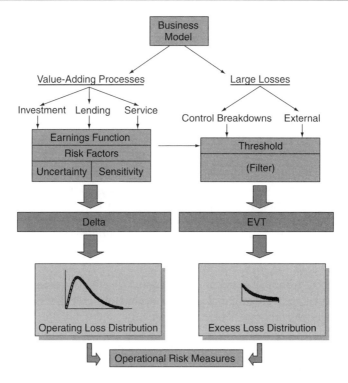

Figure 4.8 The Delta–EVT™ methodology analyses the operational risk in a business unit by separating normal operational losses in the process from large losses due to control breakdowns and external events

Table 4.3 Basic value-adding processes of the financial firm

1. **Investment**—The business unit creates earnings by buying and selling a portfolio of assets.
2. **Lending**—The business unit creates earnings by lending funds at a margin rate above the cost of funds.
3. **Service**—The business unit creates earnings by charging fees for services provided.

operating and excess loss distributions for a business unit. The analysis begins by establishing the business model of the firm with business units that include value-adding processes. These business units contribute to the earnings of the firm and their operational risk is risk to the operational income of the firm. The operational risk in each of the business units will be defined in terms of basic value-adding functions. The primary value-adding processes for a financial firm are shown in Table 4.3: The basic activities for the primary value-adding processes in a financial firm are shown in Table 4.4.

Table 4.4 Activities for the basic value-adding processes

Process	Activity
Investment	Trading, settlement, trade management
Lending	Loan origination, management, recovery
Service	Sales, delivery, customer service

4.9.2 Step 2: Determine the Risk Factors and their Earnings Function

For each of the above value-adding processes in a business unit, an earnings formula that represents earnings as a function of a set of associated factors is developed. These earnings functions include those factors that define operational risk for the business unit. In a financial firm this is reflected in the accounting for the value added by the process. Therefore, an accounting classification is natural for the risks associated with the process. The four basic categories of risk to earnings in accounting for the processes are valuation, timeliness, reconciliation, and compliance. Although sometimes considered separately, business risk can be subsumed under the valuation category of accounting risk described below (as part of the services process). These four categories are defined as follows:

1. *Valuation Risk*: Errors in the amount of the transaction (wrong amount). For instance, many transactions today are marked to the market and use a contract accounting method that defines the revenues from a transaction based on the terms of the contract and a set of market values. Models for calculating the value of a contract based on its terms and relevant market values are subject to revision and interpretation. Since they may not represent the 'true' value of the contract, there may be losses associated with errors in valuation in case of any 're-valuation'.

2. *Timeliness Risk*: Delays in processing the information (wrong time). Money has an intrinsic time value and delays in processing transactions can result in losses. The most common is a cost of carry, but market volatility can create larger losses due to delays in contract processing.

3. *Reconciliation Risk*: Errors in the account entry (wrong account). Since there are literally millions of accounts in a large financial operation, the prospect of crediting or debiting the wrong account must be considered. As with all errors, if this is not recoverable, it results in a loss. Much of it may be due to carrying cost only, and then it resembles timeliness.

4. *Compliance Risk*: Errors in the procedure used to process the transaction (wrong procedure). The contracts for financial services are subject to a number of rules and regulations, both internal and external, that govern the procedures used to originate and manage the contract. Lack of compliance with these regulations subjects the firm to unexpected variances from targets and losses such as fines and settlements.

For each accounting category an earnings function for the Delta method can be developed that reflects the corresponding factors that contribute to the risk category. For instance, model errors for securities contribute to the valuation risk, settlement failures to timeliness, and nostro breaks to reconciliation. Each of these factors has a measurable error that can be propagated to the earnings for the value-adding process based on the earnings function. An example of an earnings function that could be used to value a portfolio is given below:

$$E = \Delta V(p)$$

Investment earnings as a function of the change in portfolio value.

4.9.3 Step 3: Determine Operating Loss Distribution Using the Delta Method

Given an earnings function that relates the level of earnings to the risk factor, the Delta method uses sensitivities derived from the earnings function to propagate the uncertainty in the factor to uncertainty in earnings. The sensitivity is the change in earnings given a unit change in the risk factor. For instance, earnings may be described as 20% of sales. This means an increase of one sales dollar generates 0.2 USD in earnings and the sensitivity is 0.2. The measure used for uncertainty is the standard deviation or standard error. The formula is standard and given in Chapter 5 on Delta methodology. Given a standard error for the valuation model for a derivative and the sensitivity of earnings to the value of the derivative, the uncertainty or risk to earnings can be calculated. Such a calculation would provide a measure of operational risk due to valuation model error. The Delta method provides rules for combining uncertainties and calculating values for uncertainty of functions. Finally, a normal distribution with a mean of zero and a standard deviation as calculated by Delta for all relevant risk factors can be used as the loss distribution for the operating loss.

4.9.4 Step 4: Determine the Threshold for Operating Loss and Filter Large Losses

Assuming the operating loss has been determined using the Delta method as described above, the operating loss distribution can now be used to determine the maximum operating loss, or threshold, which is also used for the excess losses. Using a multiple of standard deviations, the maximum operating loss can be estimated for a desired confidence level (e.g. 2.33 or 99% for a normal distribution). The key questions are the unit of analysis of the loss events (i.e. whether losses are recorded for single transactions or for periods), and whether correlated losses are combined into a single event (i.e. all traded instruments are re-valued that use the same valuation model). The simplest case is transaction-based with losses not combined. This produces a loss threshold for a transaction based on the standard error calculated by the Delta method, given there is a loss. So, you may have a 2% loss rate with a 10% operating loss. Using a 2.33 standard deviation confidence interval gives a maximum operating loss of 23% relative to the earnings exposure on a transaction, given that there is a loss on the transaction. This means that any loss on a transaction over 23% of the expected earnings would be classified as an excess loss.

4.9.5   Step 5: Create Excess Loss Data Using Plausible Scenarios and Model Them Using EVT

Excess losses above the threshold are used for EVT analysis. However, it is difficult to accumulate a database of large loss events that can be used for statistical analysis. Large losses occur infrequently in any firm and an internal database of large losses would likely have few data points and thus fail to provide statistical significance. In addition, changes in the firm usually follow large losses so they are no longer relevant to existing controls. One of the alternatives is to use external data, or losses from other firms, to supplement the internal loss data. However, other firms may have very different operating environments and controls, so the relevance of external events is questionable, and some sort of scaling or other adjustment is usually required. Finally, because large losses are often shrouded in secrecy within organisations and showered with sensationalism outside it, the integrity of the data is questionable. Simple information like the size of the loss and its occurrence date are not at all clear. For instance, the Barings loss is usually cited as more than 1 billion USD on a specific day but was, in fact, a series of smaller losses that occurred over a period of more than one year (Fay 1996). Even after the collapse of Barings, actual payments and costs continued for years. Without very detailed reporting guidelines that are enforceable (e.g. GAAP standards), loss information will be plagued by such shortcomings. For these reasons, scenarios are recommended for generating extreme event databases. Scenarios can be built using models of the firm in order to make losses relevant. Since scenarios are simply plausible events, historical losses are used to generate a similar plausible event (not the actual historical event) along with its associated frequency and loss severity. Likewise, external events are internalised using scenarios, and a categorisation scheme for them is given in Chapter 7 on Delta–EVT™ Modelling.

4.10   SUMMARY

The goal of operational risk management is to decide which risks are important to the firm, and then to accept, control, or mitigate them in accordance with the risk strategy of the firm. A measurement framework enables management to identify risks, classify them, and take appropriate actions, and supports management by providing the architecture and requirements for the systems and processes needed to measure and model operational risk. Good operational risk measures provide consistent information for managing, financing, and regulating the firm. The firm's strategy should include the primary business areas, key success criteria, and a set of performance measures for them. A framework for measuring operational risk is a natural starting point for operational risk management. But it cannot be developed without a set of guiding assumptions, definitions, and methodologies embodied in a systematic approach that provides feedback and verification of the proposed risks, their level of controllability, and their impact on the firm's earnings. Initial efforts at developing a measurement framework for operational risk have not been successful given the scope and complexity of operational risk in a large organisation. Existing governance frameworks fall short of providing the required cause-and-effect relation between business activities and performance volatility. By combining process losses with rare events generated through scenarios, the proposed Delta–EVT™ methodology offers a transparent measure of risk for the business and creates a motivation to reduce process losses through improved controls and establish mitigation plans to reduce losses that could result from plausible scenarios. Delta–EVT™ provides the basic foundation needed to identify risks, determine which are controllable, allocate controllable risks to the businesses, mitigate uncontrollable risks, and provide useful quantitative feedback to management. Using a firm-wide business model and associated methodology, operational risk measurement becomes the key to linking business strategies to the business activities of the firm.

4.11 FURTHER READING

There are to date few books on operational risk. Frameworks for corporate governance control self-assessment are described in the reference documents in the earlier chapter on regulation. A good introduction to business process engineering is Champy and Hammer (1995), and Weiss (1993) provides a description of the processing for investment banking.

5
The Delta Methodology

5.1 INTRODUCTION

The Delta methodology is the calculation technique for determining the value for the assignable losses in the firm. Delta is based on error propagation, an international standard technique for measuring uncertainty due to errors and omissions. The Delta method uses *risk factors* to measure operational risk. The *uncertainty* of the risk factors is used to calculate the uncertainty in earnings using *sensitivities*, the relation of the change in earnings to a change in the risk factor. The Delta method is well established in many fields, including widespread use in financial firms where Delta–normal and Delta–gamma are two popular market risk methodologies based on the Delta method (Wilson 1996).

Delta has several important advantages as an operational risk measurement methodology. First, it enables losses to be predicted even though there is no comprehensive loss data from experience. This is important in the case where loss data have not been recorded specifically for operational losses, or where the process is new or has changed significantly. Second, it provides a clear link to business activities through sensitivities. This means it can model results from potential actions and is responsive to immediate changes in process activities. Finally, the Delta method can be validated using samples and exceptions from actual loss experience compared with the model predictions.

This chapter is mathematically oriented, making extensive use of equations and formulae. However, by taking care to work through the notation and following the examples closely it should be easily accessible to those with a basic maths background. It begins by explaining the key concepts of the Delta method, followed by a discussion of some advantages of using the Delta method, along with its limitations. Then an outline and explanation of the steps for its implementation to calculate a measure for operational risk is given. Next, detailed examples of Delta calculations for the three financial processes of investment, lending, and service are presented, and the chapter concludes with a summary of the main points.

5.2 KEY CONCEPTS OF THE DELTA METHOD

Operational risk is measured as the uncertainty in earnings due to two parts. First using the uncertainty in causal factors for losses up to a threshold and second using a large loss model for unassignable loss above a threshold. Introduced in this book, this combination of methodologies is called Delta–EVT™ and is described by the operational risk formula as follows:

$$u(E) = fu(\Delta X_1) \ldots u(\Delta X_n)) + \Phi(L_{\text{unassignable}} | L_{\text{unassignable}} > \mu)$$

Uncertainty in earnings due to operational risk is a function of the uncertainties in a set of risk factors plus a function of the distribution of unassignable losses larger than a given threshold. Note that in this chapter uncertainty in measured values is denoted by $u(\cdot)$ following the ISO standard notation, and therefore the threshold for loss has been changed to μ.

The Delta method is used to calculate the first term in the Delta–EVT™ operational risk model. This model expresses the uncertainty in earnings as a function of the uncertainty in a set of risk factors:

$$u(E) = f(u(\Delta X_1) \ldots u(\Delta X_n))$$

Delta portion of Delta–EVT™: the Delta method calculates the first term,
which is a function of the changes in several risk factors.

The Delta method for measuring operational risk is based on five key concepts that are described below. More detailed background on these ideas is available in Chapter 10 on error propagation and in the references. The key concepts are:

1. ***Earnings as a function of causal factors***. In the Delta method it is assumed that earnings are described by a series of causal factors. For a given earnings level, there is a set of causal factors whose values are used to estimate earnings:

   earnings = f(causal factors)

   Earnings described as a function of a set of causal factors.

   For example, earnings may be calculated as 20% of sales revenue minus an adjustment for rejects. By separating the causal factors into constants and volatilities, earnings can be described by a set of performance drivers that create the expected level of earnings and a set of risk factors that create volatility in the level of earnings (risk):

   earnings = f(performance drivers) $\pm$ f(risk factors)

   Earnings described as a function of
   performance drivers for level and risk factors for volatility.

   Therefore in the model earnings is calculated as 20% of sales revenue minus the variance to target cost for rejects. 'Sales revenue' is the performance driver and 'rejects' is the risk.

2. ***The risk in earnings is a random fluctuation in value caused by the uncertainty in the risk factors.*** If earnings is a function of risk factors, then the uncertainty in earnings is a function of the uncertainty in the risk factors. Given

$$E = f(x)$$

then

$$u(E) \approx f(u(x))$$

3. ***The basic measure of uncertainty for operational risk is the standard deviation of the mean, or standard error.*** In general, for any measure the standard deviation of the mean of the measured values is referred to as the standard error or simply error (ISO Guide 1993). It is calculated from a sample of n measures using the following formula:

$$\sigma_{\bar{x}} = \sqrt{\frac{1}{n(n-1)} \sum_{k=1}^{n} (x_k - \bar{x})^2}$$

where $\bar{x}$ is the mean of the measures. Note that this measure is different from the standard deviation of the measures. In fact it is related to it by the simple formula:

$$\sigma_{\bar{x}} = \frac{\sigma_x}{\sqrt{n}}$$

4. ***Uncertainties are combined using the formula for the expected value of the sum of variances.*** This formula is given for the simple case of correlation values of only 0 or 1, corresponding to independent measures and measures that are perfectly correlated. Normally this should be sufficient for operational risk measures. The complete formula can be found in the chapter on error propagation.

$$\sigma_z^2 = \sum_i \sigma_i^2 + \left(\sum_j \sigma_j \right)^2$$

Formula for combining uncertainties using standard errors where the i's are uncorrelated and the j's are correlated (perfectly) measures.

5. ***Uncertainties for functions of uncertainty measures are calculated using the law of error propagation.*** For each risk factor the sensitivity of the earnings with respect to the factor is needed. The sensitivity is the amount of change in earnings given a single unit change in the factor with everything else remaining unchanged, or the partial derivative of the earnings function with respect to the factor. Given the earnings function that expresses earnings as a function of a factor

$$E = f(x)$$

then sensitivity is defined as

$$\frac{\Delta E}{\Delta x} = \frac{\partial f}{\partial x}$$

and the formula for the uncertainty of the function of the factor is

$$u^2(E) = \sum_{i=1}^{n} \left(\frac{\partial f}{\partial x_i}\right)^2 u^2(x_i)$$

The sensitivity of earnings for a risk factor is defined as the change in earnings per unit change in the factor (with all else held constant). This is the partial derivative of the earnings function with respect to the risk factor and is used to calculate the uncertainty of a function of an uncertainty measure.

So, for the sales revenue example given earlier, the sensitivity is 0.2 since a unit change in sales revenue results in a 0.2 change in earnings. The function is usually expressed using a Taylor expansion and only the first term of the expansion is used for the sensitivity.

5.3 THE DELTA METHOD IMPLEMENTATION STEPS

The basic steps for implementing the Delta method to calculate a measure for operational risk are as follows:

1. Identify the major risk factors for earnings and their associated standard errors.
2. Determine the earnings function that relates each factor to earnings and sensitivity of earnings to the factor.
3. Calculate and combine the uncertainty measures for operational risk.

The following sections explain these steps.

5.3.1 Identifying Risk Factors and their Errors

First, we identify the factor and (possibly) partitioning. We begin by building a model that includes a factor that has a significant influence on earnings. This is shown in Figure 5.1.

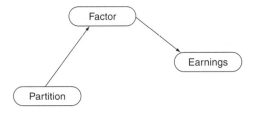

Figure 5.1   Generic factor model for earnings volatility shown with partitioning

The factor volatility may depend primarily on one of the characteristics associated with the factor. For instance, model errors are dependent on the type of instrument being valued. The risk factor errors are partitioned into several instrument groups in order to account for the differences in errors between them. A partition is a probability set that is complete and has no overlap. The sensitivity of the partition is simply the fraction of the partition for the factor. For a portfolio, the partition is simply the fraction of the portfolio that an individual asset occupies. Market risk uses this partitioning to calculate the risk in the portfolio (Elton and Gruber 1991, p. 29). The error in operational risk is an identical measure and its formula is given by

$$E[\sigma^2] = \sum_i X_i^2 \sigma_i^2$$

Formula for calculating expected variance $E[\sigma^2]$ from a partition of contributing factors X_i and their corresponding variances (ignoring correlated terms).

For operational risk the contributing factors will normally form a partition as a probability distribution on transactions or operating characteristics instead of a fraction of portfolio composition. They are usually either independent (totally uncorrelated) or perfectly correlated (correlation $= 1$) so that a simplified treatment of correlated terms is possible (see Chapter 10 on Error Propagation).

The errors shown in Figure 5.2 are relative errors, so 0.001 is the standard error relative to the exposure for an instrument. The numbers in the boxes are · the percentages for each value of *instrument type* and *model error*. Uncertainty measures in the form of standard errors of the measurement (relative errors) for risk factors will come from direct measurement or studies. For instance, the historical error in volume may be measured as the standard deviation of the

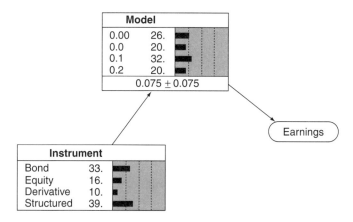

Figure 5.2 Model error factor shown with link to earnings and partitioned by instrument type

volume for several periods. Often the value of the standard error will be expressed as a percentage of the expected value or 'true' value. In addition to the measured values, there are also standards or calibration values that describe errors for risk factors. For instance, the model error for a derivative valuation model is typically expressed as a percentage error of the 'true' value at one standard deviation. So a figure of 1.4% means that the value given by the model is within 1.4% of the 'true' value 67% of the time (one standard deviation in a normal distribution).

5.3.2 Determining Earnings Functions and Sensitivity

Given an error for the risk factor, this error must be propagated to the earnings. An earnings function relates the risk factor to earnings, and the change in earnings given a change in the risk factor is calculated using this earnings function. Mathematically, we are looking for the value of $\partial f / \partial x_i$ in order to be able to describe the function for the uncertainty in the earnings for each of the factors. For a simple formula, the partial derivative is easy to see. For instance, given an earnings function for volatility in price as

$$E = (p - c)v$$

the partial derivative for volume is simply $(p - c)$. That is, for a unit change in volume, the earnings will change by the difference between the price and the cost. More complex formulae or algorithms may require a Taylor expansion or finite differencing to be performed in order to calculate the sensitivity. The Taylor approximation is

$$f(x) = f(x_0) + \left(\frac{\partial f}{\partial x}\right)(x - x_0) + \frac{1}{2!}\left(\frac{\partial^2 f}{\partial x^2}\right)(x - x_0)^2 +$$

$$\cdots + \frac{1}{k!}\left(\frac{\partial^k f}{\partial x^k}\right)(x - x_0)^k$$

Taylor approximation for the function $f(x)$ evaluated about the point x_0.

In its simplest form the sensitivity is just the difference in the valuations of the earnings function for various (small) changes in values of the risk factor about any given level of earnings. For the Delta method, this difference must be expressed in a linear combination of terms (hence the use of the Taylor approximation).

5.3.3 Calculating and Combining Uncertainty Measures

Given a set of risk factors, their associated errors, and their relation to earnings, the process of calculating their effect on earnings can be done using the following basic rules:

1. To calculate measured volatility using a sample of values, use the following formula (where $\bar{x}$ is the mean of x) (errors can also be estimated from studies or benchmarks where this calculation has already been done for the study or benchmark sample):

$$\sigma_{\bar{x}} = \sqrt{\frac{1}{n(n-1)} \sum_{i=1}^{n} (x_i - \bar{x})^2}$$

2. To calculate the error for a function of a factor, use the first term of the Taylor expansion for the earnings function as the sensitivity ($\partial f / \partial x$), and multiply by the error of the factor. Given $E = f(x)$, then

$$\sigma_E^2 = \left(\frac{\partial f}{\partial x} \right)^2 \sigma_x^2$$

3. To calculate the error for a factor that is partitioned, use the fraction of the ith partition X_i as the sensitivity along with the error for the partition as shown in the following formula:

$$E[\sigma^2] = \sum_i X_i^2 \sigma_i^2$$

4. To combine errors, group them according to their correlation (zero or one) and combine using the following formula (where the i's are uncorrelated and the j's are correlated):

$$\sigma_z^2 = \sum_i \sigma_i^2 + \left(\sum_j \sigma_j \right)^2$$

Standard errors should normally be expressed in relative terms (simply divide by the expected value or mean of the measures). This makes them unit-less and allows comparison of uncertainty between processes. Since the relative errors are typically small, they are usually converted to a percentage. Thus an error of 10% is a relative error expressing the standard deviation about the mean as 10% relative to the mean's value. To convert the relative errors to absolute amounts, simply multiply by the expected value.

5.4 CALCULATING THE THRESHOLD

As stated earlier, the Delta–EVT™ loss threshold is the value for combining the two loss distributions. It defines the intersection between operating losses and excess losses and helps determine the measures of risk that are the outputs of the methodology. The threshold is the single event loss amount that separates operating loss from excess loss, and sets the maximum loss amount for operating loss and the minimum loss amount to be included in the data set for historical excess losses. The threshold also has a large influence on the EVT methodology calculation of the excess loss distribution. In practice, there is usually a threshold for large loss that requires detailed accounting and explanation of losses over the threshold. The Delta–EVT™ threshold sets an objective level and justification for the threshold amount.

5.4.1 The Threshold Concept

Normally, the threshold will be set at a multiple of the standard error for the value-adding function of the process, defined as the coverage factor. For instance, a coverage factor of 3 provides a 99% confidence level on a normal distribution for operating losses. Given a standard error of 1%, the threshold error would be 3%, and any loss above 3% relative to the amount of the transaction would be classified as an excess loss. Often excess loss thresholds in absolute amounts are needed, and in this case a weighted average of the transaction amounts can be used. Since the standard errors are relative to the size of the transaction (or other exposure), this leads to a threshold amount that allows larger errors on smaller transactions (relative to the transaction amount). Such a practice is consistent with more advanced practices in some banking operations, where large transactions have more controls than smaller ones.

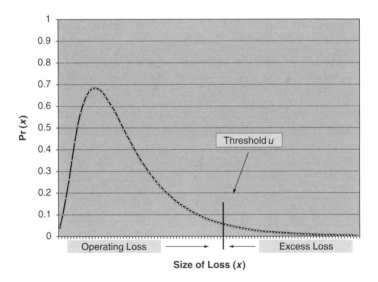

Figure 5.3 Loss event probabilities for operational risk losses. This graph shows the relation between individual losses and their probabilities. Losses below the threshold occur with a probability centred around a mean and generally resemble a Gaussian distribution. Losses above the threshold occur with a low probability, but a probability that is higher than expected by a Gaussian distribution (fat tail)

Having classified the individual large losses as excess losses, the cumulative loss distributions can be calculated using the Delta method for operating loss and EVT for excess losses as shown in Figure 5.3. Graphs of two typical cumulative loss distributions are shown in Figures 5.4 and 5.5. The threshold amount for the cumulative distribution is the coverage factor (in this case 3), and provides the

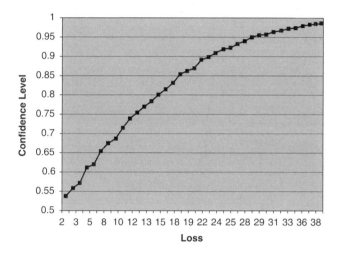

Figure 5.4   Cumulative losses calculated using the Delta method are shown in the operating loss distribution

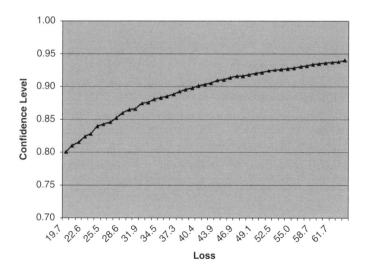

Figure 5.5   Cumulative excess losses are shown using the EVT method in the excess loss distribution. The confidence levels are expanded to show the wide variation between losses at higher confidence levels

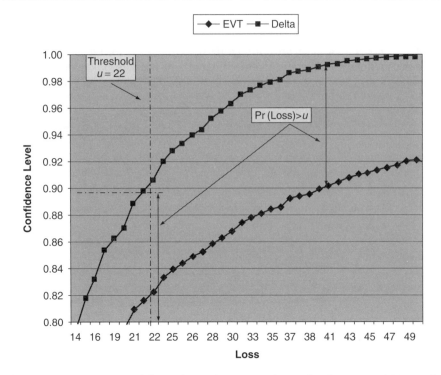

Figure 5.6 Comparison of the Delta and EVT cumulative distributions at high confidence intervals shows the difference in the amount of loss at a specific confidence level. The EVT method loss increases at a much slower rate than the Delta at high confidence levels

confidence level for the operating loss distribution. However, above this value, the excess loss distribution as calculated using the EVT methodology provides the higher confidence level needed for the large losses.

A comparison of the large losses as calculated using the EVT methodology above a coverage factor of $k = 2$ (95%) shows a more gradual increase in the confidence level for large losses using the EVT. The two distributions are shown together in Figure 5.6. Note that the Delta and EVT cumulative loss distributions converge at the threshold.

5.5 ADVANTAGES OF THE DELTA METHOD

Using the Delta method to estimate operational risk has many advantages. Some of the more important ones are as follows. First, it is a reflection of 'potential' loss and not based solely on actual loss figures. This is important because many losses may not be recorded as such, and building models on data that is incomplete is questionable at best. The second important advantage is that models reflect the quality of the operations in the firm. Thus, a firm with a better model for valuing swaps would have a lower calculation of operational risk. Third, since the error rates are relative errors based on exposures, the models are related to the size of the firm's business. Fourth, error information such as model errors is readily available (e.g. Howard and Byers 1997) and there is a good basis of public information and background on the accuracy of models such as those used for valuation and credit scoring (CMRA and Meridien Research 2000; Altman *et al.* 1994). Finally, the Delta method is well known in other fields and has been standardised by an international standards committee (ISO Guide 1993). In summary, some important advantages of using the Delta method for estimating operational risk include:

- Reflects potential loss
- Varies with quality of operation
- Varies with size of operation
- Data is readily available
- Technique is international standard

The main limitation of the Delta method is that it can only be used for assignable risk in operational processes and is not applicable to control break-downs and rare events, which is why Delta and EVT have been combined to form a complete methodology for operational risk measurement. Addressing these risks using EVT is discussed in a subsequent chapter. The assumptions of normality and symmetry of loss can be relaxed by adapting the method for use with discrete distributions and functions linked to simulation. Examples of some of these techniques are given in the modelling chapters. It should be noted, however, that many of the limitations of Delta–normal for market risk do not apply to operational risk. The error analysis techniques suggested by Markowitz (1959) were, and still are a valid approach for error analysis such as applied to operational risk.

5.6 DETAILED EXAMPLES OF THE DELTA METHOD

A series of detailed examples of calculating uncertainty using the Delta method follow. A financial firm is used, with risk categories calculated on the value-adding processes of investment, lending, and service. For each process, both the model and the calculations are discussed. The required measures are:

$$\sigma_{\text{or}}^2 = \sigma_{\text{i}}^2 + \sigma_{\ell}^2 + \sigma_{\text{s}}^2$$

Partitioning of operational risk into risk categories of investment, lending, and service.

The value-adding functions for each of the risk categories are written so that the sensitivities can be calculated. Simple functions are used here and, of course, more complex forms are possible. The basic form for calculations is risk as a function of exposure, volatility of risk factors, and sensitivity.

5.6.1 Investment Process

The Model

For investment, the sub-categories of risk are divided into volume variation, valuation error, and carrying costs (interest due to settlement failure, borrowing costs, and reconciliation breaks). These sub-categories are shown in the following formula:

$$\sigma_i^2 = \sigma_{val}^2 + \sigma_{vol}^2 + \sigma_{cc}^2$$

To determine the value-adding functions, assume earnings is a function of the value of the portfolio at time t and $t + 1$. The portfolio value is simply a function of the exposure, market values, and model used to estimate the value for each instrument. This is shown as:

$$E_p = V_t - V_{t-1} = \Delta V$$

$$V = \sum_k f(Exposure_k, MarketValues, Model_k)$$

where the subscript k refers to the instrument group in the portfolio. Using this functional form, each factor will be examined for its volatility and earnings sensitivity. The volatility of *MarketValues* is not considered because market risk is not included in the operational risk measure. This leaves the volatility of exposure and model (error), plus any correlation terms.

Assuming the model error is correlated with exposure error since model errors are related to nominal amounts (larger variation in exposures results in larger model errors), the earnings volatility equation for valuation can be written as follows:

$$\sigma_{val}^2 = (\sigma_E + \sigma_M)^2$$

Earnings volatility equation for investment valuation with contributions
from exposure and model that are perfectly correlated.

The next level of detail in the error model is built by examining each of the terms in the above equation.

5.6.2 Volume

Exposure is a function of volume and nominal amounts, so the exposure error will be simply the volatility of the volume and its sensitivity is the nominal amount multiplied by the return. The equations are given as:

$$E = VNR$$

$$\frac{\partial E}{\partial V} = NR$$

$$\Delta E = \sigma_v^2 \left(\frac{\partial E}{\partial V} \right)^2$$

$$\sigma_E^2 = \sigma_v^2 N^2 R^2$$

where

E = earnings,
V = volume,
N = nominal amount,
R = return on nominal (margin).

Earnings is a function of volume, nominal amount, and return. Each can have a volatility, but in the example only the volume volatility is used. Assuming the nominal amount N is not a single number, but a distribution of nominal amounts, the final error is a sum over the partition on N:

$$\sigma_E^2 = \sum_k \sigma_{v,k}^2 N_k^2 R^2 X_n^2$$

Error formula for volume volatility contribution to earnings volatility.

The nominal amounts are not normally distributed, so a discrete distribution is used with the fraction of the partition X used as the sensitivity. For the values of N, a histogram of nominal values and the midpoint of each histogram bar can be used. Likewise, if returns depend on products, then a partition of returns on products is also used as follows:

$$\sigma_{E,v}^2 = \sum_p \sum_k \sigma_{v,k,p}^2 N_{k,p}^2 R_p^2 X_{p,k}^2$$

Error formula for volume volatility contribution to earnings volatility
with product-dependent returns.

This implies that the volatility of volume depends on the partitioning along the nominal amounts (k subscript) and on the product partitioned along the products (p subscript). This model first partitions the transactions into buckets for nominal amounts and then into products. It propagates the relative volatility of volume to the volatility of earnings using exposure and a return. The fraction of the product and volume is denoted by X using both subscripts.

Volume Calculations

Assume the standard errors for volume by product as shown in Table 5.1. The calculation of earnings risk due to volume proceeds as follows:

$$\sigma_E^2 = \sum_k \sigma_{v,k}^2 N_k^2 R^2 X_n^2$$

Table 5.1 Table of standard errors for volume and return by product

Instrument	Value in USD	Volume error (%)	Return error (%)	Fraction
XY bond	5 000 000	2.0	10	0.27
Z bond	10 000 000	5.0	15	0.57
Widget stock	2 000 000	20.0	20	0.11
Preferred customer X	1 000 000	20.0	30	0.06
	18 000 000			1.00

$$\sigma_E^2 = ((0.02 + 0.10) * 5\,000\,000)^2 + ((0.05 + 0.15) * 10\,000\,000)^2$$
$$+ ((0.2 + 0.2) * 2\,000\,000)^2 + (0.2 + 0.3) * 1\,000\,000)^2$$
$$= 5.25 * 10^{12}$$
$$\sigma_E = 2\,291\,288$$

This represents 12.7% based on the portfolio value of 18 million USD. Likewise, the model errors are based on the nominal amount and volume to get exposure. The model error is a relative error on exposure, and since it is not related to volume, only the product partition is needed.

$$\sigma_M^2 = \sum_p \sigma_{m,p}^2 N_p^2 V_p^2$$

Error formula for model error contribution to earnings volatility.

Note that the preceding formulae propagate the relative errors of volume and models to the absolute error in earnings because the exposure figures are included as sensitivities. The relative error for earnings is simply the absolute errors divided by the exposure.

Valuation

The simplified example provided below will demonstrate the calculation of operational risk due to valuation in an investment operation. Table 5.2 includes the standard errors (relative) for traded products. The composition for one day of trading is given in Table 5.3.

Table 5.2 Given model errors for product type

Trade product type	Valuation standard error (%)
Fixed income	0.1
Equity	1.0
Illiquid	10.0
Structured	20.0

Table 5.3 One day's trading activity

Instrument	Model	Value in USD	Fraction
XY bond	Fixed income	5 000 000	0.27
Z bond	Fixed income	10 000 000	0.57
Widget stock	Equity	2 000 000	0.11
Preferred customer X	Structured product	1 000 000	0.06
		18 000 000	1.00

For the trading operation the valuation of the trade is considered using the following error model:

$$V_i = \bar{v}_i + e_i$$

Basic error model for trade transaction.

The value of the trade is given by the estimated value plus an error term. Thus, for a 20 million dollar bond we have a standard error of 0.1%, or 20 000 dollars. This means that the 'true' value lies between 20 020 000 and 19 980 000 with a 67% confidence level (two standard deviations, as the standard error is defined). For a portfolio of trades, the Delta method is applied. First, assume that all transactions using the same model are completely correlated and there is no correlation between trades valued with different models. Using the error formula given previously, we have:

$$\sigma_z^2 = \sum_i \sigma_i^2 + \left(\sum_j \sigma_j \right)^2$$

where the i subscripts are for uncorrelated errors and the j subscripts are for correlated errors. The subscript m for model and t for the transactions are used to give:

$$\sigma_p^2 = \sum_m \left(\sum_t \sigma_{t,m} \right)^2$$

For a given portfolio p, we sum over all models the errors for the transactions used for each model, and the portfolio error is given by the following formula:

$$\sigma_p^2 = (0.01 * 2\,000\,000)^2 + (0.2 * 1\,000\,000)^2$$

$$+ ((0.001 * 5\,000\,000 + 0.001 * 10\,000\,000))^2$$

$$\sigma_p^2 = 40\,625\,000\,000$$

$$\sigma_p = 201\,556 \text{ USD}$$

Operating risk due to valuation for sample portfolio.

Using three standard deviations (assuming a 99.9% confidence interval on a normal distribution) for an economic capital figure to cover model errors in the portfolio would yield 604 668 USD, or about 3.3% of the total portfolio as a figure for economic capital for operating risk due to valuation errors. Obviously other factors for the number of standard deviations could be chosen as is common with market risk economic capital calculations. However, the three standard deviations figure does not include the unexpected or excess losses due to control breakdowns and blunders since they lie outside three standard deviations. As presented in the previous chapter on the measurement framework for operational risk, unexpected or excess losses such as rare events or control breakdowns are not related to causal factors for value-adding processes. These therefore must be analysed using techniques such as EVT, and the error contribution calculated in order to determine the threshold for large losses. To determine the errors to be included in the EVT analysis, the threshold for the valuation error is set to a coverage factor $k = 2.33$ standard deviations, giving a 99% probability that the error did not come from the valuation error model described. This threshold could be for all traded products (2.6%), or it could be set for each product by multiplying the standard error for the product by the coverage factor. This idea is covered in the next chapter on EVT methodology.

Carrying Costs

The final errors for the investment process to be considered are the 'cost of carry' losses associated with settlement failure, borrowing (in order to avoid failure to deliver), and reconciliation breaks. These errors are all interest rate dependent and require a time distribution for the calculation of carrying cost. The general form is:

$$\sigma_{E,S}^2 = \sum_{i=1,n} \{\Pr(d = i | d > 0) E_T(e^{r*d} - 1)\}^2 \sigma_{(d>0)}^2$$

where

d	is the number of days delay (past due date),
$d > 0$	is a fail,
$\Pr(d|d > 0)$	is the probability of delay for d days, given a delay,
r	is the daily interest rate,
$\sigma_{d>0}^2$	is the volatility of delay, given a fail,
E_T	is the total exposure of delayed transactions.

The first summation is over the products that provide the partitioning for exposure. $\Pr(d > 0)$ is simply the probability of a settlement failure, borrow, or reconciliation break. Its volatility is propagated to the earnings volatility using the exposure and a cost of carry calculation. The total exposure is distributed across delay days using the summation. This summation is a partition over days using the probability that the delay $d = i$, given that there is a delay. Finally,

Table 5.4 Ageing report for calculation of operational risk due to cost of carry

Value in USD	Days delay	Fraction
10 000 000	1	0.5
6 000 000	2	0.3
3 000 000	3	0.15
1 000 000	4	0.05
20 000 000		1.00

the carry cost is included in the last factor for an interest rate over the number of days delay d. This general form can be used for settlement, borrowing cost, and reconciliation breaks by substituting the appropriate probabilities. Given the ageing report shown in Table 5.4, a 3.5% failure rate (not used) with a standard error of 40% and a 6% cost of carry, the calculations are shown below:

$$\sigma_{E,S}^2 = \sum_{i=1,n} \{\Pr(d = i | d > 0) E_i (e^{r*d} - 1)\}^2 \sigma_{(d>0)}^2$$

$$= (0.5 * 20\,000\,000 * (e^{0.06*1/360} - 1))^2 (0.4)^2$$

$$+ (0.3 * 20\,000\,000 * (e^{0.06*2/360} - 1))^2 (0.4)^2$$

$$+ (0.15 * 20\,000\,000 * (e^{0.06*3/360} - 1))^2 (0.4)^2$$

$$+ (0.05 * 20\,000\,000 * (e^{0.06*4/360} - 1))^2 (0.4)^2$$

$$= 1\,515\,041 \text{ USD}$$

$$\sigma_{E,S} = 1\,231 \text{ USD}$$

The settlement failure rate expected value of 3.5% is not used because it does not contribute to the variability of the earnings. The 3.5% expected value of the settlement failure can be used to calculate an expected cost for the profit and loss, but only its variability has impact on the operational risk. As before, other partitions could be used (or no partition at all if there is homogeneity throughout the business). The sensitivity of earnings to the volatility of delay is not linear since the interest rate calculation is made on the number of days. For this reason partitioning over days and weighting according to the probabilities is necessary.

5.6.3 Lending

Most banks use a statistical model to estimate the quality of a loan agreement. There are usually two parts to this rating, namely the counterparty quality rating and the facility (or instrument) quality rating. The counterparty rating is based on the ability of the counterparty to service the loan over the period, and depends upon financial factors, key ratios, and other key indicators such as management quality. The facility quality depends on characteristics like the level of subordination, collateral, and guarantees associated with the specific agreement. The credit risk associated with the loan is estimated as the probability of default and the loss given default (LGD). This is based on the difference between the outstanding value of the loan and the collateral or guarantee discounted by a recovery rate.

Analysing the errors in the process, there are two contributing risk factors to the default probability estimate, namely default model errors and credit assessment errors (shown in Figure 5.7.). Likewise, for the loss given default, the collateral valuation error and other recovery errors are contributing risk factors.

Using Figure 5.7, the simplified example of Delta calculation for credit risk is a two part formula using the assessment errors and recovery errors (assume the default model errors are small). The following formula is given:

$$\sigma_L^2 = (\Pr(q_r < q)OV_q\delta_{q-1,q})^2 + (\Pr(D_q)OV_q\sigma_{r,c})^2$$

Formula for computing the variance of loss for an individual loan based on credit quality classification error and recovery rate error.

where

q is the partition using credit quality,
$\Pr(q_r < q)$ is the probability of misclassifying the credit,
OV is the outstanding value of the loan (adjusted for recovery),
δ is the difference in default rate between quality classes,
c is the partition using collateral type,
$\Pr(D_q)$ is the probability of default for credit quality q,
$\sigma_{r,c}$ is the error in the recovery rate for the collateral type c.

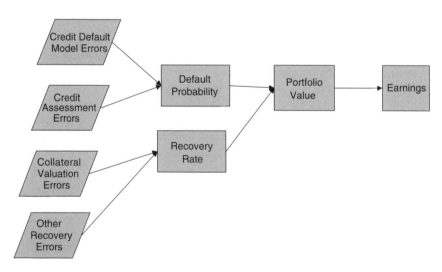

Figure 5.7 Credit process for loans showing contributions to variations in key performance measurements. Delta (Δ) represents the propagated errors

Using the above formula the error in loss given the default is calculated using the outstanding value of the loan times the error in rating classification for the rating, multiplied by the valuation error for the difference between the default rates of the rating for the loan and a rating of one classification step lower, plus the collateral value times the error for the collateral.

Calculation

For the error in assessment, assume that the rating model can correctly classify counterparties 80% of the time, and that the remaining 20% have an error of one rating classification out of ten (at some high confidence level, say 99%). This means that a loan has a 0.2 probability of being misclassified, and given that a counterparty is classified incorrectly, 99% of them are within one class away from their 'true' classification. The recovery standard error is assumed to be zero for cash, 20% for real estate, and 30% for all other assets used for collateral. For the example assume that the rating classification error is the same for all ratings (20%), and the quality rating serves as the partition. The information given in Tables 5.5 and 5.6, including rating valuation premiums, default probabilities and collateral valuation errors, is supplied for the example.

Assume the credit portfolio shown in Table 5.7 is at hand, and you want to compute the operational risk due to lending for this portfolio. The error contribution is the variance calculated for each instrument using the quality partition in the portfolio. For the total portfolio and using the preceding formula, the

Table 5.5 Default rates for loans by credit quality (example data)

Credit risk rating	Default rate (%)
AAA	0.9
AA	1.0
A	1.1
BBB	1.8
BB	4.0
B	7.0
CCC	10.0

Table 5.6 Example of collateral valuation error

Collateral type	Recovery rate (%)	Standard error (%)
Cash	100	1
Real estate	70	20
Other	40	30

Table 5.7 Lending portfolio for example calculations

Counterparty rating	Loan amount	Collateral type	Collateral amount
A	5 000 000	None	0
A	10 000 000	Real estate	8 000 000
BBB	1 000 000	Real estate	800 000
BB	5 000 000	Real estate	5 000 000
Total	21 000 000		13 800 000

calculations proceed as follows:

$$\sigma_L^2 = \left[\sum_i (OV_i * \sigma_r * \delta_{r-1,r} * (1 - R_r)^2 + \left(\sum_c \Pr(D_i)C_{i,c} * \sigma_c * R_c\right)^2\right]$$

$$\sigma_L^2 = (15\,000\,000 * 0.2 * 0.007 * 0.3)^2 + (1\,000\,000 * 0.2 * 0.022 * 0.3)^2$$

$$+ (5\,000\,000 * 0.2 * 0.03 * 0.3)^2 + [8\,000\,000\,(0.011)\,(0.2)\,(0.7)$$

$$+ 800\,000\,(0.018)\,(0.2)\,(0.7) + 5\,000\,000\,(0.04)\,(0.2)\,(0.7)]^2$$

$\sigma_L = 53\,401$ or about 0.3% of the total outstanding loan value.

Credit risk calculations normally include the tenure of loans as a partitioning because the attributes (such as default rate and exposure) vary with the time expired from the loan's origination. This (and other) improvements may be needed for the implementation of large and diverse portfolios, but the above calculation can provide important initial insight into the possible exposure of operational risk in a lending operation.

5.6.4 Service Process

Model

Suppose you are interested in the volatility of earnings due to changes in the volume for a service. You can measure the volume regularly and compute its standard error and expected value. The value function is a relation that includes volume, price/unit, cost/unit, and fixed cost as follows:

$$E = V * P - V * C - F$$

Earnings function based on V (volume), P (unit price), C (unit cost),
and F (fixed cost).

Using lower case letters to denote the expected values of the variables from the above equation, the partial derivative of the earnings function with respect to volume is given by:

$$\frac{\partial e}{\partial v} = p - c$$

and the formula for the volatility of the earnings due to volume is then:

$$\sigma_E^2 = \left(\frac{\partial e}{\partial v}\right)^2 \sigma_v^2$$

$$\sigma_E^2 = (p - c)^2 \sigma_v^2$$

$$\sigma_E = \sqrt{(p - c)^2 \sigma_v^2}$$

Calculation

For a service where the price is 100 USD and the cost is 70 USD, with a standard error for the volume of 1000 units, the volatility of earnings is:

$$\sigma_E = \sqrt{(p - c)^2 u^2(v)}$$

$$\sigma_E = \sqrt{(100-70)^2 (1000)^2}$$

$$\sigma_E = 30\,000$$

Thus 30 000 USD is the risk to earnings due to volume. For a value at risk, this standard deviation might be factored by 3–4 to provide a corresponding confidence interval based on assumptions of normality, etc. Now assume you have implemented a programme to smooth volume fluctuations over the previous year and have recorded the historical data shown in Table 5.8. Using this data, the standard deviation of earnings due to volume uncertainty would be calculated

Table 5.8 Table of volumes for a year

Month	Daily volume
Jan	33 200
Feb	29 500
Mar	34 000
Apr	27 345
May	32 650
June	28 750
July	39 765
Aug	28 456
Sep	37 340
Oct	36 322
Nov	36 786
Dec	24 530
Mean	32 387
Std Dev	4171
Std Error	426

as follows. Assume the same functional relation between the price, volume, cost, and earnings $E = V * P - V * C - F$, and a price of 100 and a cost of 70, with no fixed cost. The calculation is now:

$$\sigma_E^2 = \left(\frac{\partial f}{\partial v}\right)^2 \sigma_v^2$$

$$\sigma_E^2 = (p - c)^2 (\sigma_v)^2$$

$$\sigma_E^2 = (100 - 70)^2 (426)^2$$

$$\sigma_E = \sqrt{163\,328\,400}$$

$$\sigma_E = 12\,780 \text{ USD}$$

The reduction in the standard error due to volume from 1000 to 426 has reduced the effect on daily earnings from 30 000 to 12 780 USD. Note that the expected value of the volume would be used to generate the volume standard error in the formula if the standard error for the volume was given as a relative figure (e.g. 1.02%). This is a normal procedure since relative errors are more portable than absolute variances.

5.7 VALUE AT RISK FOR OPERATIONAL LOSSES

The Delta method can be used to generate the volatility for daily profit and loss due to operational risk in the processes as shown in this chapter. Using a 99% confidence level, three standard deviations would yield a Value at Risk (VaR) for this operational risk (3σ). This is the maximum daily loss (P&L impact) due to operational risk. It can be extended to a yearly figure by using one of several methods such as simulation or the 'square root of time' rule. The square root of time rule says that the volatility over t periods for any percentile of a distribution is simply the volatility multiplied by the nth root of t. For a normal distribution $n = 2$ and the volatility is simply multiplied by the square root of time. Therefore we have for a year's VaR:

$$\text{VaR}_{\text{year}} = \text{VaR}_{\text{day}} \sqrt{260}$$

As with market risk methodologies, the reliance on the normal distribution for the confidence level and time expansion can be relaxed by introducing other more advanced methods such as Monte Carlo simulation or other stochastic methods. Extending the loss distribution to multiple years requires developing the more advanced methods such as simulation over periods using the volatility of the exposures.

5.8 SUMMARY

The Delta method for operational risk—the Delta component in the Delta—EVT™ methodology proposed in this book—is the calculation technique for determining the value of the operational risk for assignable losses in the firm. It is based on classic error propagation and can be used to measure the risk in financial operations due to errors and omissions. It is similar to the existing Delta techniques used in market risk (e.g. Delta–normal and Delta–gamma). One of the main advantages of the Delta method is that since it relies on readily available data, it has the potential of immediate widespread application. By using the Delta method as a starting point, one of the important application challenges of EVT (developing the threshold) is overcome. The combination of Delta and EVT methodologies provides a powerful and flexible method for measuring operational risk.

5.9   FURTHER READING

See Chapter 10 on Error Propagation in Section IV for more information and references on the Delta method. A description of the Delta–normal and Delta–gamma methods for market risk can be found in Wilson (1996).

6

The EVT Methodology

6.1 INTRODUCTION

The process of determining losses due to control breakdowns and external events (not included in the Delta method) is undertaken using Extreme Value Theory (EVT). The basic approach is one of developing a loss model, but only for large losses over a specific threshold, and the starting point is a set of large loss events. Using the loss data, a loss model with separate severity and frequency distributions is built. The loss amounts over the threshold are fitted to one of a basic class of distributions in EVT, namely the Generalised Pareto Distribution (GPD). Several fitting techniques are possible, but maximum likelihood is used for the examples provided in this chapter. The frequency of loss events is fitted to a Poisson distribution using the time between loss events. These two distributions (the fitted GPD for severity and the Poisson for frequency) are combined in a Monte Carlo simulation to generate the excess loss distribution. The excess loss distribution is used along with the operating loss distribution from the Delta method to determine measurement values for operational risk.

The chapter begins with a brief description of the general form for loss models and an example using Poisson and lognormal distributions to model historical losses. Next, EVT and the method of peaks over thresholds (POT) are discussed. Then a detailed example of calculating operational risk for excess losses is presented. The individual steps of determining severity using the GPD, frequency using the Poisson distribution, and cumulative loss using Monte Carlo simulation are shown. Finally, some thoughts on data and validation for loss models are offered.

6.2 BASIC CONCEPTS

6.2.1 Loss Models

Loss model is a general term applied to a statistical model for estimating loss. Generally, a set of loss data is fitted to one or more parametric distributions (one for frequency and the other for severity) and then the overall loss distribution is generated using a Monte Carlo simulation. Loss models have been used for many years in insurance (Klugman *et al.* 1998), and have recently been applied to operational risk measurement. A single period or static loss model deals with the distribution of loss for one period. Multi-period models are required for long-term analysis and combine a frequency distribution with a loss severity distribution to extend the single period model through simulation. The loss models for operational risk are necessarily multi-period models because they deal with large losses that can occur over long intervals.

6.2.2   Data for Loss Model

Loss models can also be characterised by the source of loss data. The following are descriptions of general types of loss models based on their data sources.

Historical Loss

The actual losses are fitted to a parametric distribution for events and one for severity of loss. The firm's overall loss distribution is calculated using a two-stage Monte Carlo simulation with the fitted event and severity distributions.

Benchmark Loss

In this method a history of loss events and severity of losses by business are recorded for firms similar to the one in question (i.e. cohort group). The process is then the same as described above, with the added step of scaling events and severity based on characteristics (e.g. revenue or assets) of the cohort group compared with the firm. Using benchmark losses from other firms to calculate a candidate figure for the firm in question is sometimes referred to as the 'insurance approach'.

Subjective Loss

The subjective approach uses estimates made by experts about the frequency and severity of loss that may occur. This approach has grown out of the internal assessment processes already in place for auditing. An internal assessment is used to determine the loss data figures (usually in each business area). They are summed across the businesses to generate a firm-wide figure.

Scenario Loss

Scenario losses are based upon a set of plausible values for the firm and its environment that result in a loss event. Historical, benchmark, and subjective losses are classes of scenarios when they have been scaled to the firm. The scenario approach can provide a defined set of loss data specifically for a firm and is very flexible since it includes the other types.

Simulated Loss

Losses are simulated using a model of the process generating the loss. The simulation is run over large amounts of inputs in order to generate instances of events with very small probabilities.

6.2.3 Parametric Distributions

Loss models can also be characterised by the parametric distributions used. For example, a typical multi-period loss model has a Poisson frequency distribution and a lognormal severity. The Poisson family is used most often for the frequency, but many types of severity distributions are used, such as Negative Binomial, Burr, Pareto, and others.

6.2.4 Monte Carlo Simulation

Given the two distributions and their parameters, the overall loss distribution is then generated using a two-stage Monte Carlo simulation as follows. Given loss events L (e.g. $L \propto$ Poisson (λ)) and severity values S (e.g. $S \propto$ lognormal (μ, σ^2)), then the algorithm shown in Table 6.1 can be used to generate a loss distribution and quantile.

6.2.5 Historical Loss Model Example

In the historical loss approach, two parametric distributions are developed—one for frequency and the other for severity of losses—and fitted to actual data. After determining the parameters for these two distributions, the overall loss distribution is found using Monte Carlo simulation. In this simple example the data are

Table 6.1 Algorithm for generating the loss distribution for a multi-period loss model using two-stage Monte Carlo simulation

Repeat 10 000 times	// generate 10 000 simulations
Select L_i from L	// get number of losses
Repeat L_l times	// for each loss event
Select S_i from S	// get a severity
$R_{n+1} = S_l$	// and add severity to risk
Order R	// sort the losses

fitted with a Poisson distribution for the events and a lognormal distribution for the severity. Data for this example are given in Table 6.2.

The Poisson distribution is fitted with a λ frequency parameter and the lognormal distribution is fitted with a mean and variance (μ and σ^2) using a maximum likelihood technique. The average number of days between events is 16. Using a monthly period gives $\lambda = 2$ for the Poisson distribution. A maximum likelihood fit yields values of $\mu = 3$ and $\sigma = 2$ for the lognormal distribution. The Monte Carlo simulation for total loss proceeds in a two-stage simulation as described earlier. First, a sample from the Poisson distribution is drawn for the number of events n in the period (month), then this value for the number of events is used to sample n times from the lognormal distribution for the values of severity of these events. Twelve samples constitute the year, and another set of samples is drawn. The process is repeated several times to get a probability distribution of loss data over years. A simulation run of 100 is shown in Figure 6.1, ordered by amount of loss. A confidence level for the maximum yearly loss can be read directly from this graph (e.g. 95% is 7400).

Table 6.2 Example of loss events for the historical loss model

Loss	Date
160	01/02/00
4	01/03/00
0.8	01/04/00
6	01/10/00
2.1	02/03/00
2.7	03/11/00
1512	04/15/00
47	04/20/00
654	05/07/00
6	05/11/00
111.3	05/13/00
7.3	05/28/00
5.9	06/16/00
9.8	07/11/00
345	07/21/00
3.7	08/03/00
34	08/14/00
18.4	09/01/00
10	10/03/00
80.9	11/07/00
1.8	11/08/00
11.9	11/11/00
14.5	11/16/00
54.8	11/17/00
26.6	12/26/00

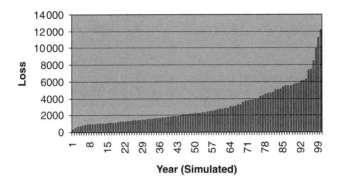

Figure 6.1 Ordered losses from Monte Carlo simulation for Poisson frequency ($\lambda = 2$) and lognormal loss ($\mu = 3$, $\sigma = 2$) distributions. The mean of the cumulative distribution is 3012 and its standard deviation is 2301

6.2.6   EVT Loss Models

Extreme Value Theory (EVT) offers a parametric statistical approach for the extreme values of data. Its roots are in the physical sciences and it has recently been applied to insurance. It provides a set of parametric distributions for the largest (or smallest) values (GEV) and excess values over a threshold (GPD) from a set of underlying losses. Because traditional statistical techniques focus on measures of central tendency (e.g. mean), they are not as accurate when estimating values very far from the centre of the data. EVT, on the other hand, deals only with the extreme values and ignores the majority of the underlying data and its measures in order to provide better estimates of the 'tails'. See Chapter 11 on EVT and the references therein for more information on extreme value theory.

The EVT methodology for operational risk is basically a loss model for large losses using a GPD for the severity. The technique for fitting the GPD to data is the peaks over threshold method (POT), where large values over a specific threshold are fitted to the GPD. The POT method has been used successfully for many years in the physical sciences and more recently applied to insurance (Reiss 1987). A theoretical explanation for the GPD can be found in Pickands (1975) and Smith (1987). A detailed description of the application of GPD is described in McNeil and Saladin (1997). The POT method uses the following basic assumptions (Embrechts *et al.* 1997):

1. the excesses of an independent identically distributed (or stationary) sequence over a high threshold u occur at the times of a Poisson process;
2. the corresponding excesses over u are independent and have a GPD;
3. excesses and exceedance times are independent of each other.

Table 6.3 Steps for EVT methodology

1. Collect loss data over the threshold along with the time of loss event.
2. Fit the excess loss amount (severity) to the GPD using maximum likelihood (or other fitting technique).
3. Fit the arrival time of loss events to a Poisson distribution using the mean inter-arrival rate (or appropriate fitting technique).
4. Use Monte Carlo simulation to generate a loss distribution from the Poisson distribution and GPD over a time horizon.

These characteristics allow the estimation of large losses using the exceedances, or excess losses over a threshold. These excess losses are fit to a GPD to determine the severity of a loss given that it exceeds the threshold. This is a conditional severity distribution for large losses. Since the number of exceedances follows a Poisson distribution, it is fitted and used to estimate the frequency of exceedances. Combining the severity and frequency distributions in a Monte Carlo simulation gives the excess loss distribution. The resulting excess loss distribution is a multi-period loss distribution for only those losses that exceed the threshold.

To implement the EVT loss model method for calculation of an operational risk measure, the steps in Table 6.3 are needed. Of course, the value of the threshold must first be determined as described in Chapters 4 and 5.

6.2.7 Fitting the GPD

To fit a GPD, one of several techniques can be used. A general discussion of fitting parametric distributions to a sample of data is beyond the scope of this book, but an excellent reference is Johnson *et al.* (1994). However, the maximum likelihood technique is a popular approach and will be presented for use in the loss models. The maximum likelihood technique optimises a likelihood function for the data. The basic idea is to find the parameters for the assumed distribution that maximise the likelihood that the sample data came from the distribution with the associated parameters. The likelihood is simply the joint probability for the data, but is usually calculated using the log of the likelihood function in order to simplify the procedure. For the GPD, the log-likelihood function to be maximised is

$$\text{LL}(\text{GPD}(X_1 \dots X_n)) = -n \log(\beta) - \left(\frac{1}{\xi} + 1 \right) \sum_n \log \left(1 + \frac{\xi}{\beta} x_n \right)$$

Maximum likelihood function (log-likelihood) to be maximised for fitting GPD to a set of data $(X_1 \dots X_n)$, where n is the number of data points.

where

    n is the number of sample data values,
    X_n is the nth sample value,
    ξ is the shape parameter,
    β is the scale parameter.

This function can be programmed into a spreadsheet and the maximisation performed on a data set quite easily. The values of the two parameters of the GPD, ξ and β, are determined. A goodness of fit test for the GPD is not easily derived, so procedures such as jack-knife or bootstrap are used to generate confidence intervals for the parameter estimates. An example is given later in this chapter.

6.2.8   Determining the Severity Distribution

Given the parameters ξ and β, the GPD distribution function can be used to calculate the quantiles of interest for a particular confidence level. This represents the severity level of the excess loss distribution at a particular quantile. The equation needed is

$$\text{GPD}(\xi, \beta, x) = 1 - \left(1 + \frac{\xi x}{\beta}\right)^{-1/\xi}$$

Formula for calculating the distribution function value for the GPD.

Note that this is the distribution of the severity of excess losses only and not the distribution of all losses. Again, this function can be programmed into a spreadsheet so that various values of loss severity at particular confidence intervals are generated. Some typical example values are given in Figure 6.2 for common values of the parameters and the loss (assume losses are in thousands).

6.2.9   Determining the Frequency Distribution

Having fitted a GPD to the amount of loss for a set of excess losses, the next step is to determine the frequency of losses using a Poisson distribution. The Poisson distribution is well known as a single parameter distribution for the number of occurrences of an event with relatively small probabilities given a relatively large sample. The formula for the Poisson distribution is

$$\Pr(x) = \frac{\lambda e^{-x}}{x!}$$

Formula for Poisson distribution of x events with single parameter λ, the arrival rate.

The fitting of the Poisson to a set of occurrences proceeds using the inter-arrival times for the loss events. That is, the average time between events can be

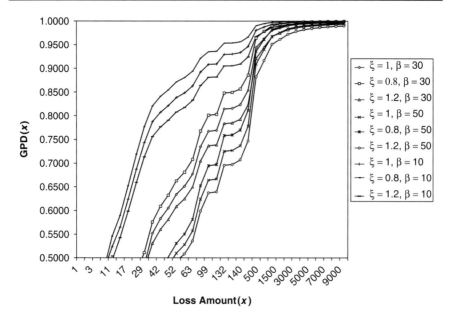

Figure 6.2 Empirical distributions sampled from the GPD with common values of the parameters and the losses (losses in thousands)

used to determine the arrival rate or lambda for the Poisson formula. (The arrival rate is simply the inverse of the inter-arrival time.) For the Poisson distribution, it can be shown that the maximum likelihood estimator for λ is given by the mean arrival rate formula below (Johnson *et al.* 1994).

$$\lambda = \frac{\sum\limits_{k} k n_k}{n}$$

Formula for estimating λ for the Poisson distribution.

where

  k is the number of events in a period,
  n_k is the number of periods with k events,
  n is the total number of periods.

A goodness of fit statistic for the Poisson distribution can be found using a simple χ^2-squared test. The test statistic is:

$$\chi^2 = \sum_{k} \frac{(n_k - n\operatorname{Pr}(k;\lambda))^2}{n\operatorname{Pr}(k;\lambda)}$$

Chi-squared test statistic for the goodness of fit of the Poisson distribution
to a set of data.

where $\Pr(k; \lambda)$ is the probability of k events for the Poisson distribution with parameter λ. The degrees of freedom are $n - 2$.

6.3   EVT LOSS MODEL EXAMPLE FOR LARGE OPERATIONAL LOSSES

Assume the table of losses shown in Table 6.4 has been accumulated for a period of one year. A graph of the large loss data is given in Figure 6.3. As expected, a simple plot of the ordered values shows them to be exponential in nature, with a heavy tail, as can be seen in Figure 6.4.

Finding the data for loss amounts using the log-likelihood formula given earlier results in $\xi = 0.779$, $\beta = 61.56$, and log-likelihood $= -17.76$. A graph of the fit is shown in Figure 6.5.

The parameters for the GPD also have errors. The standard errors for the estimated parameters are found using a technique known as bootstrapping (Efron and Tibshirani 1993). The details are not given here, but the procedure gives the standard errors for the parameters for the example as:

$$SE(\xi) = 0.38 \qquad SE(\beta) = 25$$

Standard errors for the GPD parameter estimates for the loss example.

Table 6.4   Table of large losses
(in thousands of Euros)

ID	Date	Amount
1	01/01/98	35.1
2	01/19/98	40.0
3	01/30/98	55.0
4	02/11/98	80.9
5	02/12/98	508.0
6	02/17/98	3.5
7	03/18/98	48.8
8	03/20/98	12.0
9	03/27/98	168.9
10	03/27/98	98.0
11	04/07/98	128.0
12	06/01/98	21.6
13	06/11/98	100.0
14	07/01/98	770.0
15	07/24/98	142.0
16	08/18/98	61.5
17	08/30/98	129.4
18	10/05/98	1450.0
19	10/12/98	30.0
20	10/15/98	17.0
21	10/22/98	8.0
22	11/30/98	12.0
23	12/28/98	50.0

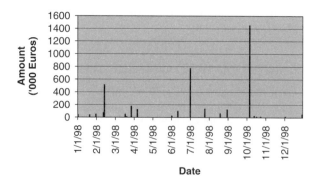

Figure 6.3   An historical graph of large loss data

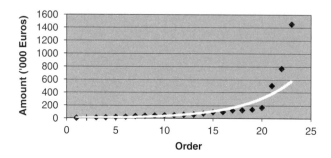

Figure 6.4   Ordered loss data showing exponential tendency with a heavy tail

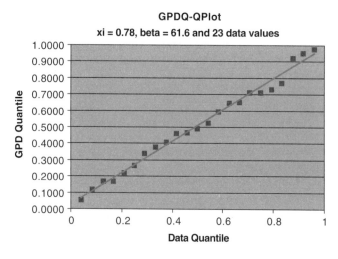

Figure 6.5   GPD fit of loss data with parameters $\xi = 0.78$ and $\beta = 61.6$

Table 6.5 Table of confidence values for the GPD using the loss example

Confidence level	Excess value
90%	397
95%	740
99%	2800

Table 6.6 Table of confidence values for the GPD showing two standard error estimates for low and high values for excess

Confidence level	Excess value	Low	High
90%	397	28	2918
95%	740	36	6791
99%	2800	57	45 148

For instance, assuming you are interested in an interval using a confidence value of 95% or 99%, you would expect to use one of the values shown in Table 6.5. Including the error analysis for the GPD, Table 6.6 is built for the confidence levels, given a two standard error (e.g. 67%) interval for the parameters. As can be seen, there is a large difference in values at the confidence limits for this distribution in the tail between 90% and 99%. Determination of the threshold as described earlier is also a key and will likely play a major role in any provisioning or capital allocation action to be taken.

6.3.1 Determining the Frequency for the Loss Model

The foregoing analysis yields a distribution for the size of a loss that can be classified as excess loss. The frequency of the occurrence of the losses is needed in order to generate the figure for the loss over a period of time. Using a Poisson distribution to fit these losses is common, and the rate of occurrence is referred to as λ (the arrival rate). Using the actual occurrences of loss, λ is determined for the distribution and the two parameterised distributions are combined in a Monte Carlo simulation in order to generate a distribution for excess loss over a period (Table 6.7). Fitting these data to a Poisson distribution gives a parameter of $\lambda = 1.9$ for monthly data. The yearly distribution is shown in Figure 6.6.

A χ^2 test for these data and a Poisson distribution with $\lambda = 1.9$ is shown in Table 6.8. The expected number of months with events of zero through five or more is calculated using the total number of months (12) and the Poisson probability for the number of events in a month (using $\lambda = 1.9$). The complete formula was given previously. The χ^2 statistic is then calculated normally using the square of the difference between the observed and expected, divided by the expected (see formula given previously). Since the value of χ^2 is below the critical value for 0.05, the Poisson distribution hypothesis is not rejected.

Table 6.7 Table of losses
for one year

Losses	Date
35.1	01/01/98
40.0	01/19/98
55.0	01/30/98
80.9	02/11/98
508.0	02/12/98
3.5	02/17/98
48.8	03/18/98
12.0	03/20/98
168.9	03/27/98
98.0	03/27/98
128.0	04/07/98
21.6	06/01/98
100.0	06/11/98
770.0	07/01/98
142.0	07/24/98
61.5	08/18/98
129.4	08/30/98
1450.0	10/05/98
30.0	10/12/98
17.0	10/15/98
8.0	10/22/98
12.0	11/30/98
50.0	12/28/98

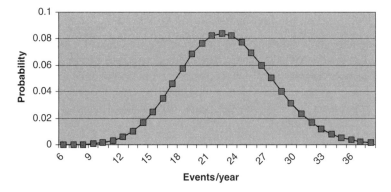

Figure 6.6 Poisson distribution for yearly events using fitted data for $\lambda = 1.9$ monthly

Using the Poisson frequency and the GPD severity to generate a loss distribution via Monte Carlo gives the final distribution, as shown in Figure 6.7. Using the yearly cumulative loss figures, the excess loss distribution can be used to determine the maximum yearly loss expected at a chosen confidence level. The figures given in Table 6.9 reflect the yearly loss distribution. These figures can be

Table 6.8 Chi-squared test for the Poisson distribution fit of data

Events	Months	Pr(Events)	Expected	x^2	Critical 0.05
0	2	0.15335	1.84	2.173606	
1	3	0.28754	3.45	2.608328	
2	3	0.26957	3.23	2.782216	
3	2	0.16848	2.02	1.978465	
4	2	0.07898	0.95	4.220725	
5+	0	0.04208	0.50	0	
10	12	1	12.00	13.76334	18.30703

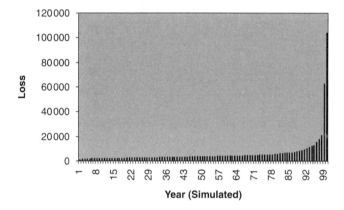

Figure 6.7 Yearly ordered losses from a Monte Carlo simulation of Poisson frequency distribution ($\lambda = 1.9$) and Generalised Pareto Distribution (GPD) ($x_i = .78$, $\beta = 62$)

Table 6.9 Figures for yearly cumulative loss distribution

Confidence level	Yearly value
90%	7764
95%	12 749
99%	62 365

used in a financing strategy to develop the provisioning and capital requirements for the business unit. For instance, to cover the excess losses in an average year at a 95% confidence level, the figure of 740 is needed (from Table 6.5). In order to account for yearly variations and cover all excess losses in 95% of the years, the figure of 12 749 is needed (from Table 6.9).

6.3.2 Value at Risk for Excess Losses

The GPD is a loss distribution for excess losses over the threshold as defined earlier. Selecting a confidence level on this distribution (say 90%) means that the excess losses (losses that exceed the threshold) in a year will not exceed the level 90% of the time. The single year is extended to multiple periods using the two-stage simulation that incorporates a Poisson distribution for the frequency of excess loss events. Using the multi-period distribution of excess losses and selecting the same confidence level has the following meaning. The total excess losses *in a percentage of the years* will not be exceeded. In the example you would need a reserve of 397 in order to cover 90% of the excess losses expected in a typical year (see Table 6.5). However, you would need a reserve of 7764 in order to cover all excess losses for 90% of the years (see table of confidence values for yearly cumulative loss). In addition, if the threshold is set so that the excess losses occur less than 1% of the time (coverage factor $k = 2.33$ for normal), then the meaning of the values relative to all losses can be stated as follows. The reserve of 397 will cover 90% of the excess losses that are over and above 99% of all losses. In other words, 99.9% of all losses expected in the typical year. The reserve of 7764 would cover all excess losses (100% of all losses) for 95% of all years. The value of the reserve required also needs to take into account the error analysis for the excess loss distribution (which may be quite large) and other factors relating to the firm's strategy and environment.

6.4 SUMMARY

The EVT methodology presented is a multi-period loss model with two important distinctions. First, it uses the Generalised Pareto Distribution (GPD) as one of the extreme value distributions to fit losses. Second, it only applies to losses over a specific threshold (excess losses). By focusing on estimates for excess loss, the EVT methodology promises to improve upon traditional parametric techniques that use all of the underlying data and measures of central tendency (e.g. means and variances). The determination of the threshold is essential in applying EVT to operational risk. When combined with the Poisson frequency distribution, a value at risk for excess losses can be estimated.

6.5 FURTHER READING

The basic application of loss models is described by Klugman *et al.* (1998), applying them mainly to insurance problems. The early works on application of EVT include Smith (1987) and Castillo (1988). For some applications to finance, see the later works of McNeil and Saladin (1997) and Cruz *et al.* (1998). See Chapter 11 on EVT for more theoretical background and references.

SECTION III
MODELLING OPERATIONAL RISK

7

Delta–EVT™ Models for Operational Risk

7.1 INTRODUCTION

The application of the Delta–EVT™ methodology to operational risk requires the development of a specific set of business models, risk factor models, loss models, plausible scenarios, and risk measures for the firm. This chapter presents a skeletal set of these components that can be used as the architecture for building an operational risk measurement system along with an in-depth example of their application. The models presented are necessarily simpler than those found in real-world applications, but they can serve as templates to build more sophisticated versions that address a firm's specific needs.

The chapter begins with a business model template and identification of the related value-adding processes and activities. Then models for measuring the operational risk associated with the business model are developed based on the Delta method. Next, techniques for building loss models are presented along with some ideas for generating large loss event data from scenarios. Finally, operational risk measures are briefly discussed and then calculated in an example based on a fictitious firm called Genoa Bank.

7.2 BUSINESS MODEL

Business models are the basic unit of analysis for operational risk. They contain the value-adding processes within each business unit in the firm, and the activities and factors within these processes that combine to form the hierarchy for the firm. Business models are obviously firm specific, but the general model given here should provide a good start for practitioners. Included in the examples are definitions of each level of the hierarchy, along with the risk models for the lowest level. To reinforce understanding of the business model, a set of basic definitions is provided as follows:

- *Business Unit.* The business unit is the unit of analysis for operational risk and will normally correspond to a profit and loss (P&L) reporting unit of the firm. It is important that a profit and loss figure (or other earnings related figure) for the unit is reported and managed so that operational risk measures can be compared and combined with performance measures.
- *Value-adding Process.* A value-adding process is a profit-making component for the business unit. It consists of the delivery of a product or service that customers of the business see as value added by the business.
- *Activity.* An activity is a major function in the value chain for the value-adding process. For example, in capital markets the trading, settlement, and management functions should normally be identified as major activities in the process.
- *Risk Factor.* A risk factor is a contributor to earnings volatility within the activity. It is a causal factor that is linked to the earnings of the value-adding process through a value function, and its volatility (random uncertainty) will be directly measured or estimated.

Figure 7.1 shows a simple business model and associated risk factors. A brief description of each of these factors is given in Table 7.1.

Many other models of the business are possible. For instance, the investment process could have trade management as one of its activities. Likewise, volume could appear as a factor for the lending origination activity. The decision of what to include will be based largely on the level of detail needed for the business model, the identification of the important factors, and the availability of relevant information concerning them. It is usually better to begin with a simple model and

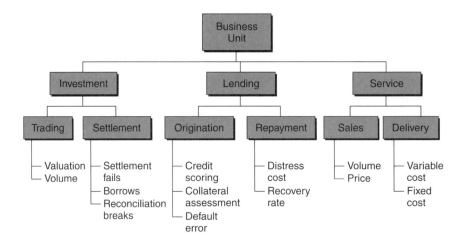

Figure 7.1 Example of a business model for a financial firm. The processes and activities of the business unit are shown in the shaded boxes. Risk factors are listed below the relevant activities

Table 7.1 Table of processes and associated risk factors from a business model

Process	Activity	Risk factor	Description
Investment	Trading	Valuation	Earnings variance resulting (primarily) from errors in the valuation model and market value errors.
		Volume	Variance in earnings due to volume changes.
	Settlement	Fails	Failure to deliver on value date.
		Borrows	Borrow due to security not on hand.
		Breaks	Unreconciled cash or securities account.
Lending	Origination	Scoring	Credit scoring error (percentage of loans scored in wrong quality group).
		Default	Error in the default rate (uncertainty in estimate).
		Collateral	Error in collateral valuation.
	Recovery	Distress	Carry cost for distressed loans (before recovery).
		Recovery	Error in recovery rate.
Service	Sales	Volume	Variance in earnings due to volume changes.
		Price	Variance in earnings due to price changes.
	Delivery	Variable Cost	Variance in earnings due to variance in variable cost.
		Fixed Cost	Variance in earnings due to variance in fixed cost.

expand it as needed to explain the significant parts of operational risk within the firm. Techniques for identifying and evaluating risk factors are further discussed in Chapter 9 on Causal Models for Operational Risk.

7.3 RISK MODELS

Risk models relate the risk factors to the activities of value-adding processes through a value function. This function is the relation between the factor and earnings, and is differenced to get the sensitivity, which is the relation between the change in the factor and the change in earnings. For each of the risk factors a value function can be written relating the factor to earnings. This function is then differenced to create the basis for the risk model equation. The total contribution to risk is often calculated by partitioning along a key characteristic group to determine the risk's volatility, such as nominal amount, product, or credit rating. This procedure is performed for each factor in the investment, lending, and service processes in the following sections. The analysis begins by considering each risk category and possible risk factors for it. Although the earnings equation is not shown it is easily understood from the differenced equation. A table then summarises the important risk factors for each category. Finally, the risk models using factor volatilities, sensitivities, and partitioning are given.

7.3.1 The Investment Process

The investment process includes the trading and settlement activities. For each of the risk categories of valuation, timeliness, reconciliation, and compliance, risk factors and their value-adding functions are considered. We assume that the risk factors to be used for the operational risk model are those given in the tables below. Risk models are then developed for these factors and shown in the following sections. Trading includes risks due to volume (exposure) and valuation (model). For the settlement activity, the value function includes operating cost, borrowing cost (in order to deliver a security that is not at hand), and interest claims (when delivery is not performed as promised). In order to provide a more complete picture of the investment settlement activity, the reconciliation breaks are also included. These are nostro and depot account breaks for the cash and securities accounts in correspondent banks. The example risk models do not include compliance risk factors.

Earnings Function (Differenced) (Table 7.2)

Table 7.2 Value-adding functions for the trading and settlement activities of investment banking

---

$\Delta E(Trading) = f(Instrument, Exposure_\varepsilon, Model_\varepsilon)$
$\Delta E(Settlement) = f(Exposure, Cost_\varepsilon, Borrows_\varepsilon, Failures_\varepsilon, Breaks_\varepsilon)$

Risk Factors (Table 7.3)

Table 7.3 Errors for the investment process

Risk category	Example risk factors
Valuation	Model error resulting from errors in the valuation model and market value errors.
Timeliness	Potential interest claims from settlement failures. Borrowing cost from short positions.
Reconciliation	Aged nostro breaks and depot breaks with correspondent banks.
Compliance	Failure to comply with internal procedures in client origination and product origination, and trading. Failure to adhere to limits.

Risk Models

- *Trading Activity*

$$\text{Volume risk}: \sigma_E^2 = \sum_k \sigma_{v,k}^2 N_k^2 R^2$$

$$\text{Valuation risk}: \sigma_M^2 = \sum_p \sigma_{m,p}^2 N_p^2 V_p^2$$

where

E = earnings,
V = volume,
N = nominal amount in currency transaction,
R = return on nominal (margin),
k = partition on nominal amount,
p = partition on product.

- *Settlement Activity*
  Settlement risk:

$$\sigma_{E,S}^2 = \sum_p \sum_{i=1,n} \{\Pr(d = i | d > 0) N_p V_p (e^{r*d/360} - 1)\}^2 \sigma_{\Pr(d>0)}^2$$

Borrowing risk:

$$\sigma_{E,B}^2 = \sum_p \sum_{i=1,n} \{\Pr(d = i | d > 0) N_p V_p (e^{r*d/360} - 1)\}^2 \sigma_{\Pr(d>0)}^2$$

Reconciliation risk:

$$\sigma_{E,R}^2 = \sum_p \sum_{i=1,n} \{\Pr(d = i | d > 0) N_p V_p (e^{r*d/360} - 1)\}^2 \sigma_{\Pr(d>0)}^2$$

where
$\Pr(d)$ = probability of d days delay,
r = interest rate,
n = maximum number of days delay.

7.3.2 Lending Process

Likewise, the two main activities for the lending process are loan origination and repayment. The main factors for each are shown in the formulae below. The risk factors in loan origination are the type of loan instrument (e.g. collateral), volume of lending (exposure), the error in the collateral valuation, and the error in the credit rating. For the repayment activity the risks are the distressed loan costs (before default), and recovery errors (ε). Here, compliance risk factors and default rate errors have not been explicitly addressed.

Earnings Function (Differenced) (Table 7.4)

Table 7.4 Value-adding functions for the loan and payment activities of the lending process

$\Delta E(Loan\ Origination) = f(Instrument, Exposure, Scoring_\varepsilon, Default, Collateral_\varepsilon)$
$\Delta E(Repayment) = f(Exposure, Recovery_\varepsilon, Distress_\varepsilon, Default)$

Risk Factors (Table 7.5)

Table 7.5 Categories and examples of risk factors

Risk category	Example risk factors
Valuation	Scoring error resulting from errors in the scoring model and input value errors. Collateral valuation error.
Timeliness	Late watchlist recognition of distressed loans, late payments on outstanding balances.
Reconciliation	Default rate error and error in recovery rate.
Compliance	Failure to comply with internal procedures in client origination and product origination, and lending. Failure to adhere to limits, or failure to achieve the targeted quality mix for loans.

Risk Models

- *Origination activity*

$$\text{Scoring risk: } \sigma_L^2 = \sum_r \left(OV_r \text{ Rr } \sigma_r \delta_{r-1,r}\right)^2$$

$$\text{Collateral assessment risk: } \sigma_L^2 = \sum_c \left(\Pr(D_r)C_{r,c} \text{ Rr } \sigma_c\right)^2$$

- *Repayment activity*

$$\text{Recovery error: } \sigma_L^2 = \sigma_R^2 \left(R \sum_r \Pr(D_r)OV_r\right)^2$$

$$\text{Distress risk: } \sigma_L^2 = \sum_r \left((\Pr(W_r) - \Pr(D_r))OV_r \sum_i (e^{\eta d/360} - 1)\Pr(d = i)\right)^2$$

where

OV = outstanding value of the loan (adjusted for collateral),

σ_r = rating error,

$\delta_{r-1,r}$ = percentage error in valuation between the rated class of the loan and one class lower,

C = collateral value,

σ_c = collateral valuation error,

r = partition using credit quality,

c = partition using collateral type,

$\Pr(D_r)$ = probability of default,

η = yearly interest rate,

$\Pr(W_r)$ = probability of being on the watchlist (in distress),

R = recovery rate.

7.3.3 Service Process

For the services process the two main activities are the revenue or sales function and the manufacturing or delivery function. The analysis calculates a business risk with the main factors of volume, price, and cost (or margin) partitioned (optionally) along the product mix.

Earnings Function (Table 7.6)

Table 7.6 Value-adding functions for the sales and delivery activities of the services process

$E(Sales) = f(Volume_\varepsilon, Product, Price_\varepsilon)$

$E(Delivery) = f(Margin_\varepsilon, Product, Volume)$

Risk Factors (Table 7.7)

Table 7.7 Causes of errors in the service process

Errors	Description
Valuation	Pricing errors, volume volatility. Cost variances.
Timeliness	Receivables, bookings failures.
Reconciliation	Cost allocation errors.
Compliance	Failure to comply with internal procedures in client origination, product origination, and service. Failure to achieve target market or product mix.

Risk Models

- *Sales activity*

$$\text{Sales volume risk: } \sigma_{E,S}^2 = \sum_k (p_k - c_k)^2 \sigma_{k,S}^2$$

or

$$\sigma_{E,S}^2 = \sum_k R_k^2 \sigma_{S,k}^2$$

$$\text{Pricing risk: } \sigma_{E,P}^2 = \sum_k \sigma_{p,k}^2 S_k^2$$

- *Delivery activity*

$$\text{Variable cost risk: } \sigma_{E,VC}^2 = \sum \sigma_{VC,k}^2 S_k^2$$

$$\text{Fixed cost risk: } \sigma_{E,FC}^2 = \sum_k \sigma_{FC,k}^2 \left(\frac{S_k}{\sum_i S_i}\right)^2$$

where

E = earnings,
S = sales volume,
N = nominal amount,
R = return on nominal (margin),
P = price,
k = product type partition.

$$\text{Margin risk by product: } \sigma_{E,R}^2 = \sum_k \sigma_{R,k}^2 S_k^2$$

7.4 LOSS MODELS

In addition to the causal models, a loss model is needed to calculate excess loss for the business unit. The loss model is a parametric statistical method based on a set of loss data. To begin, actual losses are recorded according to a classification scheme used for scenarios and risk assessment. The date of the loss event and the severity (amount of the loss) are recorded. To facilitate scenario generation, a description of the loss event in sufficient detail should be provided along with the categorisation of loss. This descriptive text is very important, as it will allow plausible scenarios to be built regardless of the classification scheme chosen (Table 7.8). Note that there is no causation attached to large losses, and so the categorisation does not have to form a partition on the losses. It is just a

Table 7.8 Large loss model database field requirements

Attribute	Description
Business unit	Name of business unit charged with loss.
Date	Date of loss event.
Severity	Amount of loss (in home currency).
Category	Assessment category for primary cause of loss.
Description	Detailed description of loss, including key factors, extenuating circumstances, and related events.

convenient way to keep track of the loss and relate it to a scenario because all losses for the business unit will be used in the same loss model.

7.5 SCENARIOS

Many rare events may not be included in the loss database because the records have not been kept for a long enough time, or there is limited experience. Nevertheless these rare events and their associated losses can be modelled using scenarios. A scenario is a loss (event frequency and severity) that is described in sufficient detail that it is considered plausible given the relevant characteristics of the business unit. Plausible scenarios are relevant because they include a description of the causal factors for the event and a measure of its frequency and severity based on the business unit's relevant characteristics. In practice, plausible scenarios are based on historical events and events in other firms that can be modified to create plausible scenarios for your firm. A comprehensive list of plausible scenarios is not available, but the assessment categories used for governance may be a good place to begin. Consider scenarios for the categories shown in Figure 7.2.

Using this categorisation and scenario losses, the frequency and severity of each loss can be specified according to the operating characteristics of the firm. For instance, maximum expected loss can be used as the threshold determining severity (it becomes the minimum) and the maximum at stake is the maximum

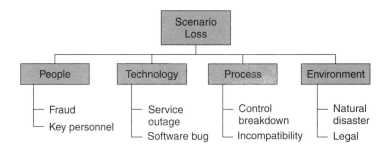

Figure 7.2 Scenario loss categorisation

unexpected loss. Although scenarios are by nature subjective, these two starting points help bound the frequency and loss values for the scenarios. Control self-assessments and loss databases that have similar categorisation and detailed descriptions can also help provide needed information for building meaningful scenarios. Models of the processes are used to scale values to the loss database and determine the frequency and severity of the loss from scenarios. Also a critical factor for severity is the estimation of the detection probability for losses (e.g. that exceed the maximum expected loss). This probability determines the cumulative loss possible over time (losses for the same loss event) that can occur. It may also help to separate the scenarios into single event large losses and protracted large losses (losses from multiple related events over some time period).

7.6   RISK MEASURES

Measures of risk are the outputs of the operational risk measurement system. They are used to measure the level of operational risk and form the basis for calculating economic capital requirements for the business unit. The measures from Delta–EVT™ are loss measures from the two loss-generating sources—value-adding processes and rare events. Given the operating loss and excess loss distributions, the risk measures are statistics from them. One of the most important risk measures is value at risk (VaR). VaR is defined as the maximum loss of a specific confidence interval over a defined period (Jorion 1997). Operational risk measures provided by Delta–EVT™ include the following.

1. *Maximum operating loss*: The value of a loss from the operating loss distribution at a specific confidence level (e.g. 95%).
2. *Value at risk*: The value of the operating losses at a specific confidence level (e.g. 95%) and for a specific period (e.g. one year).
3. *Maximum excess loss*: The value of the loss from the excess loss distribution at a specific confidence level (e.g. 95%).
4. *Excess value at risk*: The value of the excess losses at a specific confidence level (e.g. 95%) and for a specific period (e.g. one year).

7.7   IN-DEPTH EXAMPLE—GENOA BANK

An in-depth example of the calculation of operational risk measures using a fictitious firm named Genoa Bank will demonstrate the application of the essential ideas. The steps for the implementation of the Delta–EVT™ methodology for Genoa Bank are:

1. Develop the business model
2. Apply the Delta methodology

3. Determine the threshold(s)
4. Apply the EVT methodology
5. Calculate the operational risk measures.

In the remainder of the chapter these steps are performed as an example exercise using fictitious information for Genoa Bank.

7.7.1 Step 1: Develop the Business Model

Genoa Bank has only one business unit—the capital markets operation. But in that one unit, all value-adding processes are present and so the calculation of operational risk includes most of the techniques described earlier. The model and associated risk factors for the business unit of Genoa Bank are developed and shown in Figure 7.3. Other models and risk factors could be chosen, but a judgement based on all available information is made that these factors are initially the important ones. (A more detailed discussion of the techniques for determining risk factors is presented in Chapter 9 on Causal Models for Operational Risk.)

As basic background information, the income statement and balance sheet of Genoa Bank are presented below in a shortened form (Tables 7.9 and 7.10). From these, the operating characteristics that are relevant to earnings are derived, and factors for each of the value-adding processes are developed and related to earnings using the Delta method. Then the threshold for large loss is determined. Next, a loss history is given and scenarios are developed to generate a loss model using the EVT method. Finally, the loss distributions generated are used to calculate a set of operational risk measures for the business unit.

As can be seen, Genoa Bank is a reasonably-sized investment bank (over 100 billion Euros) with good earnings. The share price is probably about 100 Euros, which means the market value is over 7.5 billion Euros. Return on shareholders'

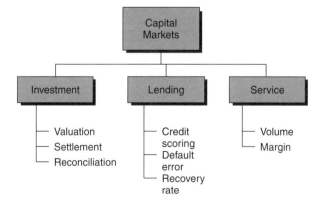

Figure 7.3 Business model for the example of Genoa Bank capital markets

Table 7.9   Genoa Bank income statement

Income statement (millions of Euros)	
Net income from securities transactions	1500
Net commissions	500
Total revenue from operations	2000
General and administrative expenses	(1200)
Net income before provision and tax	800
Net provisions for loan losses	(100)
Net income before tax	700
Income tax	(154)
Net income	546
Shares outstanding	75,324,323
Earnings per share	7.25

Table 7.10   Genoa Bank balance sheet

Balance sheet (millions of Euros)	
Assets	
Treasury operations and interbank transactions	8183
Trading securities	111 989
Securities held for sale	6434
Investment securities	978
Fixed assets	1494
Total assets	129 078
Liabilities	
Treasury operations and interbank transactions	15 343
Trading securities	90 323
Bonds and other negotiable debt securities	11 323
Accruals, provisions and other liabilities	7343
Net worth (shareholder's equity)	4200
Net income	546
Total liabilities and net worth	129 078

equity is about 13%, a healthy figure for the financial sector. The first step for calculating operational risk measures is to look into the value-adding process of investment, lending, and services that are involved in this capital markets operation.

7.7.2   Step 2: Apply the Delta Method

The next step is to apply the Delta method to each of the investment, lending, and service processes shown in the business model, beginning below with the trading and settlement activities of the investment process. For this example the assumption of Gaussian distributions for the risk is often used. The Delta method applied using the assumption of a Gaussian (or 'normal') distribution is often referred to as Delta–normal.

7.7.3 Investment Process

The additional information needed to carry out the investment analysis consists of the trading activity and product information summarised in Tables 7.11 and 7.12. There is a considerable amount of proprietary trading (about 20%). The valuation error for the investment process for proprietary trading will be calculated first. Using the values for the traded products from proprietary trading only, model errors for each type of instrument will be propagated to the earnings function. The model errors are based on the Bank of England study (Bank of England 1997) and shown in Table 7.13.

The error model for valuation of the proprietary trades can now proceed with the daily volume used to develop an error for the daily earnings due to model (valuation) error. The error for Swaps will be taken as the Bond error from the table, since the errors due to yield curve calculation are assumed to be similar. Otherwise, Derivatives will assume the Vanilla error rate and the Structured products will have an error rate of 20% from Exotic. This gives Table 7.14 for the error contribution (quantity of errors times volume squared) from valuation in the proprietary trading portfolio for a day's earnings.

As might be expected, the majority of errors are in Derivatives and Structured products, with little error in liquid market-priced products. Next the carrying

Table 7.11 Genoa Bank trading volumes

Trading volumes	
Client trading	
Transactions per day	4000
Average value per transaction	400 000
Average margin per transaction (in basis points)	300
Nominal volume per day (millions)	1600
Income per day (in millions)	4.8
Proprietary trading	
Transactions per day	1000
Proprietary trading volume per day (in millions)	400
Portfolio size (millions)	22 398
Return on portfolio	12%
Income per day (in millions)	10
Total income (EUR million)	15
Daily direct costs	(9)
Daily earnings before tax and provisions	6.1

Table 7.12 Genoa Bank traded products

Client trading	Nominal volume (millions of Euros)	%
Fixed income	680	42.5
Equities	536	33.5
Derivatives	40	2.5
Swaps	336	21
Structured products	8	0.5
Total	1600	100
Proprietary trading		
Fixed income	170	42.5
Equities	134	33.5
Derivatives	10	2.5
Swaps	84	21
Structured products	2	0.5
Total	400	100

Table 7.13 Table of model errors for Genoa Bank

Product	Std Dev. (%)
Equity	0.1
Bond	0.3
Vanilla	5
Exotic	20

Table 7.14 Valuation error contribution for proprietary trading

Proprietary trading	Volume (millions of Euros)	%	Error (%)	Error contribution
Fixed income	170	42.5	0.30	0.260
Equities	134	33.5	0.10	0.018
Derivatives	10	2.5	5	0.250
Swaps	84	21	0.30	0.064
Structured products	2	0.5	10	0.040
Total	400	100	0.157	0.632
Std Error				0.795

costs for the operation will be calculated. These costs will consist of the settlement and reconciliation costs associated with the trading activity. Again for one day's trades, the errors in settlement and reconciliation will be used to determine the variance in earnings due to these factors. Ageing reports for settlement and reconciliation are shown in Tables 7.15 and 7.16. These reports will be used to develop the error models for carrying costs.

Table 7.15   Settlement failure report for Genoa Bank

Age	%	Average/day	Cost/trade (Euros)	Failure rate	Total daily cost (Euros)
1	48.9	2445	67	0.035	5705
2	10.5	525	133	0.035	2450
3	10.2	510	200	0.035	3571
4	9.5	475	267	0.035	4435
5	4.6	230	333	0.035	2684
10	1.3	65	667	0.035	1518
30	4.9	245	2005	0.035	17 193
60	8.2	410	4020	0.035	57 688
100	2.0	100	6723	0.035	23 529
Total	100	5005	678		118 774

Table 7.16   Genoa Bank nostro breaks ageing report

Age	Accounts	Amount (thousands of Euros)	Percent of total	Average/ account	Est trades	Cost (Euros)
0 to 4	52	900 323	22.35%	17 313 904	2251	300 158
5 to 9	85	1 300 500	32.29%	15 300 000	3251	1 518 135
10 to 29	112	880 343	21.86%	7 860 205	2201	2 939 373
30 to 59	28	12 343	0.31%	440 821	31	92 921
60 to 89	25	33 923	0.84%	1 356 920	85	426 699
90 or more	23	900 433	22.36%	39 149 261	2251	15 132 974
Total	325	4 027 865	100.00%	12 393 431	10 070	20 410 260

Normally the costs resulting from claims on failures are accepted as part of the cost of doing business and are included in expenses. But there are two sides to the interest claims and reconciliation breaks. They can just as well be gains as losses, and therefore in this error analysis an expected value of zero is taken for them. Consequently, the computations are for a variance in earnings (not an expected value) and they represent an error in expected earnings due to errors and omissions. The settlement cost is simply the potential cost of interest claims for all trades whose settlement date passes the value date. It is computed based on an average rate of failure for all trades (3.5%) for Genoa Bank and the probability of a day's delay given that a trade fails. The assumption is a stationary ageing distribution for failed trades as shown in Table 7.15. A failed trade can be either a buy or sell, so the interest claim can be either payable or due. Assume the difference between paid and received interest has a standard deviation of 20% of total potential cost. This gives a settlement risk of 23 755/day and if scaled to one year using $\sqrt{260}$, the yearly settlement risk would be .383 million. For reconciliation risk, the amounts are not as straightforward.

The 'reconciliation ageing account' represents a class of accounting and record keeping errors that includes nostro, depot, and intra-system breaks (within the bank, but between accounting or reporting systems). These errors also result in losses due to incorrect hedging on wrongly reported portfolios, payment errors, and missed conversion of settlement instructions leading to trading losses. To simplify the example, the operational risk variance is computed as simply a fraction of carry cost for the nostro account for the year. In practice, this figure may be found to be a good proxy for experienced losses. Its basis is that since the breaks are two-sided (credits and debits) losses of half the amount of the entire nostro account should not occur with a 99.9% assurance level. Assuming this is a 3σ loss, 1σ is 16.5% of the total nostro account. In practice operations managers will likely have more detailed information to use for the cost of carry calculations, such as ratios of interest claims for and against, reconciliation write-offs, and ageing account variance to target.

7.7.4 Lending Process

Operational risk in the lending process is also present in the capital markets business in the form of counterparty risk. The trade agreements over long periods that are executed over the counter are especially prone to counterparty risk, or the risk that the counterparty to the trade will not fulfil the obligations. Most financial firms now have systems in place to calculate this counterparty credit risk. The operational risk measure for the lending process includes only the errors in the credit risk estimate. The main errors are in credit scores (the quality rating is in error), default rate error (the default rate is an estimate with associated uncertainty), and recovery rate error (the recovery rate is an estimate with associated uncertainty). For the calculations, the exposure for the trading counterparties and the default rates for the credit quality ratings are needed. These data are given in Tables 7.17 and 7.18. This information allows the calculation of errors in the default rate calculation and provisioning due to errors in the credit classification. For the scoring error, a probability of 0.2 will be used for misclassification of credit quality. This means there is a 20% chance that a credit will be classified in a

Table 7.17 Credit exposure for counterparties of trading business (millions of Euros)

All trading	Exposure	%	Collateral	Net exposure
AAA	734	12	43	691
AA	1893	31	290	1603
A	1222	20	233	989
Other	2343	38	540	1803
Total	6192	100	1106	5086

Table 7.18 Yearly default rates and their std dev for loans by credit quality for Genoa Bank (Moody's 2000)

Credit risk rating	Default rate (%)	Volatility (%)
AAA	0.01	0.00
AA	0.08	0.20
A	0.08	0.30
Other	1.43	1.70

rating group lower than its 'true' group. Using this simple model, the operational risk due to credit scoring is calculated (Table 7.19).

Next the default rate error is calculated partitioned on the credit quality similar to the scoring error. The results shown in Table 7.20 are for operational risk due to lending for the credit default uncertainty.

For credits that default, there is an additional error in the loss given default represented by the recovery rate error. Assuming a recovery error rate of 15% for an expected recovery rate of 38% from Table 7.22 the following calculation for error in loss given default can be estimated. The figures for the recovery rate of

Table 7.19 Operational risk due to credit scoring error of counterparties in Genoa Bank. The portfolio distribution is adjusted using a 20% probability for misclassification

	Exposure	%	Adj Exp	Collateral	Delta exposure	Default (%)	Weighted
AAA	734	9	587	43	−147	0.01	0.0000
AA	1893	27	1661	290	−232	0.08	0.0002
A	1222	22	1356	233	134	0.08	0.0002
Other	2343	42	2587	540	244	1.43	0.0060
Total	6192	100		1106	0		0.64%

Score Relative Error: 9.4%
Score Error: 3 402 160

Table 7.20 Credit default error calculations for operational risk in the lending process

	Exposure	%	Collateral	Net exposure	Default (%)	Weighted	Default error	Error contribution
AAA	734	12	43	691	0.01	0.0000	0.00%	0
AA	1893	31	290	1603	0.08	0.0002	0.20%	3029
A	1222	20	233	989	0.08	0.0002	0.30%	2933
Other	2343	38	540	1803	1.43	0.0054	1.70%	569 583
Total	6192	100	1106	5086		0.58%		575 545

Relative Error: 1.60%
Credit Error: 575 545

38% with a standard error of 1.5% (relative) are based on the table of recovery rates (Moody's 2000) (Table 7.21). The calculations are again shown in tabular form (Table 7.22), but they follow the formula for combining errors given earlier.

7.7.5 Service Process

We now show the estimates for operational risk in the service value-adding processes. The factors for volume volatility and margin error will be propagated to the earnings function. The volume volatility is calculated from the average daily trading volumes for each month of the previous year. Margin variance is taken from the cost performance figures of variance of actual to budget and found to be 7%. The monthly volatility figures for the client trading operation are shown in Table 7.23.

The formula for relating volume and margin to earnings is $E = f(m, v)$, or the change in earnings is dependent on simply the product of margin and volume.

Table 7.21 Table of recovery rates based on Moody's (2000)

Year	Recovery rate (%)
1990	28
1991	35
1992	39
1993	45
1994	30
1995	38
1996	39
1997	42
1998	45
1999	35
Mean	38
Std. Err.	0.6
Rel. Error	1.5

Table 7.22 Recovery error calculations for credit exposure in trading portfolio

	Exposure	%	Collateral	Net exposure	Default	Recovery	Recovery error	Error contribution
AAA	734	12	43	691	0.0001	0.3800	0.015	20
AA	1893	31	290	1603	0.0008	0.3800	0.015	5530
A	1222	20	233	989	0.0008	0.3800	0.015	2110
Other	2343	38	540	1803	0.0143	0.3800	0.015	2 236 100
Total	6192	101	1106	5086		38.00%		2 243 750

Recovery Error: 149 792

Table 7.23 Volume volatility calculations for daily trading volume (client trading)

Month	Daily volume
Jan	800
Feb	1800
Mar	1800
Apr	1450
May	2050
June	1400
July	1300
Aug	1000
Sep	2300
Oct	2150
Nov	1300
Dec	1850
Mean	1600
Std. Err.	39
Rel. Error	2.4%

From this basic relation the error equations for volume and earnings can be derived as follows:

Volume

$$\sigma_{E,V}^2 = m^2 \sigma_v^2$$

Margin

$$\sigma_{E,V}^2 = v^2 \sigma_m^2$$

Putting these two equations into a table and using the figures of 4000 trades per day with 2.4% relative error for the volume and 40% gross margin (from the income statement) with 7% for the relative error for the margin gives the results for the operational risk in services (Table 7.24). This error is the daily error in earnings due to volume and margin uncertainty. There are several approaches to scaling it up to a yearly figure. One of the simplest uses a square root of time argument wherein the scale factor is simply $\sqrt{t}$, where t is the number of days. So, the factor is the square root of 260 days, or about 16.1, for a yearly error of 2.3 million Euros. The example could have included partitioning of the margin and volume risk factors by product in order to provide a more accurate figure.

Table 7.24 Summary of service calculations (daily earnings in Euros)

Exposure	Volume	Income per trade	Volume error	Margin	Margin error	Error contribution	Error
4 800 000	4000	1200	0.024	0.4	0.07	20 226 996 364	142 222

7.7.6   Summary of Delta Method Calculations for Genoa Bank

To summarise the calculations so far using the Delta method, Table 7.25 shows the major factors considered for each of the value-adding processes and the resulting operational risk measure calculated.

It is not surprising that the operational risk in capital markets is dominated by valuation. Large trading exposures magnify even small model errors to create a sizeable source of risk. What is possibly more interesting is the significant amount of other operational risk and the seeming reasonableness of the figures.

7.7.7   Step 3: Determine the Threshold

For single transaction loss the standard error for the processes of investment and credit dominate, but the overall error is 13.9 (million Euros) for the year. Total revenue for the year is approximately 2000 million (from the income statement), so the error is about 0.7%. Selecting 2.33 standard deviations (a 99% confidence level for a normal distribution) for the threshold gives 1.62% (relative) as the maximum loss per transaction. Since the exposure per trade is 400 000 Euros, any loss above 6484 Euros should be classified as a large loss for Genoa Bank. In practice, a value of 5000 Euros or lower will be used.

7.7.8   Step 4: Apply the EVT Methodology

Now the extreme values relevant to the business unit of the bank can be considered using the Delta method. Assume you have been recording losses above 5000

Table 7.25   Summary of operational risk measures (yearly) using the Delta method for Genoa Bank

Summary of Operational Risk Measures (Delta)		
Euros (millions)	Standard error	Error contribution
Investment	13.26	175.92
Valuation	12.81	164.21
Settlement	0.38	0.15
Reconciliation	3.40	11.57
Credit	3.45	11.92
Scoring	3.40	11.57
Default	0.57	0.32
Recovery	0.15	0.02
Service	2.29	5.26
Volume	0.75	0.56
Margin	2.17	4.70
Total	13.90	193.10

Table 7.26 Table of losses above 5000 Euros for the Genoa Bank example

Loss('000)	Date
50	01/02/00
4571	01/03/00
24	01/04/00
212	01/10/00
31	02/03/00
10	03/11/00
25	04/15/00
17	04/20/00
1332	05/07/00
32	05/11/00
1675	05/13/00
81	05/28/00
32	06/16/00
69	07/11/00
16	07/21/00
10	08/03/00
16	08/14/00
28	09/01/00
16	10/03/00
24	11/07/00
202	11/08/00
54	11/11/00
42	11/16/00
44	11/17/00
24	12/26/00

Euros and Table 7.26 shows the losses for one year (a total of 8 638 000 Euros for the year). Using the POT method, we fit a GPD to this data using maximum likelihood fitting to generate the parameters for GPD and the resulting graph of the fit (Figure 7.4). The actual formula and technique were presented earlier in Chapter 6 on the EVT Methodology.

The values of the GPD are shown in Table 7.27. A Poisson distribution fitted to the events shown in Table 7.26 gives $\lambda = 2$ for the monthly frequency for large losses. Using the Poisson distribution ($\lambda = 2$) for frequency and the GPD ($\xi = 0.976$, $\beta = 18.1$) for the severity, a Monte Carlo simulation provides the multiple years' loss distribution shown in Figure 7.5.

Table 7.27 Values for GPD fit from excess loss data

$\xi = 0.976$
$\beta = 18.1$

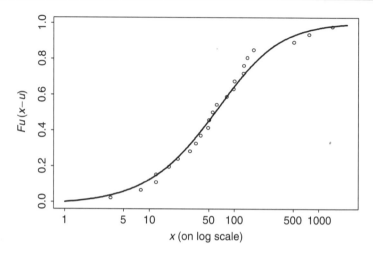

Figure 7.4 Fit of generalised pareto distribution (GPD) to excess loss data for Genoa Bank, where x is the log of the loss amount, u is the threshold, and $Fu(x - u)$ is fitted to the GPD

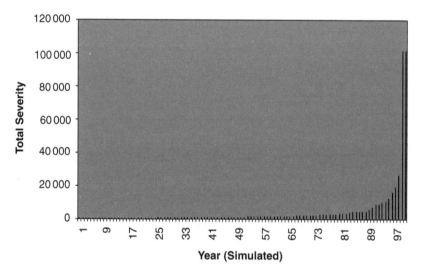

Figure 7.5 Cumulative yearly losses (ordered) for excess loss in the business unit of Genoa Bank

7.7.9 Step 5: Calculate the Operational Risk Measures

The 95% confidence level gives a value of 9.4 million Euros for the excess loss component of the operational risk measures for Genoa Bank. The final results of the operational risk calculations are shown in Table 7.28 (the large loss values in

Table 7.28 Summary of operational risk measures for Genoa Bank. Using 95% confidence levels, risk VaR is 31 million Euros (about 1.6% of revenues) and excess VaR is 9.4 million Euros (about 0.5%) for the year

	Standard error	Error contribution	95% confidence level	99% confidence level
Investment	13.3	175.9	21.88	30.90
Valuation	12.8	164.2	21.14	29.86
Settlement	0.4	0.1	0.63	0.89
Reconciliation	3.4	11.6	5.61	7.93
Credit	3.5	11.9	5.70	8.04
Scoring	3.4	11.6	5.61	7.93
Default	0.6	0.3	0.94	1.33
Recovery	0.1	0.0	0.25	0.35
Service	2.3	5.3	3.78	5.34
Volume	0.8	0.6	1.24	1.75
Margin	1.5	2.4	2.55	3.60
Large Loss			9.36	50.83
Total			40.72	95.12

the table are obtained from a 1000-run Monte Carlo simulation). As can be seen, the value for operational risk capital could be very different depending on the confidence level desired. In addition, it could be argued that the expected losses are already covered by budgets related to the losses (e.g. settlement failures). However, the risk financing strategy and the governance attitude will have the same considerations as in market and credit risk. Trading profits may offset a large portion of market losses over time, but only the losses are used to compute risk capital. In any event the actual amount of economic capital set aside will depend on the attitude and policy of the firm, but should be based on information provided by an objective measurement methodology. In short, the accommodation and pragmatic implementation decisions should be made, to the extent possible, *after* the measurement calculations.

7.8 SUMMARY

Operational risk measures include those from two loss-generating processes. The relevant measures are maximum expected loss, value at risk, maximum unexpected loss, and excess value at risk. Their calculation begins with a business model containing the value-adding process, related activities, and relevant risk factors. Value functions and their difference equations are used to propagate the variance of factors to earnings using sensitivities. Unexpected losses are modelled using plausible scenarios that combine information from actual historical losses over the threshold, external losses, and other plausible events to form the excess loss distribution. Application of the Delta–EVT™ methodology for measuring operational risk can begin with a simplified approach using formulae or causal models and loss history.

7.9 FURTHER READING

Ross (1997) provides a good background for modelling in general and gives a detailed description of partitioning for discrete variables to get the conditional expectation in his Chapter 3. See also Moody's (2000).

8
Causal Modelling

Imagine you work in credit operations and the losses in the corporate loan portfolio have increased significantly over the past few months. Your bank is evaluating the credit scoring methodology, pricing of corporate loans based on value drivers, and considering ways of improving the credit watch list management for distressed loans. You are asked to perform an analysis of the credit watch list management situation and the contribution of the increase in the number of distressed loans to this problem. You list the possible causes and the alternatives available to deal with them, and begin gathering information. The head of corporate loan origination says that distressed loans are not identified quickly enough and once they reach central credit many of them are beyond intervention. The manager of central credit management blames it on deteriorating loan quality, and claims that many of the distressed loans referred to central credit should never have been approved in the first place. Several branch managers give a variety of reasons for the increase in loan distress, including general economic conditions, lack of compliance with procedures, and the influence of 'subjective factors' in approvals and management. There is clearly no consensus among your experts, because they see only part of the process and therefore have different views of the problem and its cause. But the *real* problem is more fundamental—*you* don't have an objective, systematic way of determining the causes or contributing factors for this problem. This is where causal models for operational risk can help.

8.1 INTRODUCTION

Dealing with complex systems and their associated uncertainties requires sophisticated tools. Causal modelling, based on Bayesian decision theory, is a technique that can be used to build operational risk measurement systems and serve as the cornerstone for measuring operational risk. Causal models use *causality* as the basis for building models of the real world instead of *associations* (co-relations of states). The key point is that causal relations are one-way and associations are bi-directional. Although *causal* has the connotation of determinism and necessity, in the practical world causal relations are much more subtle. We say that 'smoking causes cancer' and 'drinking and driving causes accidents', when what we mean is that these 'causes' only make the consequences more likely, not certain. In short, any practical notion of causation requires the ability to express these various degrees of likelihood. Causal modelling based on Bayesian networks fills this need.

This chapter covers the basic ideas of causal modelling. It begins with simple definitions of causality and causal models and a review of the burglar alarm example from the Bayesian chapter (Chapter 12) to help clarify the key concepts. Then a more formal definition of the basic causal relation is motivated by a simple sprinkler example. Next the main ideas behind building and using causal models are described using a famous example from statistics known as Simpson's paradox. The paradox is described using an actual example of university admissions. The chapter concludes with examples of applications of causal models to operational risk in finance and a brief description of their use. More rigorous and detailed discussion of causal modelling, including the algorithms used for causal models (Bayesian updating), can be found in the references provided.

8.2 WHAT IS CAUSALITY?

Causality is the basis for action. Knowing 'what causes what' gives you an ability to intervene in order to affect your environment and control the things around you. It is different from correlation, or constant conjunction, in which two things are associated because they change in unison or are found together. We know that the falling barometer is associated with rain, but we do not think the barometer causes rain. Causality can lead to action, but action based on associations is tentative at best. For instance, you might postulate that there is a positive correlation between the number of fire trucks and the amount of damage caused by a fire. But you would not consider reducing the number of trucks in order to reduce the level of damage. These simple cause-and-effect relations are known from experience, but more complex situations (such as the credit operations described earlier) may not be so intuitively obvious. How then can management develop a causal understanding of its business and take appropriate action to control and manage risk?

The history of investigation into causes begins with ascribing all phenomena to supernatural creatures. Later, responsibility was given to humans as well. Eventually the scientific method (Popper 1959) introduced an approach to dealing with the physical world using controlled experiments and intervention in order to determine 'causes'. In the early part of the twentieth century, statistics was born and the notion of correlation was proclaimed by Karl Pearson as a more fundamental idea than causation (Pearson et al. 1899). To this day, statistics and its primary measure of correlation (and contingency tables) are used for analysis in business and other fields without any explicit notion of causality. In fact, although most of us are taught that 'correlation does not imply causality' and cautioned against the lurking spurious correlation, action is often based on correlation only (Huff 1991). This occurs even though we readily admit that the identification of causality is required in order to formulate a plan of action.

8.3   WHAT ARE CAUSAL MODELS?

Causal models are a way of representing the physical world and reasoning about the impact of uncertain events in it using a definition of causality based on observation and intervention. The notion of causality refers to the idea of being able to influence the value of certain variables by changing the value of a causal factor. This intervention is the primary tool of business management used to achieve the goals of the organisation. Causal modelling in operational risk embodies the mathematics and the business processes into a tool that can be used to provide measures for managing the business. It offers a way of dealing with uncertainty by developing causal relations instead of just associated ones. The advantages of building models around *causal* rather than *associated* information include:

1. The judgements needed to build a causal model are more meaningful, accessible and intuitive.
2. Dependencies that are supported by causal relations are actionable.
3. Causal models are adaptable and can respond to change quickly.

8.3.1   A Simple 'Burglar Alarm' Example

A simple example will help to clarify the key concepts. Consider the situation of your home burglar alarm sounding. The question arises as to whether a burglary is actually occurring. You begin your reasoning by considering whether you have heard any other strange noise. The 'strange noise' event impacts your assessment of the truth of an actual burglary event. You also consider the previous false alarms from your system and are prepared to discount this current alarm based on their frequency. You know, for example, that stormy weather conditions can activate the alarm. In general, you reason that *if event A has taken place, then event B has taken place with probability p*, where probability is a measure of your uncertainty. In this way most people come to a rational assessment of the potential burglary situation and can take reasonable actions accordingly. A causal model for the burglar alarm situation is shown in Figure 8.1, where the circles identify the events in the physical world that are under consideration. The arrows indicate the relation between the events. It is believed that if a Burglary event has taken place, then there is an impact on the likelihood of Alarm. The model also takes into consideration the impact of Burglary on Strange Noise. The reasoning is that if a certain event is known, then there must be an *impact* on the uncertainty of other events. Although impacts remain vague at this point, it is worth noting that the methods used update the uncertainty of the event. In other words, prior information is needed about the situation before input is gathered. In the burglary alarm example, the prior information is the likelihood of a burglary without knowing anything else about alarm soundings, strange noises, or false alarm rates.

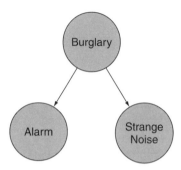

Figure 8.1   Causal model for burglar alarm situation

8.3.2   Computational Example

A computational example using the burglary scenario will show how this operates
in practice. The burglar alarm example will be used in Chapter 12 on Bayesian
Methods and is reproduced here for convenience.

Scenario for Burglar Alarm

A burglar alarm is recently installed in your home and the following information
is given about a situation relating to the alarm. The probability of a burglary in
the neighbourhood is 0.0001 (there is one burglary expected every 10 000 days).
The alarm unit is generally reliable and effective, but still a clever burglar can
disable or circumvent it 5% of the time. Because it uses infrared detectors and
magnetic switches, the alarm can be falsely triggered about 1% of the time. Your
neighbour calls to tell you the alarm is sounding. What is the probability that a
burglary is taking place?

The values for prior probabilities of Burglary and conditional probabilities
for Alarm and Telephone Call are taken from the description of the problem.
The entire example can be found in Chapter 12. A causal model for the burglar
alarm scenario showing the conditional probability tables is shown in Figure 8.2.
Burglary has a prior probability associated with it and Alarm depends on Burglary
with the conditions shown in the table to the right of the alarm node. The model
can provide the answer to the question of the probability of a burglary given an
alarm by setting the value of Alarm to True and noting the probability for the
Burglary value of True as shown in Figure 8.3.

The causal reasoning here is simple and easy to express. A burglary causes
the alarm to sound and the sounding alarm causes the telephone call from the
neighbour. Nevertheless it contains the sophisticated capabilities of measuring
uncertainty, updating the measures, and expressing the sensitivity of causal relations. Even a simple example embodies the key concepts of causal models.

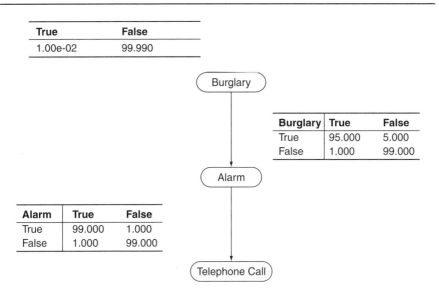

True	False
1.00e-02	99.990

Burglary	True	False
True	95.000	5.000
False	1.000	99.000

Alarm	True	False
True	99.000	1.000
False	1.000	99.000

Figure 8.2 Computational example of a causal model for the burglar alarm scenario showing conditional probability tables

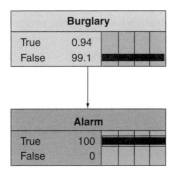

Burglary	
True	0.94
False	99.1

Alarm	
True	100
False	0

Figure 8.3 Alarm and Burglary nodes of burglar alarm model showing Alarm finding set

8.4 CAUSAL MODELLING CONCEPTS

Causal models are built using Bayesian networks and some of the following concepts apply to the underlying network. Formal definitions for them can be found in Pearl (1988, 2000).

- *Random variables.* A causal model includes a set of random variables that have a finite number of discrete values, or states (continuous variables are discretised). These states each have a probability associated with them, so that each random variable has a distribution of state values. In the example above the variables are Burglary, Alarm, and Telephone Call, each having two states (True and False).

- *Dependence*. The random variables in a causal model are linked together in a structure based on their dependency. A variable *A* is dependent on another variable *B* if a change in state of *B* causes a change in the probability distribution for the states in *A*. Each set of variables that is dependent will have an associated conditional probability value for each of the combination of possible states (i.e. the probability of state $1 - m$ for variable *A*, given state $1 - n$ for variable *B* in an $m \times n$ table). The probability of Alarm = True given Burglary = True is 0.95 shown in percent as 95.000 and given in the table to the right of the Alarm variable (Figure 8.2).

- *Updating*. Updating in the causal model is a revision of the probabilities of states for variables based on the joint probability table for variables that are dependent (i.e. connected by links in the network). An example of this table is given in Chapter 12. The algorithm for updating is given in the references.

- *Intervention*. A variable *A* in a causal model can have a finding set when the value for the probability of one of its states is set to one. The other (dependent) variables in the model will have their probabilities updated according to the update algorithm for Bayesian networks. Then the variable *A* has had an intervention. The Alarm variable is set to True to find the answer to the question: 'What is the probability of a Burglary given an Alarm?'

- *Reversibility*. A causal model can be interpreted as a series of events in the 'forward' direction, or as a series of evidence about hypotheses in the 'backward' direction. A consequence of this property is that reversing the arrows has no effect on the model representation, and it will be possible to use an event model or evidence model depending on which is most intuitively useful by simply reversing the direction of the arrows.

8.5   CAUSAL RELATIONS

Causal models are built using causal relations. Causal relations are more stable than associative relations. Consider a simple model of a sprinkler, rain, wet grass, and wet pavement. We might infer that the state of the grass is related to the state of the sprinkler and rain. When the grass is wet, it is likely that it rained or the sprinkler was on. Likewise the state of the pavement is related to rain, but is it related to the sprinkler? And is the state of the sprinkler related to rain? Most associative models would say yes to both questions, based on the data containing the information about all variables for a series of days (Figure 8.4).

The covariance matrix for these variables is shown in Table 8.1. Try to think of the associations and why the data might give these results. In so doing, you will probably use a causal model based on what you know about sprinklers, rain, wet grass, and wet pavement.

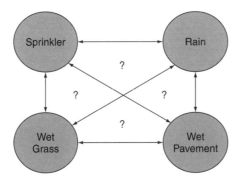

Figure 8.4 Possible relations for model variables of sprinkler, rain, wet grass, and wet pavement

Table 8.1 Correlation table for Wet Grass, Sprinkler, Wet Pavement, and Rain

	Wet Grass	Sprinkler	Wet Pavement	Rain
Wet grass	1	0.8	0.4	0.7
Sprinkler	0.8	1	−0.6	−0.7
Wet pavement	0.4	−0.6	1	1
Rain	0.7	−0.7	1	1

Using the relations between these four variables based on the covariance matrix given, we want to answer the question: 'Is the state of the sprinkler related to rain?' There is obviously no causal relationship between sprinkler and rain, but there is an associative relation because the seasonal variation of rain and plant growth influences when the sprinklers are turned on. Likewise, assuming we do not sprinkle the pavement, the wet pavement will only occur when rain is present. However, there will also be an association between wet pavement and the state of the sprinkler (spurious correlation propagated by the associated relation between sprinkler and rain). This could lead to taking the action of increasing the sprinkler 'on' time with the expectation of getting fewer wet pavements—an intervention that is totally erroneous in this case.

However, we *know* that sprinklers do not cause rain (and vice versa), and the sprinklers do not reach the pavement. A causal model for this problem is given in Figure 8.5. Here the appropriate relations are shown and the statistics will be generated based on the information contained in the model. In this model **Sprinkler** and **Rain** are independent (given **Wet Grass**), and **Wet Pavement** is related to **Sprinkler** only through **Rain** and **Wet Grass**.

It may be possible, of course, for an analyst using an associative model to come to the same results as the causal model. However, it is likely to be more difficult because it will require domain expertise, an exhaustive set of data, and the ability to identify variables that must be included for control. For example, an

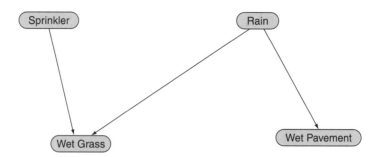

Figure 8.5 Causal model for sprinkler and rain showing model variables based on known relations

associative model might introduce a controlling variable for season to mitigate the Sprinkler and Rain—sprinklers are used more in the summer because it rains less in summer. It seems more straightforward to use a causal model to capture this knowledge and use it to build an effective solution quickly. The point of this exercise is that we know how to build this model because we rely on causal relations between the variables of interest. Had the labels been Greek letters, there would have been much more opportunity for error in building the model. We often use our understanding of causality naturally to influence the way we build and use associative models. Causal modelling makes this step explicit.

Determining causal relations from associated ones is not simple. Intuitively we use the ideas of temporal ordering of correlation and a third (intervention) variable to determine causation. Observing things change together over time and noticing states occurring at the same or relatively same time (conjunction) creates a set of temporally ordered associations. We use the temporal ordering of correlation (and conjunction) as a rough qualification for causes (causes do not create historical effects) and we call these temporal associations possible causes. These associated relations are the beginning of causal relations. But the intervention variable is key. Once we have a set of possible causes, we need a way to classify them as genuine causes or spurious correlations. Potential causes may be classified into spurious associations and genuine causes (relative to your model) as follows.

Spurious Association

Given two variables *a* and *b* that are independent, the discovery of a third variable *c* that is associated with both *a* and *b* rules out any cause-and-effect relation between *c* and either *a* or *b*. The reason is that any cause of *a* or *b* would be propagated to the relation between *a* and *b*, since the presence of a common cause implies dependence among the effects. If sprinklers are independent of rain, and wet grass is associated with both sprinklers and rain, then wet grass cannot be a cause of either sprinklers or rain.

Genuine Cause

Consider two variables *a* and *b* that are dependent. The discovery of a third variable *c* that makes the two variables *a* and *b* conditionally independent qualifies *c* as a genuine cause. To understand what is meant by conditionally independent, consider that a barometer reading is associated with rain, but low pressure is a third variable that makes the association between the barometer and rain conditionally independent (once we know that there is low pressure our knowledge of the barometer reading does not add anything). The low pressure rules out the barometer as a cause of rain. Since the knowledge of low pressure makes the association between barometer and rain independent (conditionally independent, given low pressure), low pressure qualifies as a genuine cause of rain (in our model). The formal concept of conditional independence is as follows:

Conditional Independence. X and Y are conditionally independent given Z if

$$\Pr(x|y, z) = \Pr(x|z) \text{ whenever } \Pr(y, z) > 0$$

This means that the probability of *x* given *y* and *z* is the same as the probability of *x* given *z*, or, knowing the value of *y* adds no more to the information about *x* after the value of *z* is known.

The formal definitions of potential cause, genuine cause, and spurious association are summarised from Pearl (2000). Given temporal information (i.e. assuming the context *S* is defined earlier than *X*), the following definitions are given.

Potential cause. Every variable preceding or adjacent to variable *X* has a potential causal influence on *X*. In the causal model graphical representation, the potential causes are the variables that occur before the variable *X* in the graph. Graphically, *Y* is a potential cause of *X* if there is a path from *Y* to *X*.

Genuine cause. A variable *X* has a genuine causal influence on another variable *Y* if there exists a variable *Z* such that:

1. *Z* and *Y* are not conditionally independent given *S*, and
2. *Z* and *Y* are conditionally independent given $S \cup X$.

Spurious association. Two variables *X* and *Y* are spuriously associated if they are dependent in some context *S*, if *X* precedes *Y*, and if there exists a variable *Z* satisfying:

1. *Z* and *X* are not conditionally independent given *S*, and
2. *Z* and *Y* are conditionally independent given *S*.

The above formal definitions may seem complicated at first, but in practice causal relations are often much easier to identify.

Using causal models can help solve some of the more difficult problems quickly and easily and generate useful results for management and control. Sometimes these models are difficult to identify using associative relations. The next section shows how causal models can be used to overcome one of the most pervasive problems in statistics, Simpson's paradox. The paradox is, incredibly, that *any* statistical measure (based on associative relations) can be *reversed* by introducing an appropriate new variable into the model.

8.5.1   Simpson's Paradox

One of the most perplexing and famous problems in statistics is called Simpson's paradox. It is named after E.H. Simpson who described the phenomenon in Simpson (1951), but was probably first encountered much earlier. The problem is embodied in a report of the 1973 admission statistics for the University of California at Berkeley. The question arises whether the admissions process for the university is 'fair', or does it discriminate based on the gender of the applicant? A table of the summary of statistics for 1973 admissions is shown in Table 8.2.

Given the difference between 45% and 34% in admission success rates, one does not have to perform a detailed analysis to see the *prima facie* evidence for discrimination in admissions. With a large sample of over 4000 the difference could not be subject to so much random variation. On further investigation, the admission rates for individual departments within the university are examined. These statistics are given in Table 8.3.

Table 8.2 Summary of statistics for 1973 Berkeley admissions

	Total	Male	Female
Applied	4526	2691	1835
Admitted	1826	1198	628
Rate	40%	45%	34%

Table 8.3 Berkeley admission statistics broken down by department

Dept	Male			Female		
	Applied	Admitted	%	Applied	Admitted	%
Dept1	825	512	62	108	89	82
Dept2	560	353	63	25	17	68
Dept3	325	120	37	593	202	34
Dept4	417	138	33	375	202	54
Dept5	191	53	28	393	94	24
Dept6	373	22	6	341	24	7
Total	2691	1198	45	1835	628	34

Looking at the data for each department, a rather astounding fact emerges. In most individual departments the admission rate for females is, in fact, higher than the rate for males. And in the two departments where the rates for males are *higher*, the difference is only minor. How can it be that the overall university rate is significantly higher for males, but the individual departments have higher rates for females? Using these data a case could be made for discrimination against females based on the overall figures and against males using the department figures. But obviously these arguments are contradictory, so this model is flawed. But how?

The answer is that the gender of the applicant is only associated with the admission status and not a cause of it. There is another factor that is the cause and it influences both the admission status and the gender. (Hint: In this case it's the department.) Using causal models, it is easy to explain this phenomenon.

Consider the following model of Admission, Gender, and Department using the data given above (Figure 8.6). Note that the variables are given explicitly as Gender, Admitted, and Department. Within the variables the possible states are shown (Gender[Male,Female], Admitted[True,False], and Department[Dept1...Dept6]). The links between the variables denote a relation between the variables and two variables with links are dependent (the direction of the arrow gives the order). This model explains admission in terms of gender, so you can read 'the state of Admitted depends on the value for Gender', and 'the Department applied to depends on the value of Gender'. Variables that have no connection are independent, or conditionally independent, given their parents (the node higher up in the hierarchy or opposite direction of the arrows). Using this model you can set a value for any of the variables (intervene) and the model will update the values of the other variables in the model. So, given

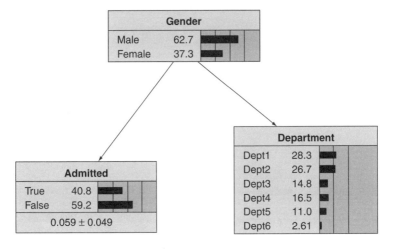

Figure 8.6 Causal model for Berkeley admissions problem using summary statistics

that Gender = Female, the updated Admitted variable is shown in Figure 8.7. As can be seen, the admission probability given that the Gender is Female has dropped to 34.2%. This is significantly below the average. And, if you select Gender = Male, Figure 8.8 shows the result that there is a significant advantage to being male.

These are the same figures shown in Table 8.3. The problem with this model is, of course, that the department in the university sets the standards for admission and determines whether or not an applicant is admitted, and the simple model shown above does not include the effect of department on admissions. This is clear because there is no dependency link between Department and Admitted.

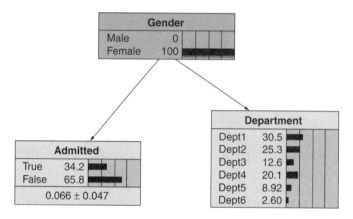

Figure 8.7 Berkeley causal model updated with Gender = Female

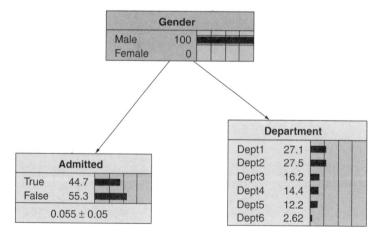

Figure 8.8 Berkeley admissions model with Gender = Male showing higher admissions probability

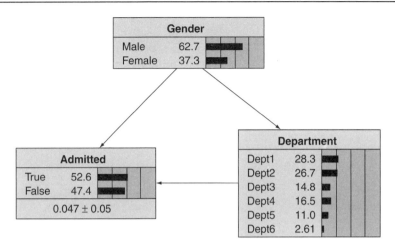

Figure 8.9   Berkeley admissions model showing dependency between Department and Admitted

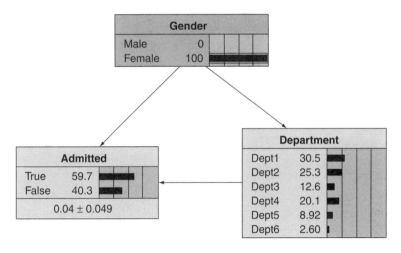

Figure 8.10   Berkeley complete causal model showing Female admissions higher

A revised model with this link is shown in Figure 8.9. Note that the probability of being admitted has now changed because the probability of being admitted depends on the department applied to as well as the gender.

This model makes more sense to most people, as it is understandable that the department will influence the probability of being admitted through the setting of standards, demographics, budgets, etc. Given this new model, the same question regarding gender is answered quite differently, as shown in Figures 8.10 and 8.11. In these two diagrams you can see that the probability of being admitted is

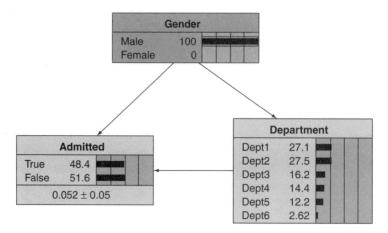

Figure 8.11 Berkeley complete causal model showing Male admissions lower

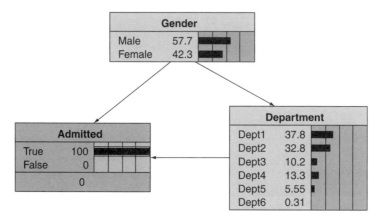

Figure 8.12 Berkeley admissions model with Admitted = True showing distribution of Department admissions rates

actually higher for females than for males (59.7% versus 48.4%). The explanation for the conflict between this result and the overall summary statistic is because departments with higher admissions rates also had a higher number of male applicants. This fact can be shown by setting the value of Admitted = True and looking at the distribution of Department as shown in Figure 8.12. As can be seen from this diagram, the probability of being admitted to Dept1 or Dept2 is very high, and any application to Dept6 is likely to be rejected. Therefore, publishing a figure for the probability of admission based on equally likely department admissions is obviously incorrect. This type of analysis is relatively simple to do using a causal model.

8.6 USING CAUSAL MODELS

Causal models support management in two ways. First, they facilitate measurement of the uncertainty associated with the processes. Second, they provide information about the effects of possible interventions. These two analytical capabilities are the key ingredients in supporting decisions using causal models. The models can be 'trained' like a neural network by entering historical data incrementally and updating the probabilities. The models then provide immediate multi-factor coefficients similar to a generalised regression. The advantages over neural networks and regression techniques include ease of understanding (since, unlike a neural network, the variables are explicitly described), and computational tractability (since, unlike regression techniques, the dependencies are explicit and extraneous covariances are eliminated). A possible disadvantage is that special domain expertise may be required to describe the structure of the model a priori. Using causal models for operational risk measurement:

1. brings transparency to the cause-and-effect relation between the business activities of the firm and the volatility of earnings;
2. can be used by both mathematicians (to analyse complex business relations) and the business manager (to take actions and make strategies); and
3. takes the abstraction out of complex situations by visualising the relations graphically rather than through mathematical equations.

In the remainder of this chapter an example of a causal model for settlement risk is presented and its ability to measure the risk, provide information on possible intervention, and generate scenarios and simulations is described. Finally, some practical issues in implementing causal models are described.

8.7 CAUSAL MODEL FOR SETTLEMENT RISK

An example of a simple causal model for the settlement risk processing model in an investment bank is shown in Figure 8.13. The variables that represent factors related to settlement loss are identified in the boxes and their possible values are grouped into categories shown by the associated histograms with the 'percent of' values in each category. The expected value of a numerical variable is shown in the bottom of the box along with a two-sided variance. The model has been trained with sample transaction data for an investment banking operation.

Settlement loss (shown in the box at the bottom) depends on the exposure due to the transaction and the amount of delay. Likewise, exposure depends on the average value of a transaction and whether it is a buy or sell. Delay depends on a number of factors related to the transaction, including the exchange, domicile, counterparty, product, and daily volume. Using this model, it can be seen that 79% of transactions have no settlement loss and that the expected value of settlement loss is 0 Euros (with a large variance 1.7e +005). This is to be expected as

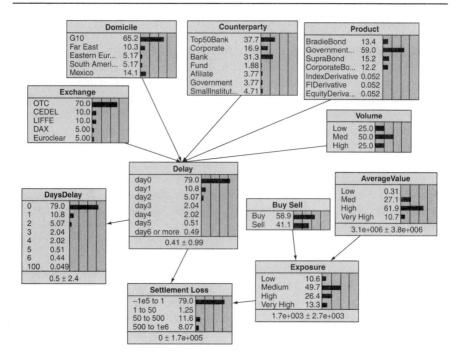

Figure 8.13   Simple causal model for settlement risk

normally settlement failures would occur a small percentage of the time (less than 10%) and carry costs might average less than 1000 Euros for the failed trades. Other factors include information such as the observation that 65.2% of transactions are from G10 countries.

8.8   ASSESSING POSSIBLE INTERVENTION

Because the model is easy to understand and the underlying probabilities update *in situ*, it is possible to perform sensitivity analyses interactively. After setting the value of any variable, the network's probabilities are updated and the results of the intervention are immediately available. Thus, to see the settlement loss for only Mexico trades, one can set the value for the domicile variable to 'Mexico' and all other nodes in the network are immediately updated to reflect their conditional probability given that the domicile is Mexico (Figure 8.14).

Interestingly, the network also works 'backwards' so that to see where the large settlement losses are coming from, one simply sets the Settlement Loss variable's node value and all other nodes are immediately updated. As previously mentioned, the model is trained using actual data, and can also be 'run forward' to simulate data from the network. A simulation generates a set of data that have the same probabilities as the network.

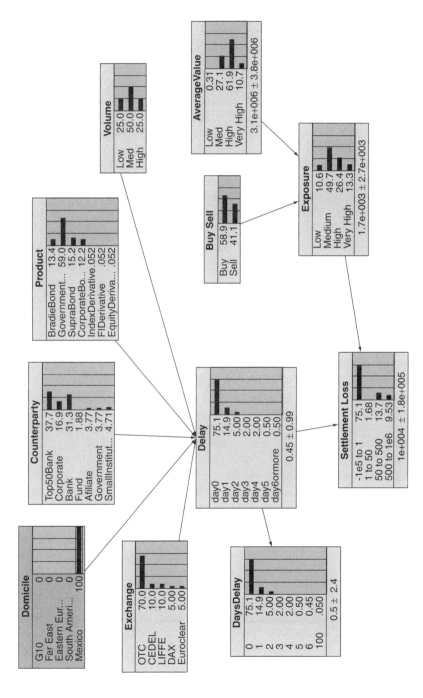

Figure 8.14 Settlement model with finding for Domicile as Mexico entered

8.9 SCENARIO AND SIMULATION WITH CAUSAL MODELS

Causal models based on Bayesian networks can easily generate scenarios and simulation using the information contained in the network. In order to generate a scenario, likelihoods are entered into the relevant nodes in the network. A likelihood is defined as

$$l(A) = \frac{\Pr(A)}{\Pr(\overline{A})}$$

or simply the probability of the occurrence of an event divided by the probability that an event will not occur. The relative likelihood is the probability of an event divided by the probability of another event and these figures can also be used to create a scenario. For instance, given the two values, True and False for a successful settlement event, one can say that True is 10 times more likely to happen than False. This results in a probability setting for the values of $\Pr(A) = 0.909$ and $\Pr(notA) = 0.091$ approximately. Many individuals may be more comfortable estimating likelihoods than estimating probabilities directly. This is important as the complexity of the models increases and scenarios become more complex.

8.9.1 Simulation Using Causal Models

Monte Carlo simulation is a well-known technique for generating a statistic from any arbitrary distribution. The technique of Gibbs sampling is used for causal models because they embody a full joint probability table. Gibbs sampling is a method of performing Markov chain Monte Carlo simulation where the proposed distribution is the actual distribution, and thus all generated samples are accepted (Gilks *et al.* 1996). It amounts to sampling from a full joint probability model. The key to Gibbs sampling is being able to construct the full joint probability model. This full probability model is embodied in the conditional probabilities included in the Bayesian network underlying the causal model. The result is excellent performance for simulation using causal models. The performance of a causal model for simulation depends primarily on the number of nodes and particularly the number of links between them. Normally a causal model will have a specific purpose and use that will allow minimisation of the number of interconnections of nodes. Given a fairly complex network of 25 nodes (Figure 8.15), the times shown in Table 8.4 using a laptop PC can be expected.

Table 8.4 Timing for causal model performance

Generate 10 000 Monte Carlo scenarios using Gibbs sampling: *less than 10 seconds*
Train using 10 000 transactions: *less than 60 seconds*

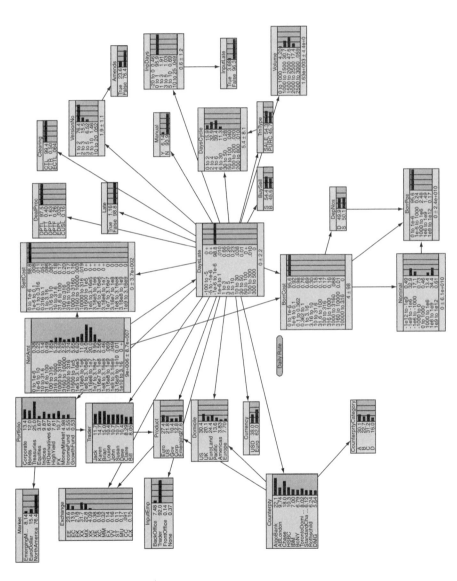

Figure 8.15 Fairly complex model used for benchmark performance figures

8.10   PRACTICAL ISSUES

8.10.1   Where Do the Probabilities Come From?

The probabilities in the causal models described above have come from the relative frequencies of events. Calculating probabilities in this way gives an empirical model and requires enough data to generate good results. In addition to data-driven probabilities, subjective probabilities using assessments and probabilities from parametric distributions can also be included. Parametric distributions and subjective probabilities are added to the graphical model using special nodes that contain equations or explicit parametric distributions. This is useful for developing loss models. Categories and ranges for variables outside the observed empirical values can also be added. These adjustments add information from sources outside the bounds of the empirical model and increase the robustness of the simulation and scenario testing. For example, to add a random error into the settlement process a new node that contains a normal distribution, described by its mean and variance, could be linked to the settlement delay node. The delay would then not only depend on the transaction factors, but also on the random error value. As a result, even though no delays greater than six days were observed, the random error variable could introduce additional possible values so that a range of 10–30 days would be considered.

8.10.2   Implementation of Causal Models

In production, the model can be connected to data sources for transactions that are used to train the model. Given a trained model, the daily reporting and monitoring of transactions consists of comparing the new incoming transactions with the trained model. Outliers and anomalies are reported as exceptions and daily statistics for causes of errors, failures, and losses can be generated from the model. Periodically the model needs to be retrained in order to take into account any changes in the transactions and processes over time. Because of their good performance in training and simulation as described earlier, causal models can be linked to high volume production system processes.

8.11   SUMMARY

Causal modelling is a powerful tool for building representations of diverse problem domains and incorporating a wide range of input information. They are able to represent problems graphically and encode large numbers of variables and relationships in compact form. Because causal models are graphical, they are more easily understood by domain experts, and because they are based on causal relations, domain experts can participate fully in their construction. Since casual relations can be based on categorical data as well as numerical data, and subjective probabilities as well as objective (e.g. property or frequency) probabilities, they are applicable to a wide range of problems. The application of causal models is now widespread in fields such as oil exploration, medical systems, and nuclear risk. There are many tools available to build and evaluate causal models, and a number of excellent references.

8.12 FURTHER READING

The original work on causal modelling is Pearl (1988) and it is still a basic reference for Bayesian networks and their interpretation as causal models. The recent work by Pearl (2000) deals more directly with the idea of causality. See Shafer (1996) for a nice introduction to probability trees and their use in modelling and inference. A practical description of causal modelling is given in Jensen (1996). Implementation of causal models can be found at `http://support.microsoft.com/support/tshoot` and various tools are also available (see for example `http://www.norsys.com`, `http://www.hugin.com`, and `http://www.mrc-bsu.cam.ac.uk/bugs`).

9
Causal Models for Operational Risk

9.1 INTRODUCTION

Causal models are an important tool for implementing a systematic approach to managing operational risk. They enable the efficient and effective implementation of the operational risk framework and methodologies introduced earlier to support operational risk management. Building causal models for operational risk involves identifying key risk factors and building risk models for them using the sensitivities of earnings and correlation between factors. This implies an understanding of the causes of earnings volatility in order to predict and control risk. Thus, causal models are used to develop a clear way to directly influence the earnings volatility and support the goals of operational risk management. Using the extensibility of causal models, operational risk can be analysed at the appropriate level of detail for finance, management, and control. Causal models also serve as an implementation tool to help identify risk factors, calculate sensitivities, and partition volatility using characteristics of the risk factors. In addition, they simplify the generation of loss distributions and scenario-based excess loss events. In summary, causal models are well suited to the measurement and analysis of operational risk.

This chapter is about building causal models to implement the proposed measurement framework for operational risk. First, the main advantages of causal models for operational risk are summarised from an earlier chapter. Next, the steps for building a causal model for operational risk are presented, broken down into those associated with building and training causal models and those for using the trained model. A section on implementing causal models for operational risk provides the practitioner with general guidelines and a summary of the basic steps, followed by an in-depth example using (again) the fictitious Genoa Bank to clarify the key concepts and show some sample calculations. Then, for the more experienced practitioner, advanced uses of causal models for operational risk, such as models for compliance and consistency, are discussed and examples presented. The chapter concludes with a brief summary.

9.2   ADVANTAGES OF CAUSAL MODELS FOR OPERATIONAL RISK

Causal models are a way of representing the physical world and reasoning about the impact of uncertain events in it using a definition of causality based on observation and intervention. The advantages of using causal versus other models for operational risk were presented in Chapter 8, and the main points are summarised as follows:

1. The judgements needed to build a causal model are more meaningful, accessible and intuitive.
2. Dependencies that are supported by causal relations are actionable.
3. Causal models are adaptable and can respond to change quickly.

Casual models are generally easier to understand and interpret because relationships are represented graphically rather than textually. Causal models expand the framework ideas into an illustration of the relation between the risk factors, activities, and value-adding processes that make up the operations of a business unit. With causal models in place, it is easier to see the impact of the operational risk structure than with a list of earnings functions or calculated end results and this makes them useful as a medium for discussion with business managers. Building a causal model for operational risk begins with the measurement framework and the Delta–EVT™ methodology.

9.3   BUILDING A CAUSAL MODEL FOR OPERATIONAL RISK

Up to this point in the book it has been assumed that the important risk factors for calculating operational risk measures have been known. This certainly may not be the case in many real-world applications, but using causal models helps the task of identification and evaluation of factors. Causal models can serve as an implementation tool to help identify risk factors, calculate sensitivities, partition volatility, and to simplify the generation of loss distributions and scenario-based excess loss events. Building causal models for operational risk involves seven steps, which are presented in this section in two groups, namely those steps associated with building and training causal models and those for using the trained model. *Building and training* the causal model involves using the information generated from developing a business model guided by the proposed measurement framework to create a causal model structure that can be calibrated with empirical or analytical data for the nodes to get to a trained model. *Using* the trained causal model requires adding other information to generate the operating loss distribution and associated measures for operational risk.

9.3.1   Getting a Trained Model

A trained causal model follows the business model part of the measurement framework. It contains all the processes, activities, and risk factors of the business model along with their volatilities and sensitivities. The four steps to getting a trained model are described as follows:

Steps 1 and 2: Start with the measurement framework, and put it into a causal model structure. These are the steps for identifying what is related to what. The causal model structure can be thought of as the top-level causal model for the framework because it makes explicit the link between operational risk, value-adding processes, activities, and risk factors. A causal model for operational risk is dominated by the risk factors because they are the 'causal' part of the method-ology. Figure 9.1 shows the completed structure with the addition of external loss. Although this is not a causal factor because it is not generated by the value-adding processes, it must be added because it is another source of loss (as discussed in the framework chapter).

Steps 3 and 4: Collect data on causal model nodes, volatilities and sensitivities, either analytical or empirical, and train the model using one of two approaches. Once the causal model structure is built, the next step is to train the model. This can be done either empirically or analytically.

- The empirical approach means to train the model with empirical data. Transac-tion-level (historical) data are input into the causal model structure to produce a trained model. The Bayesian network underlying the causal model enables the calculation of volatilities and sensitivities that are then stored as condi-tional probabilities in its structure in order to end up with a final trained model. Transaction-level data come from historical values for the factors. Figure 9.2 shows the empirical path which uses historical data to train the model
- The analytical approach means calibrating the model with analytical data to get a trained model. The analytical data, in the form of volatilities and sensitivities, are input directly into the causal model structure. From the trained model, simulated data can then be generated. In this case volatili-ties and sensitivities come from other sources such as studies or benchmarks. Figure 9.3 shows the analytical path, which starts with volatilities and sensi-tivities for training the causal model that then enables the generation of simulated data.

Whether one takes an empirical or analytical approach to train the model depends on the availability of accurate data, and so in general the choice is more or less dictated by existing information at hand. Usually both paths are available and a combination of the two approaches can be used. Figure 9.4 shows a trained

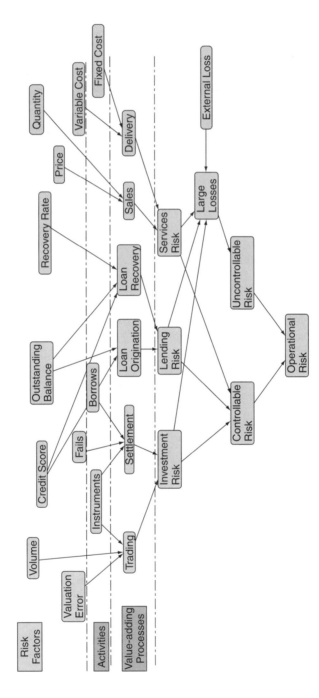

Figure 9.1 Causal model structure showing the risk factors, activities, and value-added processes for a financial firm

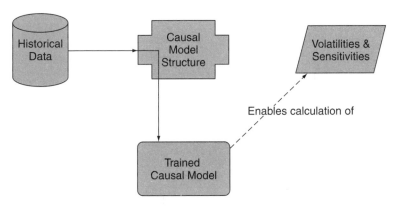

Figure 9.2 Determining volatilities empirically in order to develop a trained causal model

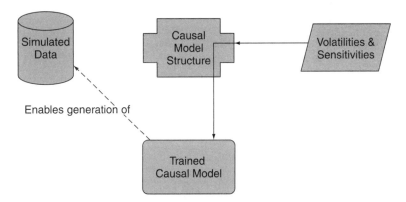

Figure 9.3 Starting with volatilities and sensitivities to train the model analytically

causal model structure for Genoa Bank, a fictitious company introduced earlier in Chapter 7 to demonstrate the concepts.

9.3.2 Using the Trained Model

Now that the causal model is trained, there are three more steps that need to be completed which are associated with *using* the trained model. The first two correspond to the Delta and EVT parts of the Delta–EVT™ methodology introduced with the measurement framework. The third serves as a way of testing the importance of the risk factors and, in general, the validity of the model. The three steps are summarised as follows.

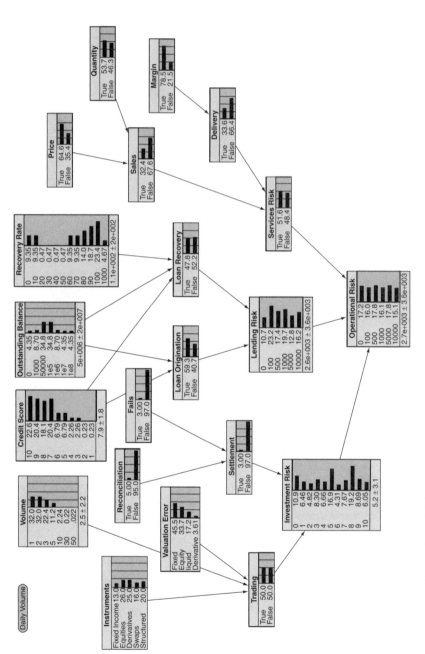

Figure 9.4 Trained causal model for operational risk containing volatilities, sensitivities of risk factors, and showing distributions of values for Genoa Bank

Step 5: Generate an operating loss distribution. This is where the maximum expected loss and value at risk measures of operational risk will come from. Using the causal model that has now been trained with the historical data (empirically), a loss distribution using Monte Carlo simulation and the Bayesian network underlying the causal model can easily be generated. This simulation goes quickly because the probability distribution is already completely contained in the Bayesian network subject to the categorisation and quantization chosen for the nodes.

Step 6: Generate scenario losses that contribute to the excess loss distribution. Using a model with appropriate causal factors, specific values for some of the factors can be chosen in order to generate stress points for operational risk excess losses. For instance, in the trained causal model for Genoa Bank presented in Figure 9.1 above, the daily Volume (node in the upper left corner) can be set to a very large value in order to generate extreme values for the loss distribution using the causal model.

Step 7: Evaluate the risk factors. This is how to determine if the risk factors chosen are indeed the important ones and thereby validate the model. The sensitivities of the losses to risk factors are an important measure to validate the significance of the risk factors in the model. Other tests are based on more traditional statistical measures like contribution to variance.

Once all seven steps are complete, the end result is an operational risk measurement model that can be incorporated into a production management information system (MIS) and used to provide decision support for management. Following are general guidelines and a summary of the basic steps.

9.4 IMPLEMENTING CAUSAL MODELS FOR OPERATIONAL RISK

This section provides the practitioner with general guidelines and a summary of the basic steps used to implement causal models.

9.4.1 General Guidelines

General guidelines for building causal models for operational risk include the following.

1. *Start with the model and involve the business manager.* The process of causal modelling is begun not by collecting the data but by developing the model. Good data are expensive and it is important to narrow down the possible factors before data collection. Candidates for key factors should come from the existing expert knowledge within the firm. The identification of value-adding processes, main activities, and factors affecting performance are business analysis tasks, not mathematical ones. This means that building the

structure of the causal model requires business involvement. Business unit managers have the expert knowledge to build a causal model by identifying the processes, activities, and risk factors and linking them together in a hierarchy of dependencies.

2. *Use a tool.* Operational risk measurement and modelling is complex. Building causal models and providing management information from them requires an iterative approach to modelling and a systematic approach to implementing an MIS. Good tools that enable causal models to be built and tested quickly are needed, and once a good model is developed, the tool must be capable of incorporating the model into a production system. Otherwise, the process may become mired in data gathering, the search for the perfect model, or the implementation issues for a production MIS.

3. *Validate using a utility measure on actual data.* The test of any model is validation using actual data. Beware of tests that produce measures of accuracy with no corresponding evaluation of the accuracy required of the model. Simple scoring schemes can be devised to reinforce the accuracy of the model in calculating volatilities and sensitivities based on established objectives in order to provide regular feedback to management on the performance of the model in terms of its usefulness.

9.4.2   Summary of the Basic Steps

Given the foregoing discussion, a summary (and Figure 9.5) of the basic steps in causal modelling for operational risk are:

1. Identify the value-adding processes, activities, and factors affecting performance.
2. Build a causal model structure reflecting the dependencies and hierarchy of the processes, activities, and factors.
3. Collect data on causal model nodes (volatilities and sensitivities), using either analytical or empirical techniques.
4. Train the causal model to develop volatilities and sensitivities.
5. Use the trained causal model to generate an operating loss distribution.
6. Generate scenarios for factors and simulate excess loss events.
7. Evaluate the model factors in order to identify important risks.

Because operations are continually changing, operational risk modelling is an ongoing effort. New factors can be considered and the models revised and re-validated using the above procedure in an iterative fashion. In the following section, an in-depth example for the fictitious Genoa Bank (as in Chapter 7) is used to show the application details for the above steps and underscore the benefits of causal modelling for operational risk.

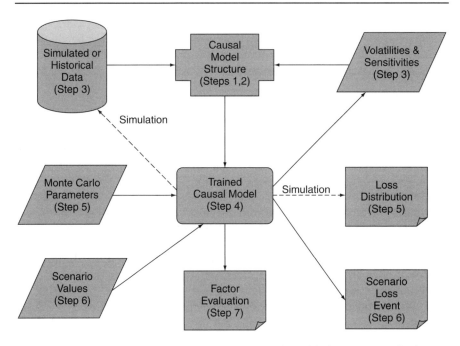

Figure 9.5 Seven basic steps to implementing causal models for operational risk

9.5 EXAMPLE CALCULATIONS: GENOA BANK EXAMPLE USING CAUSAL MODELS

The example starts with the capital markets business unit for Genoa Bank, given here in the form of a causal model. To the extent possible, the same structure and values used for the Genoa Bank example in the Delta–EVT™ modelling chapter (Chapter 7) have been used, and the same three value-adding processes for a financial firm are included, namely investment, lending, and service. For clarity, each of the processes is shown separately with an associated causal model diagram. The factors for the model are generally toward the top of the diagram with the risk measures at the bottom. Each box displays the distribution of values for the factor or measure using a value and percentage figure with a corresponding horizontal bar chart. At the bottom of the node is the expected value (mean) for the variable and its standard deviation (for continuous variables). Exponential notation is used for large values (e.g. 2e5 is 2×10^5 or 200 000). The mean and standard deviation depend to some extent on the quantization error when selecting the discrete values used for the distribution. The nodes of the model are connected with arrows showing (conditional) dependency between the factors and measures (factors not connected are conditionally independent). Constants (e.g. carry costs) do not have an associated distribution and are shown in nodes with their name only. They can be set to one of several possible values for modelling and simulation. There may be some difference between the figures calculated using the equations in Chapter 7 and the causal approach herein which are due to the quantization error and the fact that the causal models use discrete distributions that are not necessarily normal (Gaussian).

9.5.1 Investment

The trained causal model for the Genoa Bank example investment process is shown in Figure 9.6. Here, investment risk depends on trading risk, reconciliation risk, and settlement risk, and is simply the error combination of these figures. Trading risk depends on valuation error, and settlement risk depends on interest claim risk. The factors for valuation error are the instruments and proprietary volume of trading. For each of the instruments, the valuation error is calculated using the constant node for the instrument valuation error (e.g. equities err) and the proportion of its proprietary volume from the Instruments node. For reconciliation risk, the factors are nostro ageing and nostro amount. Interest claim risk depends on the fails rate and the days of settlement delay. Its value (as well as the value for reconciliation risk) is calculated using a simple interest rate exponential formula using the constant cost of carry (carry cost). The values calculated by the causal model can be compared with the values for the Delta methodology (i.e. Delta–normal) using the summary of operational risk measures in Chapter 7. The careful reader may notice that the values are slightly different between the approaches. For example, the causal model value for settlement risk is 0.3 million Euros compared with 0.4 million Euros (using Delta–normal), and 3 million Euros compared with 3.4 million Euros (using Delta–normal) for reconciliation risk. The overall risk using the causal model is 13.6 million Euros versus 13.3 million Euros in the Delta–normal model. The overall difference of 2% and the reconciliation difference of 10% reflect the quantization chosen and non-linearity and deviation from normality of the loss function and its distribution.

9.5.2 Lending

The trained causal model for the Genoa Bank example lending process is shown in Figure 9.7. For the lending model, lending risk depends on default risk, scoring risk, and recovery risk. Default risk is calculated using the standard error of the default probabilities for each loan quality rating. These errors and the associated default probabilities are given constants. They are applied based on the total exposure and distribution of credit quality. Scoring risk depends on the score quality distribution which is the credit quality distribution adjusted for the scoring error. Recovery risk depends on the recovery rate and associated recovery rate error. These values are very similar to those values calculated in Chapter 7

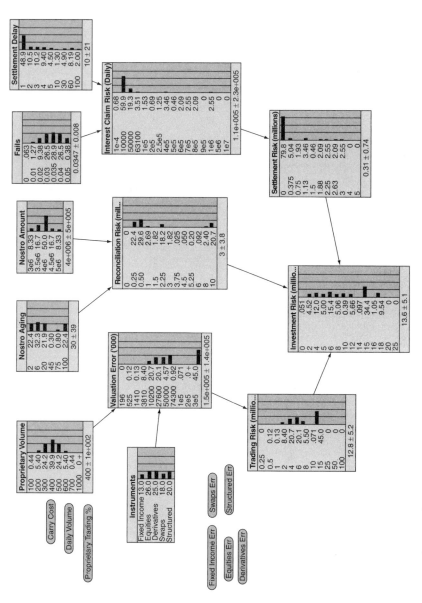

Figure 9.6 Causal model for operational risk in the investment value-adding process of Genoa Bank

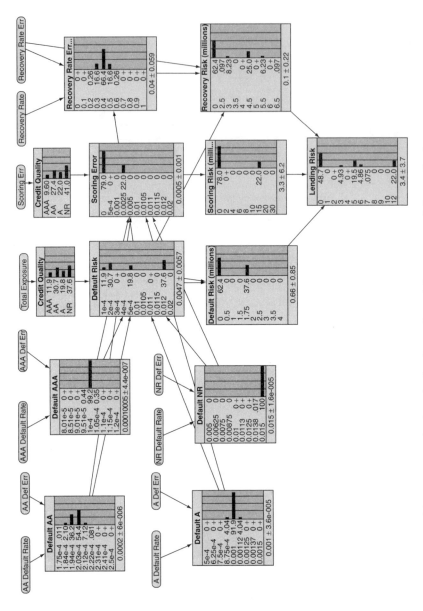

Figure 9.7 Causal model for operational risk in the lending value-adding process of Genoa Bank

using Delta–normal. The causal approach calculates an overall lending risk of 3.4 million Euros compared with 3.5 million, with the largest relative difference in recovery risk (this is the smallest contributing factor). Scoring risk is 3.3 million Euros with a causal approach versus 3.4 using Delta–normal, and default risk is 0.66 million Euros using the causal model compared with 0.6 using Delta–normal.

9.5.3 Service

A trained causal model for the service process of the Genoa Bank example is shown in Figure 9.8. The service process risk is a simple model that only uses

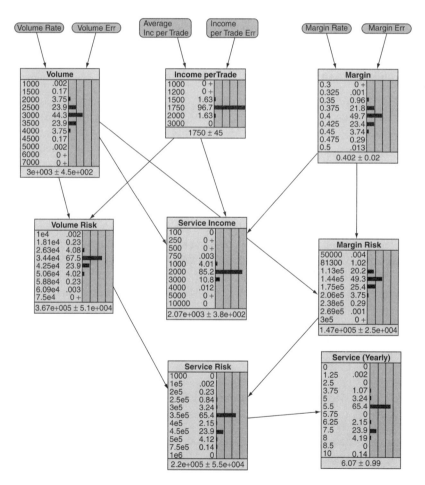

Figure 9.8 Causal model for operational risk for the services value-adding process of Genoa Bank

volume risk and margin risk as key components of service risk. The factors are simply volume, income per trade, and margin. Each of these distributions is generated from a two-parameter normal distribution using calculated means and standard deviations for the factors. These are shown in the constant nodes at the top of the diagram. In addition to calculating the service risk, the service income is also shown, along with its corresponding distribution. The total value for service risk (yearly) is calculated using the causal model as 2.2 million Euros compared with 2.3 using Delta–normal. To compare the components, multiply the values in the causal model by 16 ($\sqrt{260}$) to get the yearly risk figure shown in Table 7.25 given in Section 7.7 of Chapter 7. Volume risk is thus 0.6 million Euros (.0367× 16) compared with 0.8 using Delta–normal. The margin risk of 2.4 million Euros (0.147× 16) in the causal model is more than the 2.2 million Euros using Delta–normal.

9.6 ADVANCED USES OF CAUSAL MODELS FOR OPERATIONAL RISK

Causal models are a general tool that can be applied to many complex modelling problems. For instance, they can also be used with loss data to implement the EVT methodology and for advanced process monitoring. Advanced uses of causal models for process monitoring include models for efficiency and effectiveness and models for compliance and consistency. These can be thought of as second-level causal models because they are developed as derivatives from the top-level model. In Section 9.6.2 on advanced models for efficiency and effectiveness, detail models are discussed. Detail models are for managing operational risk efficiently and for determining assignable causes to improve the efficiency and effectiveness of the value-adding processes engaged in by the business unit. The examples provided include the banking activities of settlement and loan origination and their factors of fails and credit score, respectively. In Section 9.6.3 on advanced models for compliance and consistency, process models are discussed. Process models aid audit and control of the value-adding processes in the business unit by testing for compliance and consistency. The two examples that are briefly discussed are a process model for compliance in setting up a new client for trading and a consistency model for a loan watchlist.

9.6.1 Causal Model for Loss Data and EVT

Up to now causal models have been used for only the Delta methodology, but they can also be applied to EVT. The basic approach is to fit a GPD function to the data by using the Bayesian network to calculate the parameters of ξ and β for the GPD. This is an empirical Bayes estimation and more on the various techniques of Bayesian parameter estimation can be found in technical works such as Press (1989) and Berger (1985). The causal model is made up of the data from the historical losses (loss data) and the GPD probability distribution function value is generated from the data using the two parameters ξ and β. The parameters are selected so that the GPD function updates the parameters for the given loss data in order to 'fit' the distribution to the data (Figure 9.9).

9.6.2   Transaction Models for Efficiency and Effectiveness

For the risk manager and business manager, the top-level models such as those discussed earlier in this chapter provide the information needed to plan and allocate resources. However, for the operations manager, a more detailed model is needed to manage the day-to-day operations and provide the measurement and feedback in order to fine-tune the processes. For instance, settlement fails are the cause of the carry cost and provide enough detail for financial planning, but the operations manager is interested in the causes of these fails and must model at a more detailed level. In this section two detailed causal models for transactions are presented, one for capital markets and the other for credit operations. The first is a transaction attribute model for settlement. It is based on the trade characteristics and process performance indicators of a capital markets settlement operation, and can be used to evaluate settlement performance and risk at a detailed transaction level. The second is a credit scoring model and can be used to validate the credit origination process based on a set of loan applicant characteristics.

Model 1: Settlement Model for Trading Transactions

In general, settlement is the culmination of a trade, and consists of exchanging securities and cash under a defined set of terms and conditions. Using a trading business as an example, a simple transaction attribute model for monitoring the settlement risk in operations will be built. For the transaction model the attributes of the transactions must be specified. In this case a trade will be identified by the attributes shown in Table 9.1.

The passing of the value date without the trade being settled is a settlement failure, and this is a key factor in the operational risk measurement of the trading

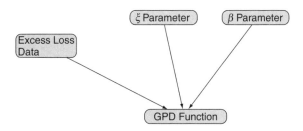

Figure 9.9   Causal model showing empirical Bayesian estimation of the GPD parameters ξ and β for the EVT methodology

Table 9.1 Transaction attributes for trade in the bond trading business activity model

Attribute	Description
Trade date	Date the trade was made
Value date	Date the trade is due to settle
Product	Type of product traded
Counterparty	Name of counterparty of trade
Trader	Trader who made the trade
Valuation error	Uncertainty measurement for value
Valuation method	Model used for valuation error
Amount	Net amount of trade
Clearing method	Method of settlement
Settled status	Status of settlement

business. The simple causal model for failures is built by formulating a 'naïve Bayes' network (a Bayes network with all attributes contributing to the settlement failure), as shown in Figure 9.10.

This simple model has the transaction attributes as factors and settlement failure as the measure. All the factors are connected to the simple measure. (Since a Bayesian network is invariant with respect to the arrow direction, the arrows will often point outward to minimise the size of the tables that have to be stored and increase the computational performance.) Since Settlement Cost is a function of the Cost of Carry, this model is expanded by including the number of days delay past the value date (Days Late) that the trade actually settles and by computing a Cost of Carry for the funding during the delay period. The expanded model is shown in Figure 9.11.

Note that Days Late has replaced Settlement Fails as the key measure. This is because once the number of days late is known, settlement failure is also immediately known (i.e. Days Late >0 implies Settlement Fails = True). The

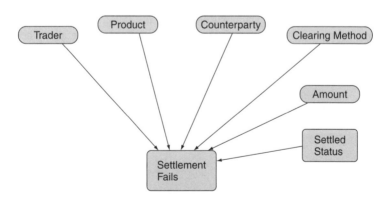

Figure 9.10   Simple settlement attribute model using the 'naïve Bayes' network

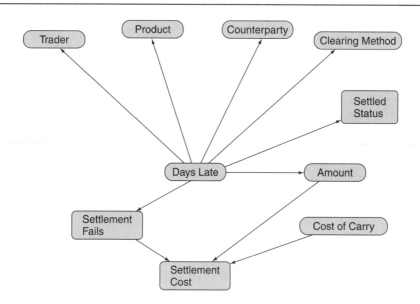

Figure 9.11 Expanded settlement attribute model with arrows 'out' and including Days Delay and Cost of Carry

Settlement Cost depends on the Days Late, the amount of the transaction, and the Cost of Carry (an interest rate). Since there is no parent for Cost of Carry, this must be input into the model directly as a constant. Also interesting is the lack of dependency between Trader and Product. It is assumed that most traders only trade in certain products and that there would be a strong relationship between these factors. As long as there is no interest in predicting trades from products (or vice versa) these links can be omitted with no effect on the ability to understand settlement failures and associated costs. Later, if there is an interest in detecting anomalous trades in portfolios, these links must be included because of their obvious importance to inferences that might be made. As the last step, Borrowing Cost is incorporated into the detailed model for settlement. The borrowing cost depends on whether or not a trade is late, and is distinguished by a negative position for the instrument. Trade Value is used for both interest cost due to late settlement and borrow cost due to borrowing to deliver. The complete detail model structure is shown in Figure 9.12.

The probabilities in an attribute model are usually populated using frequencies based on historical transactions. Using a database of transactions, the conditional probabilities are computed by the network using the frequencies occurring for the combinations of variables included in the model structure. For each variable the values for that variable (or range of values if the variable is continuous) that occur are recorded and their frequencies of occurrence are used to compute conditional probabilities for the dependencies. There is a set of values that occurs

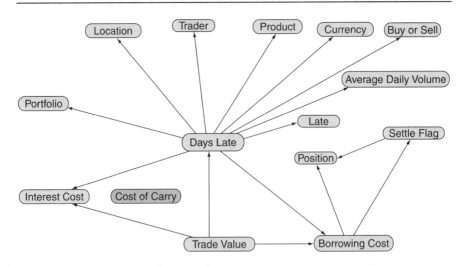

Figure 9.12 Complete model for settlement showing interest cost and borrowing cost

and the frequencies of occurrence for them are stored in the model for each of the variables in the structure. For each dependency there is also a set of conditional probabilities between the two variables for each of the values they take on. Given a settlement failure frequency of 2%, then Settlement Fails = TRUE with probability of 0.02 and Settlement Fails = FALSE with probability of 0.98. A calibrated model using several days of transactions might look like the example in Figure 9.13. In the model it can be seen that Fred has traded 5.84% of the trades and that the location shown as GB has had 24.9% of the trades. Overall, about 2% of the trades are late, but you may also inquire as to how many of George's trades are late by setting a finding on the Trader variable for George and viewing the Late variable. In doing this it can be seen that George has a significantly worse settlement rate than the firm taken as a whole (6.57% versus. 2.02%) as shown in Figure 9.14 with Trader = George, and node labelled Late.

An even more interesting question is: 'Given that a trade is late, what attributes is it likely to have?' This is calculated by the model by setting the finding of Late = TRUE, and the results are shown in Figure 9.15. Using this figure you can see the values of the variables that contribute most to settlement failure can be identified (Late = TRUE). By comparing this figure and the previous one for all settlements, you can determine the relative contribution to being late for each of the variables in the model. For instance, the US location had 24.9% of failed trades (Figure 9.15) and only 13.7% of all trades (Figure 9.13), showing a significant propensity to fail more than the average. By calculating such differences over all nodes and measuring the change in Late, a sensitivity table for contribution to Late can be developed (Table 9.2).

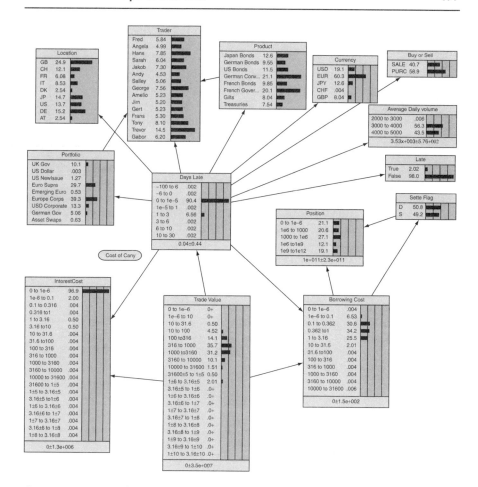

Figure 9.13 Trained Settlement Attribute model showing percentages for all values (ranges) of variables

In practice models can be more complex, but the ones presented here can provide a good overview of the activity and lead to some initial measures, discussion, feedback, and improvement of the measurement and modelling effort for operational risk at the operating unit level.

Model 2: Credit Scoring Model for Loan Origination

Credit scoring is a technique for assigning a quantitative credit risk measurement to individuals or institutions for the purpose of pricing and making loan approval decisions. It is used extensively in retail banking for credit cards and car loans, and most recently has been applied to home mortgage loans. It is also used

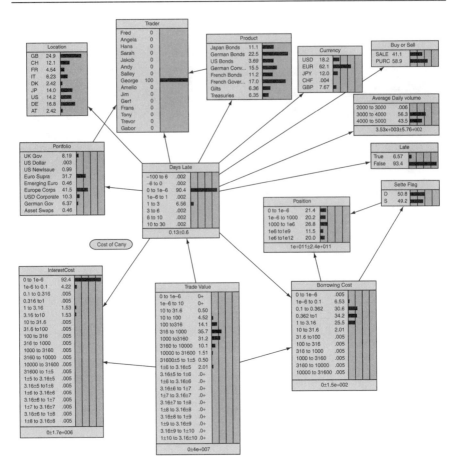

Figure 9.14 Settlement attribute model with Trader = George showing three times the average settlement failure

for loan origination in commercial banking. A classic commercial retail credit scoring model generates a score of between 400 and 800 based upon lifestyle, credit history, financial condition, and other credit experience of retail applicants. A model is structured with factors that are relevant to loan repayment and the model is trained with existing loan data. Such a model is shown in Figure 9.16 and a brief description of the factors is given in Table 9.3.

The node in the centre of Figure 9.16 shows the credit score for existing loans. Typically a score of 650 would be 'good' credit quality and scores above and below are grouped so that expected repayment problems can be identified using the ranges. Figure 9.17 shows an example model trained with a set of loan data. The causal model shown can provide key insights into the process and can be used to answer the following operational questions:

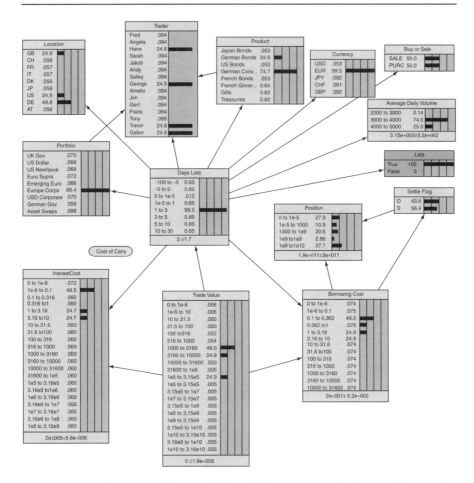

Figure 9.15 Settlement attribute model with the **Late**=True finding set showing the contributing factors to late settlement

- What are the most important factors determining credit worthiness?
- What is the volatility of the credit score?
- What is the score for a particular application?
- Which loans have the strongest credit scores?

Assuming the model has been built and trained with existing loans as shown in Figure 9.17, it can now be used to answer some of the questions posed. For example:

- *What are the most important factors determining credit worthiness?* Setting the Credit Score node to 700 (see Figure 9.18) shows the factor contribution

Table 9.2 Late sensitivity to other nodes in the causal model using a quadratic score

Node	Score
Days Late	0.019742
Interest Cost	0.014565
Trade Value	0.00286
Product	0.000936
Trader	0.000815
Portfolio	0.000625
Borrowing Cost	0.001311
Location	0.000544
Currency	0.000273
Position	0.000137
Daily Volume	7.07e-05
Buy or Sell Flag	1.46e-05
Settle Flag	8.3e-06

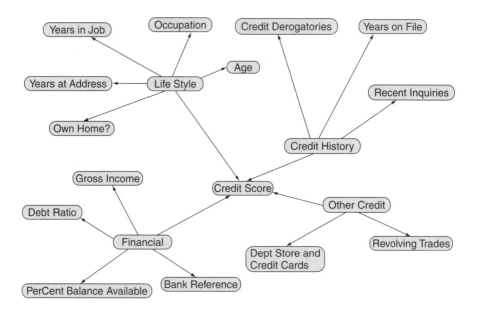

Figure 9.16 Demonstration model for credit scoring

to being granted credit (assuming a score of 700 is the cut-off). It can be seen that the Lifestyle node has gone from an average value of 194 (credit scoring model trained with existing loans) to a value of 230 (more than 15% increase), while the other nodes have not increased nearly as much. Clearly, the lifestyle of the applicant is an important factor in granting loans using this

Table 9.3 Table of credit scoring factors and their descriptions

Factor	Description
Years in Job	Number of years at present job
Years at Address	Number of years resident at present address
Own Home?	Whether the applicant owns a home
Occupation	Applicant's occupation
Debt Ratio	Ratio of outstanding debt to total gross income
Gross Income	Yearly gross income
Percent Balance Available	Per cent of credit card limits or retail limits used
Bank Reference	Current account, savings account at banks
Credit Derogatories	Worst credit action to date (e.g. late payment, collection, bankruptcy)
Years on File	Number of years of credit history on file with central agencies
Recent Inquiries	Number of recent inquiries as to credit worthiness with central agency
Revolving Trades	Credit with revolving accounts
Credit Cards	Number of credit card or major department store credit accounts

model. A complete table of node contributions can be built using sensitivities as shown earlier.

- *What is the volatility of the credit score for loans granted?* The mean credit score is 648 with a standard deviation of 86. The volatility is the standard deviation (86) and, if assuming a normal distribution, 95% of the loans would have a score of at least 448. The actual distribution shows 0.89% of loans with a score of 450 or less. To reduce the credit scoring compliance risk, the volatility of the score for loans granted must be reduced. Assuming a cut-off value of 650, about 42% of the loan portfolio is below the cut-off point. Of course this analysis assumes no migration of scores after the loan is granted.

Because the causal model includes categorical variables and weightings, it is useful for credit scoring applications. Indeed, with a causal model the non-linearity of credit scoring is easily accommodated and often better results can be achieved than with traditional discriminate analysis. For a more in-depth discussion of credit scoring methodologies, see Caouette *et al.* (1998).

9.6.3 Process Models for Compliance and Consistency

In addition to improving the efficiency and effectiveness of processes, causal models can also be used to measure compliance and consistency. Compliance means following specific procedures that are described in documents for the process. Consistency means following a pattern of action with few exceptions, even though the pattern has not been explicitly prescribed. In this section two

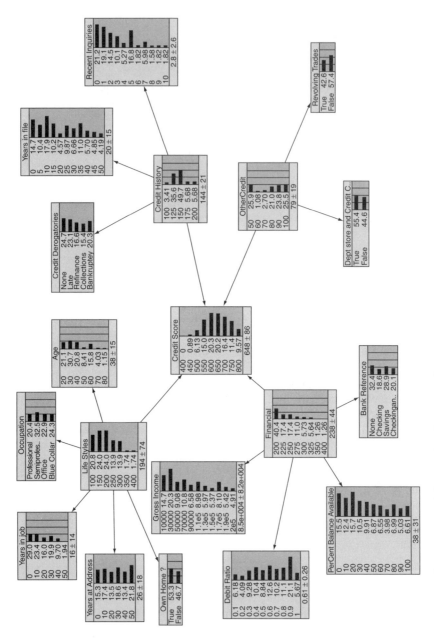

Figure 9.17 Credit scoring model trained with existing loans

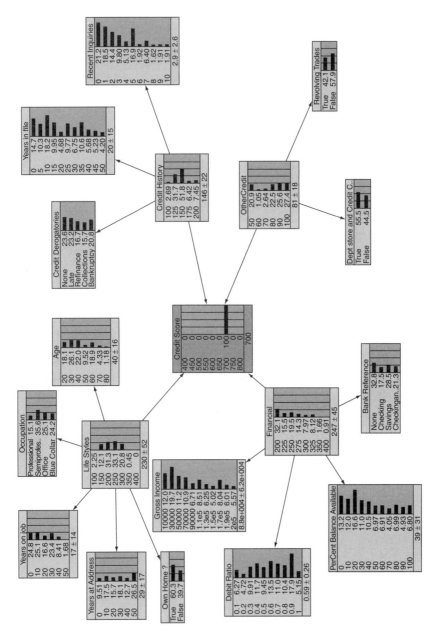

Figure 9.18 Credit scoring model showing factors contributing to being granted credit

models are shown that are aimed at measuring compliance and consistency in processes. The first is a model for compliance in trade origination and covers the process required to set up a new client for trading. The compliance measures for the control points in the process are measured using elapsed time to completion. In the second model the consistency of management for distressed loans is modelled. This model is used to evaluate the consistency of putting loans on a 'Watchlist', where central credit management's objective is to avoid default and improve recovery rates for loans that are in danger of defaulting (but are not yet in default). The measure is based on the characteristics of a loan that puts it onto the Watchlist, and loans on the Watchlist are compared with loans that are predicted by the model in order to create an exception list of inconsistencies.

Model 1: Trade Process (Compliance)

In the capital markets area, three of the main processes in the value chain are trade origination, trade settlement, and trade management. Origination is the start of a new trade, including new client set-up and new product set-up. Settlement is the completion of the trade and includes confirmation, delivery, and payment. Trade management is required for ongoing events that affect the completed trades such as corporate actions or interest payments due. Each of these processes has a set of steps that are required and these steps generally depend on the type of product being traded and the client or counterparty being dealt with on the trade. A simple causal model for the process of setting up a new client is shown in Figure 9.19.

Most capital markets operations have detailed procedures that cover the steps required in each of these stages, and specific control points that require verification and checking before the process can proceed. The first control is to determine

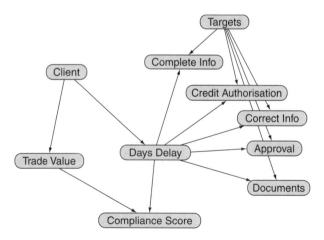

Figure 9.19   Causal model for measuring compliance of setting up a new client process

if the client information is complete. Incomplete client information can result in the trade settlement being delayed, with subsequent charges for interest due. The second check is a credit authorisation for the client in order to ensure the client can fulfil payment obligations to the bank. The third check is for correct client information because the same settlement problems can occur if the client details are incorrect. The next check is management approval for the new account, which is also a double check in order to ensure the client is able to meet any payment obligations. The last control check is to ensure that the legal documentation is completed so that any transactions entered into with the client are legally binding. These control points are often probed by a control self-assessment using a questionnaire via a survey or in a moderated forum. However, for risk measurement, a more objective count of successes and failures, or timely completions, is used.

The compliance model is calibrated using targets for delay for each of the process steps. Then existing client transaction data are input to determine the elapsed days between each of the process steps as well as Trade Value. These figures are then compared with the Targets. The variances to target are ordered and provided as a list of compliance exceptions. In addition, the volatility of the delay can be used as a measure of compliance risk and to estimate potential future failures. A compliance model such as this can be used to generate specific exceptions for operations and audit follow-up, measure overall compliance risk for risk management, and identify key factors contributing to it (possibly by adding a detail level attribute model as discussed earlier for Days Late).

Model 2: Watchlist Process (Consistency)

On both the commercial and private sides of the lending business most banks maintain a so-called 'Watchlist' for loans that for some reason or another require close monitoring. Usually individual credit managers keep a list of such loans, which they report to a central credit department. The decision of the credit manager to include a loan on the Watchlist is based on many interrelated factors, and thus can be very complex. Moreover, many factors influencing the decision are 'soft', and their relevance and weighting are difficult to determine accurately. In addition, there is usually a large number of outstanding loans (thousands of commercial clients and usually more in retail) which makes efficient regular monitoring of all factors extremely difficult.

A central credit department may develop an aggregate Watchlist by collecting those of individual credit managers (a 'bottom-up' process). However, it does not provide a consistent, systematic overview of the entire credit portfolio. Since early systematic identification of critical loans is key to avoiding potential defaults and improving recovery rates, an alternative is for the central credit department to develop a list of critical loans independently of the credit managers based on the key causal factors of distress (a 'top-down' process). This is a good example of an advanced use of a causal model for operational risk. Such a system can provide an overview of the entire portfolio, and credit managers can be made aware of key risks based on the causal model.

It is significant that the model can be calibrated to reflect current practice. The model is trained using historical data and then used to predict loans that should be put on the Watchlist. The 'list of exceptions' (loans with a high probability of being on the Watchlist but that are not on it) can then be reviewed by credit managers. In this way, earlier recognition of every loan that should be on the Watchlist may lead to a reduction of operational risk by reducing the volatility of both the default and recovery rates. A simplified Watchlist causal model is shown in Figure 9.20, where the node in the centre shows how many loans (in percent) are placed on the Watchlist. For the purposes of this example model, the factors influencing Watchlist membership are (clockwise from the bottom): Credit Score (1–10); industry Sector, each of which has its own credit rating (A–E); location of issuing Branch; Overdraft Utilisation; Credit Tightening; Amortisation Lengthened; and Performance Outlook. The task of the modeller is to determine how the various possible values of these factors influence the inclusion of a loan on the Watchlist.

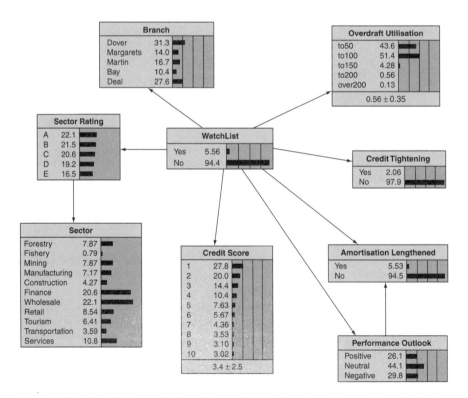

Figure 9.20 Simplified credit Watchlist model for detecting distressed credits before default

Once the trained model has been developed, the probability of a subject loan being on the Watchlist can be measured by setting the values of the model to match those of the loan. Figure 9.21 shows the probability of a specific loan being on the Watchlist (approximately 44% given the loan's attributes). Loans with a high probability of being on the Watchlist can be reviewed. Factors and branches can also be analysed to determine if there are systematic errors in the Watchlist process.

In practice, the model is trained with a set of loans that are on the Watchlist along with a set that are not. The resulting model is used to predict the probability of being on the Watchlist for the rest of the loans in the portfolio. It is then a simple matter to order the loans that are not on the Watchlist by probability and select the high probability loans for an exception list and submit them for further investigation. This provides a list of loans that, given the pattern of characteristics for the Watchlist process, should be on the Watchlist (with a high probability), but are not. Using such a model large numbers of loans can be reviewed quickly in a central location on a regular basis and exceptions forwarded to the appropriate credit manager for further review.

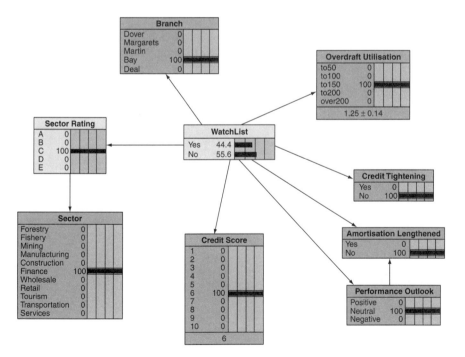

Figure 9.21 Watchlist probability estimate for a specific loan in the Finance sector, score 6, Bay Branch, with 100%–150% overdraft utilisation, neutral performance outlook, and no credit tightening or amortisation lengthening

9.7   SUMMARY

Causal models are an important tool for implementing a systematic approach to managing operational risk. Building causal models for operational risk starts with the business model of the proposed measurement framework introduced in Chapter 4. The key is to build a causal model structure that can be trained and calibrated to generate operational risk measures. This is a complex process, and it is important to have business management involvement, use an appropriate tool, and validate the models using a utility measure on actual data. An example using the fictitious Genoa Bank provides the practitioner with material to study the techniques and evaluate the calculations at a more relaxed pace.

9.8   FURTHER READING

Several tools are available commercially that can help to implement causal models, and the figures in this book were captured from models created by Netica® from Norsys Corp (http://www.norsys.com). The application of causal models to operational risk is relatively new and information is available via the website http://www.genoauk.com. More advanced applications of causal models are available by studying the detailed discussion of loss models for implementing EVT, transactions models for improving business unit efficiency and effectiveness, and process models as aids to compliance and consistency.

SECTION IV
MATHEMATICAL FOUNDATIONS

10

Error Propagation

Suppose you want to determine the 'true' height in millimeters of a new door for your home. Using a carpenter's rule the upper frame of the old door measures between the marks of 2743 and 2744 mm. Should you estimate somewhere in between (e.g. 2743.5 mm) or select 2743 because it's the mark on the rule that is closer to the edge? The *precision* of the measurement rule has introduced *uncertainty* in the measurement because the marks on the rule are a finite distance apart and the edge of the door has aligned in the gap between them. A carpenter friend advises to select the closer mark and assume that the height is between 2742.5 and 2743.5. He also advises 'measure twice, cut once', so you take a second measurement, but now it's between 2744 and 2745. Maybe you're not holding the ruler straight. So you measure three more times to get a series of five measurements. The problem now is the *randomness* in the procedure of measuring, so you take the average of these to get 2742.8 and you attach the plus or minus 0.5 mm uncertainty to it. But now you wonder if maybe you're measuring a different spot on the door. So, this time you measure the left side and find that the upper edge lies between 2741 and 2742. This means the height is now 2741 (the closer mark) and assumed to be between 2740.5 and 2741.5. You're using the same rule so the measurement has the same precision, but the door is not the same height in all places. The problem is now the *definition* of the measurement. Is it the height in the middle of the door? The minimum or maximum height? The average height? Your carpenter friend advises that height is the maximum of the three measurements at either side and in the middle. You now have a door height of 2742.6 (plus or minus 0.5 mm precision) using the minimum of each average of five readings taken at the left, middle, and right side. Satisfied, you order the door and fit it. Six months later it's winter and you notice a cool draft coming under the door. You re-measure the door and find it is now 3 mm shorter! In a panic you call your carpenter friend, who explains that the new door has dried out since you measured for it last summer and the reduced moisture content has caused it to shrink by 3 mm. The *environment* or *context* of the measurement has changed and the door height has now even more uncertainty in it. This example may seem a bit contrived, but it demonstrates that sources of uncertainty are difficult to specify even in relatively simple situations. Without an understanding of the sources of uncertainty and the risks involved (errors in the measurement) even though you take great care to get the 'right' answer, you may still get it wrong.

10.1 INTRODUCTION

Within the context of measuring operational risk, error propagation is the technique for relating errors and omissions in business activities to the volatility in performance. Understanding error propagation supports the basic idea put forth in this book that errors and omissions in the activities associated with value-adding processes cause operating losses within a business. Since relatively small mistakes can lead to large losses, the Delta method is proposed to measure the uncertainty in the activities and link this uncertainty to the resulting volatility in earnings. This chapter presents the theory of error propagation, a fundamental tool in error analysis and the theory upon which the Delta method is based. It is a common misconception for the layperson to think of errors as mistakes, but here 'error' is the term used for *uncertainty in measurement* and not necessarily mistakes. This important distinction lays the foundation for a discussion of the basic concepts of measurement, the sources of uncertainty, and the theory of error propagation. This chapter begins with an overview of measurement standards and the organisations that sponsor and promote their use, and a discussion of the importance of measurement error and its effect. Next, basic concepts of error modelling are explained, followed by discussions of direct and indirect measurement and the need for error propagation. Then the use of error models to establish intervals for measures and for classifying blunders is presented. Finally, the art of getting good measures requires a dialogue with business managers to capture the characteristics of measures and criteria for evaluating them, and the chapter closes with some thoughts on other measurement topics that support this objective.

10.2 MEASUREMENT STANDARDS

The authoritative guide for expressing uncertainty in measurements is certainly the *Guide to the Expression of Uncertainty in Measurements* (ISO Guide or GUM) (ISO Guide 1993). The document is available from the International Standards Organisation and many of its affiliate organisations. Much of the following information on the GUM is available from the US National Institute of Standards and Testing (NIST) web site. The ISO Guide is the result of an effort by the ISO Technical Advisory Group on Metrology (TAG 4) using the following terms of reference:

> To develop a guidance document based upon the recommendation of the BIPM Working Group on the Statement of Uncertainties which provides rules on the expression of measurement uncertainty for use within standardisation, calibration, laboratory accreditation, and metrology services;
> The purpose of such guidance is:
>
> • to promote full information on how uncertainty statements are arrived at
> • to provide a basis for the international comparison of measurement results.

The ISO Guide includes 'general rules for evaluating and expressing uncertainty in measurement that can be followed at various levels of accuracy and in many fields—from the shop floor to fundamental research'. It includes detailed definitions and formulae for the expression of uncertainty in measurements from a broad spectrum, including:

- Maintaining quality control and quality assurance in production;
- Complying with and enforcing laws and regulations;
- Conducting basic research, and applied research and development, in science and engineering;
- Calibrating standards and instruments and performing tests throughout a national measurement system in order to achieve traceability of national standards;
- Developing, maintaining, and comparing international and national physical reference standards, including reference materials.

The GUM has found wide acceptance throughout the world. In the United States the National Conference of Standards Laboratories (NCSL) has prepared and widely distributed Recommended Practice RP-12, *Determining and Reporting Measurement Uncertainties*, based on the GUM. ISO published the French translation of the GUM in 1995, German and Chinese translations were also published in 1995, and an Italian translation was published in 1997. Translations of the GUM into Estonian, Hungarian, Italian, Japanese, Spanish, and Russian have been completed or are well underway. GUM methods have been adopted by various regional metrology and related organisations including:

- NORAMET   North American Collaboration in Measurement Standards
- NAVLAP   National Voluntary Laboratory Accreditation Program
- A2LA   American Association for Laboratory Accreditation
- EUROMET   European Collaboration in Measurement Standards
- EUROLAB   A focus for analytic chemistry in Europe
- EAL   European Cooperation for Accreditation of Laboratories

Moreover, the GUM has been adopted by the National Institute for Standards and Testing (NIST) and most of NIST's sister national metrology institutes throughout the world, such as the National Research Council (NRC) in Canada, the National Physical Laboratory (NPL) in the United Kingdom, and the Physikalisch-Technische Bundesanstalt in Germany. Most recently, the GUM has been adopted by the American National Standards Institute (ANSI) as an American national standard. Its official designation is ANSI/NCSL Z540-2-1997 and its full title is *American National Standard for Expressing Uncertainty—U.S. Guide to the Expression of Uncertainty in Measurement*.

10.3   IMPORTANCE OF MEASUREMENT ERROR

It may be argued that such precise measurement and understanding of the uncertainty surrounding it is not important in most business cases. However, think of those instances where measurement errors are propagated through a succeeding calculation. For example, one of the great motivators for an accurate timepiece was not the desire to know the time, but to know one's position at sea. This requires measuring both latitude and longitude. By beginning at about the exact moment of noon and measuring the angle of the sun, a simple hyperbolic equation can compute the latitude of ships at sea. But computing the longitude requires knowing the exact time at the sun's apex (noon). The problem is that a time error of a few seconds creates a position error of several nautical miles, enough to ground a vessel. Over long voyages of many weeks, timepieces of the sailing era simply were not accurate enough and this error problem became one of the great challenges of the eighteenth century (Sobel 1996). The study of the accuracy of calculations that are based on uncertain measurements is called *error propagation*. In some cases errors are correlated and can accumulate, such as when a commuter bus travels in heavy traffic causing it to be late at the first stop and even later at subsequent ones. In other cases the errors may be uncorrelated and can partially 'cancel out', such as when measuring the room perimeter by adding together the individual measurements of the surrounding walls. For financial firms large portfolios of securities and loans can create the potential for relatively small errors in valuation models or credit scoring to generate large losses. Consider a portfolio of 100 000 swaps, dealt on a margin of 50 basis points each (hundreds of a percent). They require a combined accuracy of 99.95% in valuation, settlement, and management *just to break even*. In brokerage and retail the volumes are sometimes so high that small errors and cost overruns can destroy a significant part of the profitability of the business. In fact, a review of historical losses shows that large losses are usually generated by smaller losses over time. The accumulation of undetected errors can, over long periods, result in substantial loss to the firm.

10.4   BASIC ERROR MODEL

In general, the result of a measurement is an estimate of the quantity being measured and a statement of the uncertainty in the estimate. These two terms are reflected in the basic error model that is expressed mathematically as follows:

$$x_i = \bar{x} + e_i$$

Basic error model for measurement of true value of x.

where the true value of x is given by the measurement (or estimate) of x plus an error value e.

The analysis of uncertainty in performance measures (such as earnings) begins by developing a function for a value-adding process and then examining the key factors that contribute to performance and their associated errors (uncertainties). A similar technique is used when the volatility of interest rates is used to calculate the market risk of an instrument using its pricing formula. In general, given a function $q(x)$, the uncertainty δq can be found using

$$\delta q = \frac{dq}{dx} \delta x$$

where the derivative dq/dx is referred to as the sensitivity of q to x. Uncertainty in q is related to the relevance or sensitivity of q to x and the uncertainty in x. For multi-factor models, the uncertainty in q is related to the sensitivity of x to q and the sensitivity of y to q, along with the dependency between x and y (correlation). There is a common source of uncertainty for correlated x and y. For example, if q is the valuation error of a portfolio and x and y are the instruments in the portfolio, then dependency is assumed if x and y use the same pricing model for valuation. (Often it is enough to categorise x and y as correlated or uncorrelated.)

10.4.1   Representation of Errors

To understand the basics of error propagation, errors can be represented in one of two ways. First an *absolute* error can be supplied, such as when the height of the door is between 2742.5 and 2743.5 mm. In absolute terms the height is 2743 ± 0.5 mm. However, often a more useful way to represent the error is as a *relative* error that depends on the amount of the measurement, such as $x = \pm 5\%$. This means that the measurement is between $0.95x$ and $1.05x$. More often, a statistical measure such as standard deviation of the mean will be used for the measurement uncertainty. By convention, measures are quoted with two standard deviation errors (ISO Guide 1993), so assuming a normal distribution the 'true' value should lie within the quoted error boundary some 68% of the time. This is a casual interpretation, but error boundaries and confidence limits are discussed at some length later. Given that uncertainty in measurements is expressed as two standard deviations of relative error about the quoted figure, the next topic is how this error can affect the calculations of subsequent quantities of interest.

10.4.2   Sources of Errors

Uncertainty in measurements comes from many components. Some of them can be evaluated using statistical distributions on the results of direct measurements. Others are evaluated from assumed probability distributions based on subjective inputs. In both cases the standard deviation will be used as the measure of the uncertainty. Uncertainty measurements that are the result of a calculation on a series of direct measurements are called Type A uncertainty measures (or random errors). Another way to measure uncertainty is to use a subjective figure for the standard error. This figure can be based on historical measures, cohort group statistics, or expert knowledge. The term subjective is used to differentiate it from a measured value, and not intended to mean a 'guess'. Instrument calibration and measurement standards use a subjective value for the errors introduced regularly by many physical phenomena. Uncertainty measures based on subjective information are referred to as Type B measures (or systematic errors). The error value can be categorised as due to one of three causes:

1. Systematic errors (Type A)
2. Random errors (Type B)
3. Blunders.

Systematic and random errors have to do with the measurement tool and its use. Repeated errors due to the precision of the measurement tool are systematic, while non-repeatable errors due to the measurement process are considered random. Blunders are due to breakdowns in controls or simply carelessness in the performance of a task by humans. Systematic errors are identified by estimating the precision of the measuring device using a second measuring device with higher precision or sampling multiple devices. Random errors are estimated using repeated measurements and calculating the appropriate statistic. Systematic errors cannot be calculated using repeated measurements. Blunders show up as outliers in a sample of measurements. Although notions of systematic and random errors have been replaced by Type A and Type B as described above, it may still be useful to think of the sources of errors in this way.

10.5 DIRECT MEASUREMENT

Some items of interest may be measured directly, such as sales. In other cases input factors such as revenue, costs, and expenses are measured directly and a functional formula is used to calculate the required measurement (e.g. profit). One way to determine profit volatility would be to try to measure it directly. In this case we have a series of observations of profit (say daily) and we calculate the estimate for profit as the sample mean of these observations using a formula such as

$$\overline{p} = \frac{\sum_{i=1}^{n} p_i}{n}$$

Formula for calculating profit estimate from a series of profit measurements.

The uncertainty associated with this measurement is estimated using the standard deviation of the mean as follows:

$$\sigma_p = \sqrt{\frac{1}{n(n-1)} \sum_{k=1}^{n}(p_k - \overline{p})^2}$$

Formula for calculating profit error (volatility) from a series of profit measurements.

The estimate of profit has uncertainty surrounding it that is measured by its standard deviation. The standard deviation for profit is a measure of risk. Often we are concerned with an interval around the profit estimate that has an associated confidence that the true profit will lie within the interval. By assuming an underlying parametric distribution for profit we can define an interval of profit using a coverage factor such as is current practice in market risk to determine value at risk (Jorion 1997).

10.5.1 Coverage Factors

For a measure of uncertainty that defines an interval for the measurement, error analysis uses the idea of coverage: for any measurement taken the true value should lie within some multiple of the error for the measurement. For example, if the error is 1% for a measurement of 100, then a coverage factor of three would mean that the coverage is from 97 to 103. The coverage is the coverage factor times the error. The coverage factor k is chosen on the basis of the desired level of confidence to be associated with the interval (and an assumed underlying distribution). For a specific confidence limit, we assume a distribution (say normal) and use the Z factor for this distribution to compute an appropriate multiple for the standard deviation. For instance, for 99% using the normal distribution, $Z = 2.33$, and the value of the risk measure (value at risk) is 2.33σ (i.e. $k = 2.33$).

10.6 INDIRECT MEASUREMENT

Many items of interest, such as operational risk, cannot be measured directly, and in many cases there is a need to predict the uncertainty of a measurement in the future. Indirect and predictive uncertainty measures can be generated from models of the measurement under study. Often there is a simple functional relationship between the measure of interest and a set of measurements it depends upon (which are easier to measure or predict). Profit, for example, may be calculated as

$$Profit = Revenue - CostofGoods - Expenses$$

and the values for *Revenue*, *CostofGoods*, and *Expenses* can be measured and used to calculate *Profit*. In this case there is a functional relationship between profit and the other values as:

$$Profit = f(Revenue, CostofGoods, Expenses)$$

In general, given

$$y = f(x_1, x_2, \ldots, x_n)$$

and ignoring any correlation, the error σ_y^2 is given by

$$\sigma_y^2 = \left(\frac{\partial f}{\partial x_1}\right)^2 \sigma_{x_1}^2 + \left(\frac{\partial f}{\partial x_2}\right)^2 \sigma_{2_1}^2 + \cdots + \left(\frac{\partial f}{\partial x_n}\right)^2 \sigma_{x_n}^2$$

The values of $\sigma_{x_i}^2$ are the individual factors for y and $\partial f/\partial x_n$ are the sensitivities of y to the factors. Using the above formula, errors for a measurement of interest can be found. In practice, the values of the partial derivatives are found using a Taylor expansion for the function as shown in Section 10.6.2 (using the law of error propagation).

10.6.1   Effects of Correlation on Measurement Error

Up to this point, correlation has been ignored. Correlation is the degree to which changes in one measure are associated with changes in another. Correlation is important to operational risk because of the 'portfolio effect', meaning that the total operational risk is less than the sum of the individual risks. For example, suppose we measure two doors x and y. We are interested in the total height $x + y$ and the associated uncertainty. Let us assume that the uncertainty in the two measurements is given as $x \pm 2\%$ and $y \pm 2\%$. It is easy to see that our total measurement will be $x + y$ and that the error will be between 2% and 4%. We might say 4% because this is the maximum error and would be a conservative estimate for the total error. In fact, we can say that the error must be less than or equal to 4%. On the other hand, we might reason that the errors will tend to offset each other or 'cancel out' and the total error will be closer to 2%. We reason that the two measurements are not totally independent because the same procedure and instrument were used for both. How then should we decide between the two alternatives? The difference depends on how much we think the errors are related to each other. In other words, how much correlation is there between the two errors? Correlation occurs because we are using the same rule to measure, the same procedure for measurement, or other systematically repeatable phenomena related to the measurements. If the two measurements are not correlated (i.e. completely independent), then we would say the total measurement error is 2.8%, whereas if they are perfectly correlated, we would estimate the total error as 4%. The calculation is as follows. It can be shown that the general formula for two measurements is

$$\sigma_z^2 = \sigma_x^2 + \sigma_y^2 + 2\sigma_x\sigma_y \, \text{cov}(x, y)$$

where σ_x is the error for the measurement x (the standard deviation is implied). The simple cases of $\mathrm{cov}(x, y) = 0$ and $\mathrm{cov}(x, y) = 1$ are the most useful for large numbers of measurements. In these cases the formula for combining errors reduces to

$$\sigma_z^2 = \sigma_x^2 + \sigma_y^2 + 2\sigma_x\sigma_y$$

$$\sigma_z^2 = (\sigma_x + \sigma_y)^2$$

for correlated errors, and to

$$\sigma_z^2 = \sigma_x^2 + \sigma_y^2$$

for uncorrelated errors. For the general case, the formulae above can be expanded by simply adding the errors and then squaring the sum for the correlated errors, or squaring the errors and adding the sums for the uncorrelated errors. So, the total error is given by

$$\sigma_z^2 = \sum_i \sigma_i^2 + \left(\sum_j \sigma_j\right)^2$$

for all uncorrelated errors i and all correlated errors j. The derivation of this formula is given later in the chapter using expected value operators. Although this formula is sufficient for many general applications, the law of error propagation is the general formula for calculating composite errors, and is given below.

10.6.2   Law of Error Propagation

Basic concepts and definitions for this approach generally follow those given in ISO standards *Guide to the Expression of Uncertainty in Measurement 1993* (ISO Guide 1993). The standard error for a measurement is defined as the standard deviation of the measurement's expected value. The method of combining measurement uncertainties from various factors and accounting for their correlation is known as the *propagation of uncertainty*. The basic formula uses the sensitivities (partial derivatives) of the factors to calculate the standard deviation of the estimate. It is based on a Taylor approximation for the uncertainty in terms of factors such as

$$R = f(X_1, X_2 \ldots X_n)$$

Formula for the uncertainty value using factors based on Taylor approximation.

Using the Taylor approximation's first term, the uncertainty for the measure is found using the general formula below:

$$u^2(r) = \sum_{i=1}^{n} \left(\frac{\partial f}{\partial x_i}\right)^2 u^2(x_i) + 2\sum_{i=1}^{N-1}\sum_{j=i+1}^{N} \frac{\partial f}{\partial w_i}\frac{\partial f}{\partial w_j}\sigma_i\sigma_j\rho_{ij}$$

Formula for the calculation of combined uncertainty from many factors. Also known as the 'general law of error propagation' (ISO Guide 1993).

where $u(\cdot)$ denotes the uncertainty in the value, r is the risk measurement, x is the factor, and f is the functional relationship between x and r. The partial derivative term is known as the sensitivity to the factor. This formula also explicitly considers correlation between factors ρ_{ij}.

10.6.3 Expected Value

The ideas presented above can also be understood in terms of expected value. Risk in its basic form is a measure of the expected value of the variance. Just as the expected value of a random variable can be used as an estimator for performance, the expected value of its variance can be used to measure operational risk. The expected value of a random variable X is defined as

$$E[X] = \sum_i x_i \Pr(x_i)$$

Expected value for random variable.

The expected value of the variance of a random variable is given by

$$E[(X - \mu_x)^2] = \sum_i (x_i - \mu_x)^2 \Pr(x_i)$$

$$E[(X - \mu_x)^2] = \sum_i (x_i^2 - 2\mu_x x_i + \mu_x^2) \Pr(x_i)$$

$$E[(X - \mu_x)^2] = \sum_i x_i^2 \Pr(x_i) - \sum_i 2\mu_x x_i \Pr(x_i) + \sum_i \mu_x^2 \Pr(x_i)$$

Note the following:

$$\sum_i \Pr(x_i) = 1$$

$$\sum_i x_i \Pr(x_i) = \mu_x$$

Substituting and combining terms gives:

$$E[(X - \mu_x)^2] = \sum_i x_i^2 \Pr(x_i) - 2\mu_x^2 + \mu_x^2$$

$$E[(X - \mu_x)^2] = \sum_i x_i^2 \Pr(x_i) - \mu_x^2$$

$$E[(X - \mu_x)^2] = E[X^2] - \mu_x^2$$

The derivation of the combination formula for variance is also easy to derive using expected values. Consider the combination of the variance of two random variables X and Y:

$$E[(X + Y - \mu_{x+y})^2] = E[(X - \mu_x + Y - \mu_y)^2]$$

$$E[(X + Y - \mu_{x+y})^2] = E[(X - \mu)^2 + (Y - \mu_y)^2 + 2(X - \mu_x)(Y - \mu_Y)]$$

$$E[(X + Y - \mu_{x+y})^2] = E[(X - \mu)^2] + E[(Y - \mu_y)^2] + 2E[(X - \mu_x)(Y - \mu_Y)]$$

$$E[(X + Y - \mu_{x+y})^2] = \sigma_x^2 + \sigma_y^2 + 2\sigma_{xy}$$

Consider the following expressions that define the correlation of X and Y:

$$\rho_{XY} = \frac{\sigma_{XY}}{\sigma_X \sigma_Y}$$

$$\sigma_{XY} = \sigma_X \sigma_Y \rho_{XY}$$

Substituting in the above equation for the combination of variance gives:

$$E[(X + Y - \mu_{x+y})^2] = \sigma_x^2 + \sigma_y^2 + 2\sigma_x \sigma_Y \rho_{XY}$$

and for the case of perfect correlation, the correlation factor is equal to one. Substituting and rearranging terms results in the equation for correlated errors:

$$E[(X + Y - \mu_{x+y})^2] = \sigma_x^2 + \sigma_y^2 + 2\sigma_x \sigma_Y$$

$$\sigma_{XY}^2 = (\sigma_X + \sigma_Y)^2$$

The formula for uncorrelated errors is just the above with a correlation coefficient of zero:

$$E[(X + Y - \mu_{x+y})^2] = \sigma_x^2 + \sigma_y^2$$

$$\sigma_{XY}^2 = \sigma_X^2 + \sigma_Y^2$$

Given a covariance matrix, the correlation terms can be used in the equations given above. Matrix algebra formulations for multiple combinations are given in several books on portfolio analysis, e.g. Elton and Gruber (1991).

Finally, the expected value of the function of a random variable is not the same as the function of an expected value. In order to propagate errors, the expected value of the function of a random variable is developed using a Taylor expansion of the function (usually the first term only). Given a function

$$\sigma(f(X)) = \sigma_x \frac{\partial f}{\partial x} + \frac{1}{2}\sigma_x^2 \frac{\partial^2 f}{\partial x^2} + \cdots$$

and using only the first term of the Taylor expansion and squaring it gives the variance

$$\sigma^2(f(X)) = \sigma_x^2 \left(\frac{\partial f}{\partial x}\right)^2$$

Expanding the equation for multiple variables in the function gives the general formula for errors from a function of several variables (disregarding any correlation):

$$\sigma_y^2 = \left(\frac{\partial f}{\partial x_1}\right)^2 \sigma_{x_1}^2 + \left(\frac{\partial f}{\partial x_2}\right)^2 \sigma_{z_1}^2 + \cdots + \left(\frac{\partial f}{\partial x_n}\right)^2 \sigma_{x_n}^2$$

Consider the example of calculating the error in a variance estimate as given in Deutsch and Eller (1999). Given the formula for the sample variance as

$$\sigma_{\text{var}(x)}^2 = \left(\frac{n}{n-1}\right)(E[X^2] - (E[X])^2)$$

and letting:

$$z_1 = E[X] \quad \text{and} \quad z_2 = E[X^2]$$

the formula now becomes:

$$\sigma_{\text{var}(x)}^2 = \left(\frac{n}{n-1}\right)(z_2 - z_1^2)$$

The sensitivities are:

$$\frac{\partial f}{\partial z_1} = -\left(\frac{n}{n-1}\right)2z_1$$

$$\frac{\partial f}{\partial z_2} = \left(\frac{n}{n-1}\right)$$

The approximation for the error in the calculated variance is given by

$$\sigma_{\text{var}(x)}^2 = \left(\sigma_{z_1}\left(\frac{\partial f}{\partial z_1}\right)\right)^2 + \left(\sigma_{z_2}\left(\frac{\partial f}{\partial z_2}\right)\right)^2$$

$$\sigma_{\text{var}(x)}^2 = \left(\sigma_{z_1}\left(\frac{n}{n-1}\right)2z_1\right)^2 + \left(\sigma_{z_2}\left(\frac{n}{n-1}\right)\right)^2$$

$$\sigma_{\text{var}(x)}^2 = \left(\frac{n}{n-1}\right)^2 (4z_1^2\sigma_{z_1}^2 + \sigma_{z_2}^2)$$

And finally, substituting back the original values for z_1 and z_2 results in

$$\sigma_{\text{var}(x)}^2 = \left(\frac{n}{n-1}\right)^2 (4E[X]^2\sigma_{E[X]^2}^2 + E[X^2]^2\sigma_{E[X^2]}^2)$$

The above formula for the variance of the variance estimate shows how sensitive the error in the value for volatility is to the number of observations in the sample. The number of samples affects the first factor clearly, but also remember that the variance of the estimates for error factors for the expected values will vary with the sample size.

10.6.4 Error Propagation Example

A simple example will help to further clarify the basic concepts of error propagation. Assume we are interested in the volatility of earnings due to changes in volume. We can measure the volume regularly and compute its standard deviation and expected value. For the earnings we will use a function of volume, price/unit, cost/unit, and fixed cost as follows:

$$E = V * P - V * C - F$$

Earnings function based on V (volume), P (unit price), C (unit cost), and F (fixed cost).

Using lower case letters to denote the expected values for the variables from the above equation, the partial derivative of the earnings function with respect to volume is given by

$$\frac{\partial e}{\partial v} = p - c$$

and the formula for the volatility of the earnings is

$$u^2(e) = \left(\frac{\partial e}{\partial v}\right)^2 u^2(v)$$

$$u^2(e) = (p - c)^2 u^2(v)$$

$$u(e) = \sqrt{(p - c)^2 u^2(v)}$$

For a service where the price is 100 USD, the cost is 70 USD, and the standard deviation for volume is 1000 units, the volatility of earnings is

$$u(e) = \sqrt{(p - c)^2 u^2(v)}$$

$$u(e) = \sqrt{(100-70)^2 (1000)^2}$$

$$u(e) = 30\,000$$

The standard deviation of earnings is thus 30 000 USD. For a value at risk, this standard deviation might be factored using a coverage factor k of 3–4 to provide a corresponding confidence interval based on assumptions of normality, etc. Thus, for a business where the error values above were relative would result

Table 10.1 Table of values for operational risk example

Revenue	= 2 million USD
Profits	= 600 000 USD
Error	= 30 000 USD
99% VaR	= 69 900 USD

in the following values: a two million USD revenue business generating 600 000 USD in profits having 69 900 USD for value at risk due to volume volatility at a 99% confidence interval (see Table 10.1).

10.7 IDENTIFYING MEASUREMENT OUTLIERS

One of the uses of error analysis is to identify 'blunders' in measurements. Blunders are those measurement values that lie outside a proposed model for the measurement. In most cases this means values that are greater (or less) than a multiple of three standard errors (using a normal distribution and a 99.9% confidence interval for testing). This assumes the process of measurement is relatively stable and corrections for systematic errors and biases have been taken into account. In this case many of the error models use a normal distribution to approximate the distribution of error. Given a normal distribution with a mean of zero (after correction for biases) and a standard deviation equal to the calculated error, any measurement values that are greater (or less) than three standard errors would be rejected with a 99.9% confidence limit. Such values occur due to misplaced decimal points, mistyped digits, control breakdowns, and other 'blunders' in the process. One might be inclined to attempt to find outliers in the process losses using the losses themselves and applying statistical techniques to determine a threshold for losses. In practice, this cannot be done without error propagation as shown by the following example.

Classical statistical techniques approach the problem by assuming a mixture distribution and expressing the amount of contamination of the second distribution. Following Barnett and Lewis (1995), the following hypothesis is assumed:

$$H : x_j \in (1 - \lambda)F + \lambda G$$

Mixture model hypothesis for contaminated sample (from two distributions).

where λ is the proportion of values in the sample that come from each of the distributions. This model can be interpreted as trying to explain the expected losses due to errors and omissions and unexpected losses due to control breakdown in a process. The original mixture model discussion is from Tukey (1960) who describes the example of 1000 observations from a contaminated sample at $\lambda = 0.01$ for two normal distributions, $F \sim N(\mu, \sigma^2)$ and $G \sim N(\mu, 9\sigma^2)$. Some typical percentiles of the two distributions are shown in Table 10.2. The two distributions are indistinguishable for all practical purposes for values between 2.5 standard deviations.

Another method of determining outliers is described in Chapter 11 on extreme value theory. It deals with determining the threshold for peaks over threshold (POT) methods used in the application of extreme value theory. The mean excess function is a purely statistical method and also a difficult technique to apply in practice. On the other hand, the method of using error propagation models for determining outliers associated with processes has gained wide acceptance

Table 10.2 Table of probabilities and percentiles for trying to distinguish two normal distributions from a contaminated mixture sample

Cumulative probability	Percentile of F	Percentile of $(1 - \lambda)F + \lambda G$
0.25	-0.67σ	0.68σ
0.05	-1.64σ	-1.67σ
0.01	-2.33σ	-2.41σ
0.006	-2.51σ	-2.64σ

in the engineering and quality control fields. The reason is that it reflects the design of the underlying process that creates the errors and its application is well understood.

10.8 OTHER MEASUREMENT TOPICS

There are many ways to measure and measurement theory and its application is a wide field of study. Getting good measures is an art, not a science. One of the key requirements is being able to discuss with business managers the characteristics of measures and the criteria for evaluating them. In this final section, several related ideas are presented that may be useful when implementing systems for measuring and modelling operational risk.

10.8.1 Reliability and Accuracy

Understanding and eliminating all the biases in measurement can seem at first to be a daunting task. Fortunately, the simple measures of reliability and accuracy can be used to help determine if the biases have been removed. In review, reliability is the extent to which the results of the measurement are reproducible, and accuracy is a measure of how well the measurement reflects the values of interest. The simple idea of a target pattern is used to clarify these two concepts (Figure 10.1). On the left, both the accuracy and reliability are high. In the middle,

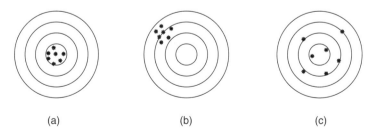

(a)   (b)   (c)

Figure 10.1 (a) High accuracy and reliability; (b) high reliability with low accuracy; and (c) high accuracy with low reliability

reliability is high and accuracy is low. On the right, the reliability is low but the accuracy is high.

10.8.2   Uncertain Sensitivities

Error propagation techniques are familiar to scientists and engineers and are widely used. In business a common situation occurs when the item of interest is not measurable and there is no clear functional relation between the item being measured and the item of interest. Often it is expedient to use an existing measurement and hypothesize a relation to the item of interest. Indeed, it is sometimes the case that measurements are chosen for convenience of measuring and not for their relevance to the item of interest. In these cases we are interested in estimating the partial derivative shown above. That is, we want to understand the *relevance* of the measured value to the value of interest. The underlying measured value's error is the *credibility* of the value. So, in mathematical terms, the credibility of the measurement is the error in its value, and the relevance of the measurement is its partial derivative with respect to the value of interest (sensitivity). These terms, *independence*, *relevance* and *credibility*, provide a way of talking about measurements in general, whether or not they are tied to numerical or other methods of measuring values of interest. In most cases we will estimate the relevance from existing data or using an expert opinion.

10.8.3   Benchmarks

Often it is convenient to use benchmark data to supplement a lack of information for decision-making. Such data are available from several sources and consultants spend a lot of resources undertaking benchmark studies. The same characteristics apply to benchmark data as to other measurements. The credibility, relevance, and independence of the benchmark data must be determined. Often this is straightforward as in the case of accounting benchmarking where the credibility is defined by generally accepted accounting standards followed by audits, the relevance is determined by standard industry classification codes, and the independent auditing affiliate of the accounting society publishes the information. However, there are many more 'benchmark' studies whose data are not verifiable and any statements regarding credibility, relevance, and independence are heroic at best. For these reasons and others, in most mid-to-large firms, in-house data can probably be used to build more useful models than benchmark information.

10.9   SUMMARY

This chapter presented the theory of error propagation, a fundamental tool in error analysis and the theory upon which the Delta method is based. Since measures are estimates they have an associated uncertainty and measurement error is a way of expressing this uncertainty. The standards put forth in the *Guide to the Expression of Uncertainty in Measurements* (ISO Guide or GUM) (ISO Guide 1993) have been adopted and promoted throughout the world as the authority for expressing uncertainty in measurements. Basic error models are a way of representing the 'true' value using an estimate and associated error. One method of determining the uncertainty is to make a series of direct measurements and compute the estimate using the expected value of the sample, and then calculate the uncertainty using its standard deviation. However, since direct measurement of operational risk is not possible, indirect measurement and its associated error propagation techniques are used. With indirect measurement, an error model is developed for the measure of interest using factors that contribute to its estimation and their functional relation to the measure. Errors from the factors are propagated to the measure using the general law of error propagation or one of its approximations. The roots of error propagation can be explained using expected value operators. An error model is also useful for identifying outliers or control breakdowns when actual data are compared with the model prediction using appropriate statistical tests. In the end, getting good measures is an art that requires attention to such issues as reliability, accuracy, and independence to understand the extent to which the results of the measurement are reproducible, unbiased, and reflect the values of interest. Dialogue with business managers to capture the characteristics of measures and criteria for evaluating them is essential because managers are the ones who are involved in the daily activities and whose performance is often judged by the results.

10.10 FURTHER READING

Taylor (1982) is a nice introduction to error analysis. The *Guide to the Expression of Uncertainty in Measurements* (ISO 1993) is the official standard for definitions and methodologies relating to errors, error analysis, and error propagation. One of the longest-lived applications of error propagation is probably in the nuclear industry and its application is described in detail by Avenhaus (1977).

11

Extreme Value Theory

Your job is to determine the height of the breakwater for a coastal town. The breakwater must hold back the largest waves in order to protect the seaside buildings. You have data for the last few years that include the highest waves on the coast, and know that you must build the breakwater higher than the maximum wave height in your data set. But how much higher? Doubling the wave height would be conservative, but the town council will never agree to the added cost. You must be able to defend the value of height you select and convince the council that the money is well spent. Since your data cover the last seven years you reason that a value equal to the maximum height in the data set might be good for seven years, but the council have told you that they do not want the waves over the breakwater for at least 20 years. Even with your background in statistics and some good analytical tools your information on the distribution of wave heights is of no interest because it's only the *maximum* that is important. If you knew the characteristics of the distribution of the maxima, you could use it to determine the recommended breakwater height. Extreme value theory addresses just this problem.

11.1 INTRODUCTION

Extreme value theory (EVT) deals with the distribution of maxima (and minima) for a random variable. EVT is an important tool for reliability and failure analysis of many physical systems. In the techniques described in this book for measuring and modelling operational risk, EVT is proposed as a way to estimate excess value at risk. Just as the maximum wave height determines whether or not the breakwater is flooded, the maximum financial loss can be used to determine whether or not the firm's equity is exhausted. If the maximum loss for a given period (say a year) is known, then a firm can set aside capital to mitigate the financial impact. EVT has its roots in the Fisher–Tippet distribution (Fisher and Tippet 1928), but its application to engineering was pioneered by Gumbel (1958). Embrechts *et al.* (1997) have described the theory in detail and its application to financial firms (primarily insurance). Castillo (1988) provides a good introduction to EVT, and several examples for physical systems.

EVT is applied in many fields, including structural engineering, ocean engineering, hydraulics, pollution, meteorology, material strength, and highway traffic.

The theory is well developed for physical processes and presents a viable alternative to traditional loss models for rare events and control breakdowns associated with operational risk. The application of the Delta method to finance is not new, but the application of EVT to finance is relatively recent (Cruz *et al.* 1998) and for this reason a theory chapter has been devoted to it. The chapter begins with an overview of the basic concepts behind EVT and examples of its use as an important tool for reliability and failure analysis of physical systems. It continues with an analogous problem regarding the stock market crash of 1987 which leads to a discussion of excess loss and threshold. Next, descriptions of time-dependent losses in the context of a classic insurance actuarial model and the follow-on application of EVT to internal losses for financial institutions are presented. The chapter concludes with a brief summary.

11.2 BASIC CONCEPTS

The application of extreme value theory (EVT) has its roots in engineering. Consider the problem introduced earlier of building a breakwater that will keep back the sea. It is obviously insufficient to build the breakwater to the average water level of the sea because the land protected by the breakwater would be flooded about half the time. Using the historical maximum level of the sea is an obvious choice, but should the breakwater be only a few inches above the historical maximum, or more? And if more, then how much more? Such questions are answered using concepts from EVT. In applying EVT you want to ensure that the operating conditions (in this example, the sea height) is less than the capacity of the element (the breakwater height) over some very long time period t. This idea can be expressed using the following simple formula:

$$O_t \leq C_t \quad \text{for any time } t$$

Extreme value conditions for operating conditions O and capacity C.

The problem described is concerned with the maximum height of the sea in a period t for some number of periods. A related problem is the number of times a particular height will be exceeded (exceedances). Using a binomial distribution for Bernoulli trials (exceeded or not exceeded), it can be shown that the mean number of exceedances ($\bar{r}$) for a sample of n past observations of an independent identically distributed (i.i.d.) variable is given by

$$\bar{r}(n, m, N) = \frac{Nm}{n + 1}$$

where

n is the number of periods in the sample,
m is the order statistic of interest (e.g. $m = 1$ for maximum), and
N is the design number of periods.

This result depends on the i.i.d. random variable and uses the idea that exceedances follow a Poisson distribution. An approach to the solution of the breakwater problem might be to examine the maximum yearly sea heights for the last 50 years and build the breakwater so that it would be exceeded only once in 20 years. The calculation then becomes:

$$\bar{r}(50, 2, 20) = \frac{20 * m}{51} = 1$$

and $m = 2.55$ or the second highest value.

11.2.1 EVT and Maximum Loss

The theory of extreme values is described in detail in the references given in this chapter. Here a brief description of its use in determining maximum loss (and later exceedances of a threshold) is given. Maximum loss is important in those instances where historical losses are recorded and the maximum loss per period for several periods is available. However, risk measures such as value at risk require knowledge of the maximum cumulative loss for a period (not the maximum loss). In the Delta–EVT™ methodology excess losses over a threshold are used to determine the risk measure for financial operations.

One of the most interesting findings of EVT is that there are only three types of non-degenerated distributions that satisfy certain conditions required for the limiting distributions of maxima and minima. These are the Frechet, Weibull, and Gumbel distributions. The general form that combines these three into one equation is called the generalised extreme value (GEV) distribution and is given by

$$H_\beta(x) = \begin{cases} \exp(-(1 + \beta x)^{-1/\beta}) \\ \exp(-\exp(-x)) \end{cases}$$

Formula for the generalised extreme value (GEV) distribution.

where β is the shape parameter and $\beta < 0$ corresponds to the Weibull, $\beta > 0$ to the Frechet, and $\beta = 0$ to the Gumbel distributions. Location and scale parameters can also be added for fitting to raw data (shown in the examples below). Gumbel (1958) shows several manual techniques for fitting data to these distributions, but today the most prevalent technique is a maximum likelihood fitting with (optionally) probability weightings.

11.2.2 Detailed Example of EVT Maximum

Below is a detailed example adopted from Castillo (1988) to demonstrate the application of EVT. A set of wind data for the last 50 years is given as shown in

Table 11.1   Maximum yearly wind speed in mph at a specific location for fifty years

Index	Speed (mph)	Index	Speed (mph)	Index	Speed (mph)
1	22.64	21	23.75	41	24.04
2	24.24	22	25.45	42	25.66
3	25.99	23	26.69	43	26.89
4	27.12	24	27.69	44	28.12
5	28.58	25	29.12	45	29.48
6	30.18	26	31.55	46	32.54
7	32.98	27	33.86	47	35.21
8	36.82	28	38.09	48	38.82
9	38.96	29	42.99	49	33.61
10	45.24	30	54.75	50	98.16
11	22.8	31	24.01		
12	24.74	32	25.55		
13	26.63	33	26.88		
14	27.43	34	27.71		
15	28.88	35	29.45		
16	31.31	36	31.57		
17	33.83	37	34.64		
18	37.23	38	38.26		
19	38.9	39	43.66		
20	47.91	40	69.4		

Table 11.1. These figures are the maximum wind velocity at a particular location in miles per hour (mph) for each of 50 consecutive years. A Frechet distribution will be fitted, and the parameters for it determined. Then the parameterised distribution will be used to determine some possible values for the wind speed at specified confidence levels. A plot of wind speed data yearly maxima and the formula for the Frechet probability distribution are given in Figure 11.1. (Note that the data are only the maximum values taken from the set of values for each year.)

$$\Pr(x) = \exp - \left(\frac{\sigma}{x - \lambda} \right)^{\beta}$$

Formula for the Frechet probability distribution.

The analysis of the maxima begins using the formula for the Frechet distribution with the parameters β, σ, and λ representing the shape, scale, and location, respectively. Setting $\lambda = 0$, the shape and scale values are determined using maximum likelihood and examined in a probability plot. This was done with a simple spreadsheet algorithm and is shown in Figure 11.2 for $\beta = 4.5$ and $\sigma = 28$.

Using the formula for the Frechet distribution with the fitted parameter values shown, the wind speed for a particular probability value can be calculated. For instance, the wind speed at a 95% probability is 54 mph, and at a 99% probability

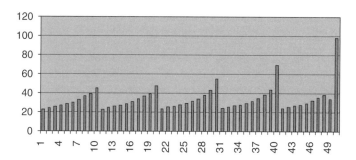

Figure 11.1 Plot of wind speed data yearly maxima

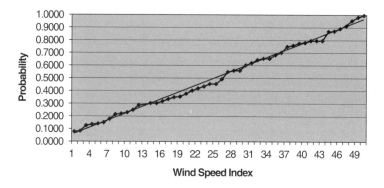

Figure 11.2 Plot of wind data to the Frechet extreme value distribution ($\beta = 4.5$ and $\sigma = 28$)

it is 78 mph. Of course, there are errors associated with the estimates of the parameters that have not been considered.

11.2.3 S&P 500 Analysis using EVT

An analogous problem is given by McNeil (1998) regarding the market crash of 1987. Consider the case where a set of data is available for maximum yearly loss in a financial process for the last 20 years. We want to determine the level of loss that would be exceeded in only one of every 50 years (2% quantile). Using the maximum likelihood technique, a Frechet distribution for the maxima described by the 20 data points would be fitted. The data and associated graph for the daily percentage fall of the S&P 500 index are shown in Table 11.2 and Figure 11.3. McNeil computes the expected value for the maximum fall as 7.4% with an uncertainty expressed in a confidence interval around (4.9%, 24%). On Monday 19 October 1987 the S&P fell 20.4%. This is perhaps one of the most notable examples of the application of EVT in finance.

Table 11.2 *Standard and Poor's 500 Index* maximum yearly fall in percent (1960–Oct 1987)

Year	Percentage fall
1960	2.268
1961	2.083
1962	5.575
1963	2.806
1964	1.253
1965	1.758
1966	2.46
1967	1.558
1968	1.899
1969	1.903
1970	2.768
1971	1.522
1972	1.319
1973	3.052
1974	3.571
1975	2.362
1976	1.797
1977	1.626
1978	2.009
1979	2.958
1980	3.007
1981	2.886
1982	3.997
1983	2.697
1984	1.821
1985	1.455
1986	4.817
1987	5.254

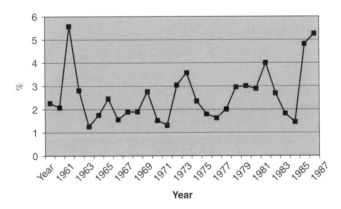

Figure 11.3 Graph of *S&P 500* maximum daily fall from 1960 through October 1987

11.3   EXCESS LOSS DISTRIBUTION

Excess losses are defined as those losses that exceed a threshold. The problem presents itself when you are interested in the distribution of losses over a specific amount instead of the maximum loss. Recall that in the preceding discussion of extreme value for maxima that we found the probability that the maximum would be exceeded in a particular year (e.g. one out of 50), and not how many times it might be exceeded or by how much. Typically the application of excess loss would be the case of an operation that includes 'small' losses in the profitability figures and provides a reserve for 'large' losses. Given a threshold value for discriminating large losses, the excess loss technique can be applied to determine the size of the provision needed. This is the basic idea of the EVT methodology presented in Chapter 6.

Pickands (1975) has demonstrated that the conditional cumulative distribution function (cdf), $G(x)$, of a function that lies in the domain of attraction for maxima of an extreme value distribution (e.g. Frechet) for $x - u$, given $x \geq u$, for some threshold u large enough, is given by

$$G(x) = 1 - \left(1 + \frac{cx}{a}\right)^{-1/c}$$

Distribution of excess for a function that lies in the domain of attraction for
Frechet EVT.

(For $c = 0$ the value is given a limiting sense.) This fact allows the estimation of c from a sample. The distribution is known as the generalised Pareto distribution (GPD) and is used in the peaks over threshold (POT) model (see Chapter 6). It has been shown that the POT model offers a unifying approach to modelling the tail of severity distributions in insurance loss (McNeil and Saladin 1997). The technique uses the GPD to model loss severity. The GPD's cdf is of the form:

$$G_{\beta,\sigma} = \begin{cases} 1 - (1 + \beta x/\sigma)^{-1/\beta} & \text{for } \beta \neq 0 \\ 1 - \exp(-x/\sigma) & \text{for } \beta = 0 \end{cases}$$

Formula for the cdf of the GPD.

The value for β determines the type of distribution: for $\beta < 0$ the model gives the type II Pareto distribution, for $\beta = 0$ it is the exponential distribution, and for $\beta > 0$ it is a reparameterised Pareto distribution. The distribution is sensitive to the threshold value u used to filter the data that in financial applications defines the minimum value of the loss qualifying for 'large losses'. The theorem assumes a 'sufficiently high threshold', and there are several techniques for determining the value of the threshold.

11.3.1   Threshold for the POT Model

Determining the threshold value is key to the successful application of the POT method. In Chapter 5 the Delta methodology was described and it was shown how it can be used to determine a threshold for financial applications. Several authors (Embrechts *et al.* 1997, McNeil 1998) have suggested using the mean excess function to determine the value of the threshold for GPD, but this can present several difficulties. The mean excess function is the sum of the excess amounts divided by the number of points exceeding the threshold and is given by

$$e(u_n) = \frac{\sum_{i=1}^{n}(x_i - u)}{\sum_{i=1}^{n}1_{(x_i>u)}}$$

Mean excess function for sample x and threshold u.

A plot of thresholds from 0 to $\max(x_n)$ will be a straight line with positive gradient when the distribution follows the GPD because the GPD excess function is linear. It is given by

$$e(u) = \frac{(\beta u + \sigma)}{(1 - \beta)}$$

Excess function for the GPD showing linearity.

where $\beta > 0$ is assumed and the reparameterised Pareto distribution will be fit. In practice it is often difficult to find the threshold easily and some practical interpretation is needed for it. For instance, McNeil and Saladin (1997) examine the threshold for almost 5000 property losses and present values at $u = 100$ or $u = 300$, with corresponding parameters for the GPD, as shown in Table 11.3.

Using a GPD to establish excess loss distribution at a confidence limit (say 95%) would differ by a factor of almost 3 (in McNeil's data, a difference of 1277 versus 3313 for the 95% value of each GPD, respectively). This demonstrates the GPD's sensitivity to the threshold value and shows that in practice the mean excess technique may not provide a satisfactory threshold determination. An alternative interpretation of the threshold and its determination using error analysis of processes is described in Chapter 5.

Table 11.3 Table of GPD parameters for different thresholds (McNeil and Saladin 1997)

	$u = 100$	$u = 300$
β	0.747	0.814
σ	118.4	261.4

11.3.2   GPD Threshold Sensitivity

In this section the sensitivity of the GPD to threshold values is explored further by using a known distribution and comparing the fits and resulting confidence level values for several different thresholds. Consider a series of losses generated from a lognormal distribution with $\mu = 3$ and $\sigma = 2$ (Table 11.4). Using these simulated lognormal losses, an arbitrary threshold u is selected and then a GPD is fitted to the losses. The results for thresholds of $u = 0$, $u = 10$, and $u = 50$ have been fitted and the corresponding probability plots are shown in Figures 11.4, 11.5, and 11.6. The mean excess plot for this data is shown in Figure 11.7. As described earlier, one of the ways to determine the proper threshold value u is to use the mean excess plot (McNeil and Saladin 1997). Unfortunately, it seems to provide very little benefit even in this fairly straightforward and simple case.

There could be an argument made for a threshold of zero as the mean excess plot shows linearity throughout the range of thresholds. On the other hand, the fit and a threshold of zero is not as good as the fit at the higher thresholds (which is expected from the theory). Assuming a confidence level of 90%–99%, Table 11.5 shows the results of selecting a particular threshold, and then using the GPD fit for that threshold in order to determine the value of the excess distribution at the chosen confidence level.

Table 11.4   Losses generated from a lognormal distribution ($\mu = 3$, $\sigma = 2$)

No.	Loss	No.	Loss
1	1	21	20
2	1	22	26
3	1	23	30
4	1	24	31
5	1	25	31
6	2	26	32
7	3	27	33
8	4	28	36
9	6	29	37
10	6	30	38
11	7	31	51
12	8	32	59
13	8	33	59
14	8	34	100
15	9	35	101
16	11	36	176
17	12	37	193
18	15	38	208
19	18	39	907
20	19	40	1092

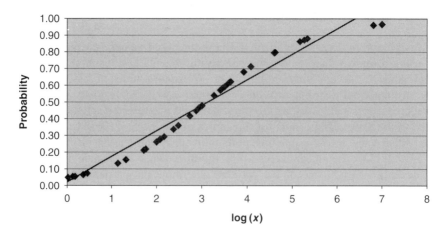

Figure 11.4   Fit (propability plot) of GPD to lognormal loss data with threshold $u = 0$

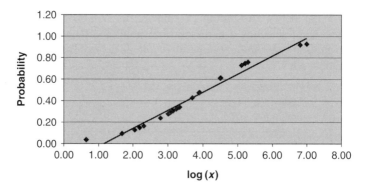

Figure 11.5   Fit (propability plot) of GPD to lognormal loss data with threshold $u = 10$

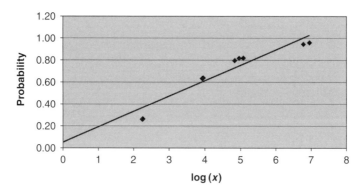

Figure 11.6   Fit (propability plot) of GPD to lognormal loss data with threshold $u = 50$

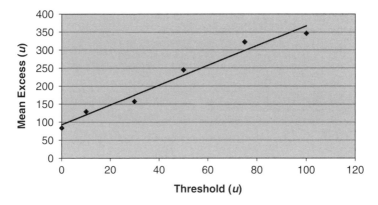

Figure 11.7 Mean excess plot for lognormal data showing the linearity of the mean excess function

Table 11.5 Some typical values that might occur using GPD fits for various thresholds at different confidence levels (shown without error values)

Threshold	ξ	β	Confidence level		
			90%	95%	99%
0	16	0.8	300	700	5000
10	40	0.8	675	1650	12 500
50	20	0.8	1000	3000	45 000

The determination of the proper threshold is currently a stumbling block for applying EVT in practice. Using maximum likelihood fits and fitting over a range of thresholds for the above data, the possible parameter values for the GPD are shown in Figures 11.8 and 11.9.

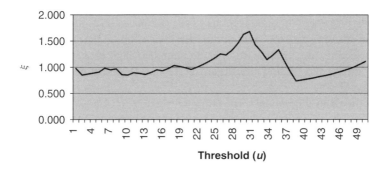

Figure 11.8 Plot of GPD parameter ξ for various thresholds

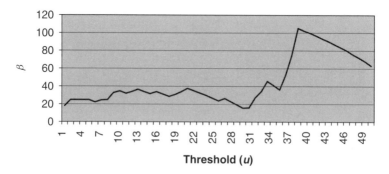

Figure 11.9 Plot of GPD parameter β for various thresholds

As can be seen the parameters are stable up to a threshold of around 25. Any threshold up to this value will produce similar fits, but there is no clear indication as to why one threshold should be preferred over another. Even when there is some evidence for a particular threshold on an analytical basis (such as the mean excess function), there still remains the question of the interpretation of the meaning of this threshold in application. Without a defensible argument for the threshold there could be differences of several orders of magnitude in the resulting provision values for a given loss data set. The Delta methodology offers an alternative to the mean excess function and a practical interpretation of the threshold as a maximum operating loss.

11.4 TIME-DEPENDENT LOSSES

The analysis using EVT has been for a specific period, and the results could be applied by extrapolating to multiple periods. However, a better solution is to introduce time dependence by considering the frequency of events separate from their severity. To this end, EVT loss distributions can be combined with Poisson or other event frequency distributions to produce a stochastic loss model for processes or organisations. The two parametric distributions can be combined using a Monte Carlo simulation that couples the event frequency to the loss severity distribution (two-stage sample). This is a basic form for the actuarial model and is shown in Figure 11.10 in a Bayesian network diagram for illustration.

EVT is used in this model to develop the severity of the loss distribution. The time of the loss events is used to develop a frequency model based on the Poisson distribution (Figure 11.11). The Poisson distribution has been widely used for events resulting from processes (e.g. birth–death processes) and is characterised by its single parameter, λ, representing the mean arrival rate of the events. The variance of the Poisson distribution is also equal to this value.

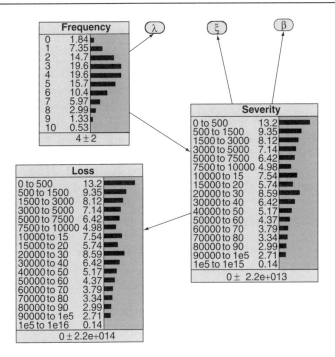

Figure 11.10 Model using Poisson frequency and EVT severity to generate loss distribution

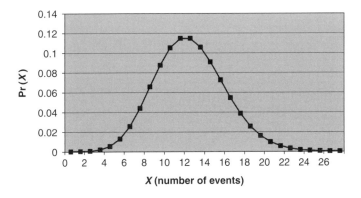

Figure 11.11 Poisson distribution plot with mean arrival rate $\lambda = 12$

Given a fit of the event frequency of occurrence to a Poisson distribution, and the determination of the EVT distribution for the severity, the loss distribution is generated using a Monte Carlo simulation from the two parametric distributions. The combination of EVT and Poisson constitutes a classic actuarial model and is also discussed in Chapter 7.

11.5 EVT APPLIED TO INTERNAL LOSSES

By now it should be clear that EVT can be applied to internal loss data for financial institutions. Assume we are given a set of internal losses that are considered 'large' losses, and we want to determine the cumulative excess loss (over a threshold) for the period at a specific confidence level. Given a reasonable number of large losses (say 20–50), we will fit a GPD distribution using maximum likelihood and determine the shape and location parameters for the fitted distribution. Using these parameters, the values for excess loss over the threshold for several confidence limits will be determined. The procedure is to fit a generalised Pareto distribution (GPD) using the peaks over threshold (POT model).

Assume the table of losses (Table 11.6) has been accumulated for some period (say one year). A simple plot of the values (Figure 11.12) shows them to be exponential in nature (which is expected). The question to answer is: What is the expected loss over the threshold at a particular confidence level? The POT method will be used to determine the answer.

Table 11.6 Table of large losses (in thousands of Euros)

Event	Loss	CumLoss	Log(Loss)	Log(CumLoss)
1	1	1	0	0
2	1.5	1.5	0.4055	0.4055
3	3.1	3.1	1.1314	1.1314
4	8.2	11.3	2.1041	2.4248
5	11	22.3	2.3979	3.1046
6	13	35.3	2.5649	3.5639
7	16.6	51.9	2.8094	3.9493
8	22	73.9	3.0910	4.3027
9	29	102.9	3.3673	4.6338
10	37	139.9	3.6109	4.9409
11	42	181.9	3.7377	5.2035
12	46	227.9	3.8286	5.4289
13	52	279.9	3.9512	5.6344
14	56	335.9	4.0254	5.8168
15	63	398.9	4.1431	5.9887
16	83	481.9	4.4188	6.1777
17	99	580.9	4.5951	6.3646
18	100	680.9	4.6052	6.5234
19	132	812.9	4.8828	6.7006
20	133	945.9	4.8903	6.8521
21	140	1085.9	4.9416	6.9902
22	175	1260.9	5.1648	7.1396
23	500	1760.9	6.2146	7.4736
24	775	2535.9	6.6529	7.8383
25	1500	4035.9	7.3132	8.3030

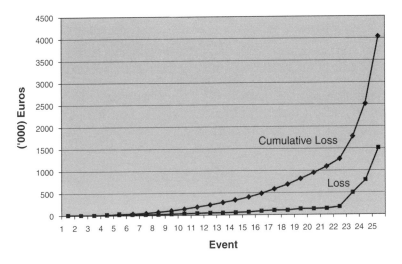

Figure 11.12   Graph of large loss data

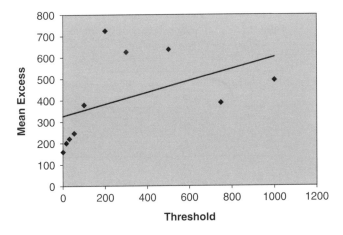

Figure 11.13   Mean excess plot for internal loss data showing non-linearity

11.5.1   Peaks Over Threshold Method for Internal Loss Data

The peaks over threshold (POT) method can be applied to the internal loss data. The threshold has possibly already been determined by the data set at 1000 Euros. A look at the mean excess function for some other possible thresholds for the data is shown in Figure 11.13. This plot shows that the mean excess function does not appear linear, indicating an expected poor fit to the GPD. Nevertheless, fitting the data to the GPD will be a useful exercise to see how

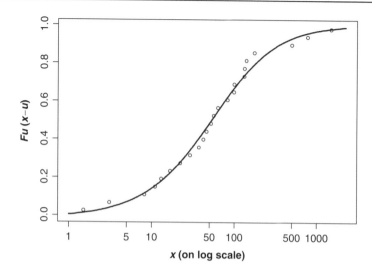

Figure 11.14 Fit of internal data to GPD using maximum likelihood fit ($\xi = 0.765$, $\beta = 57$) and showing logarithmic fit curve

Table 11.7 Table of excess values (approx.) at selected confidence limits for GPD using internal loss data ($\xi = 0.765$ and $\beta = 57$)

Confidence limit	Excess value
90%	375
95%	675
99%	2500

sensitive the application of EVT distributions is to the methods and assumptions. The method of 'eyeballing' the fit by simply judging the linearity of Q–Q plots or other 'known shape' distribution is useful for an overview of the results. The GPD plot uses all data (i.e. threshold = 0 was used because the data have been filtered for a threshold of 1000 Euros). A plot using the fitted parameters of $\xi = 0.765$ and $\beta = 57$ is shown in Figure 11.4 along with a logarithmic 'fit' curve. As suspected, the fit is not good, but further analysis is needed in order to understand the sensitivity of the GPD distribution.

Assuming you are interested in an interval using a confidence value of 90%, 95%, or 99%, we would expect to use one of the following values shown in Table 11.7. As can be seen there is a large difference in values at the confidence limits for this distribution in the tail between 90% and 99%. The figure of 2500 (thousand) for 99% is about the same as the cumulative loss less the maximum, and almost twice the maximum loss amount. Some possible effects

Table 11.8 Table of excess values (approx.) at selected confidence limits for GPD using internal loss data with one standard error for parameters ($\xi = 1.165$ and $\beta = 87$)

Confidence limit	Excess value
90%	1 100
95%	2 500
99%	16 000

due to threshold determination were discussed earlier using the lognormal fits. Standard errors for the parameters of the GPD are almost 50%, so using only one standard error gives figures quite a bit larger, as shown in Table 11.8.

As with any other parametric technique, getting good data and a close fit to one of the standard distributions is important. In addition, in the POT method determining the threshold is a critical initial step in the process. These two factors are key to the methodology and will likely play a major role in any decisions to be taken based on an analysis using EVT.

11.6 SUMMARY

Extreme value theory is well developed for physical processes and well suited for application to financial loss due to operational risk. Its focus on extreme events and exceedances makes it ideal for developing models for economic capital and insurance plans. Unfortunately its sensitivity to cut-off values and accurate data sometimes make it difficult to apply. Nevertheless, EVT presents a viable alternative to traditional loss models for rare events and control breakdowns associated with operational risk. For inclusion in a loss model it can be used for the severity of loss and then coupled with the Poisson distribution or otherwise given a stochastic component for frequency of occurrences. Although comprehensive loss data are generally not available, large loss data are much more readily at hand since there are relatively few occurrences and they are generally well documented. The application of EVT to large operational loss data from processes has many advantages. It is a well founded theory for physical processes, complements error propagation theory, and requires a relatively small dataset.

11.7 FURTHER READING

Gumbel (1958) is one of the first books on applications of EVT with many heuristics to 'fit' data to distributions. A solid reference is Embrechts *et al.* (1991) with coverage of the methods and applications of EVT to mostly insurance, and references to the application of EVT to operational risk can be found in the EVT Methodology chapter (Chapter 6) in Section II of this book. Castillo (1988) provides a practical introduction to EVT and its use in the physical sciences along with software. Weiss and Thomas (1997) is an applications-oriented text that also includes software.

12
Bayesian Methods

Thomas Bayes (1702–1761). Reproduced from Bayesian Statistics by S. James Press 1989 Wiley, Reprinted by permission of John Wiley & Sons Inc, New York

In the eighteenth century many learned men were trying to determine the existence of God using various rationales. One idea was that since there was so much 'order' and 'predictability' in nature, there must be a divine being who had designed it. Given this environment, it does not seem unusual for a Presbyterian minister from Tunbridge Wells, England, to be involved in such ideas as 'inverse probability'. In 1763 an article by Thomas Bayes entitled 'Towards Solving a Problem in the Doctrine of Chances' appeared in the *Philosophical Transactions of the Royal Society*, published posthumously, that outlined how to solve the 'inverse probability' problem. The *Doctrine of Chances* was a book published by DeMoivre (who was working in England) that presented various problems and their solutions (as was the style of the time since Bernoulli and Hyugens). Up to this time, probability was thought of as a set of properties that gave rise to certain frequencies for certain events, and the probability of the sample to be expected was calculated using these frequencies. An 'inverse probability' was one where the sample was given, but the probabilities needed to be calculated. The problem was initially stated by Bernoulli (reproduced here later) and a general solution was given by Laplace (1814). However, the basic theorem is still known as Bayes' formula. In the words of Sir Harold Jeffreys, 'On the rare occasions when anybody mentions it, it is called common sense and left at that' (Jeffreys 1960).

12.1 INTRODUCTION

In this chapter we present an overview of Bayesian decision theory, which is important to operational risk analysis because it addresses the problem of how to make decisions under uncertainty, and important to operational risk measurement because Bayesian networks form the basis for causal models. Bayesian decision theory includes an uncertainty calculus and provides the foundation for assigning uncertainties to the components of the causal models. Many more specific references are provided in the section on Further Reading for the reader who wishes to pursue this topic further. A good reference for Bayesian decision analysis theory is Berger (1980), and there are many good books on the philosophy, such as Jeffreys (1960). This chapter is sprinkled with examples, some of them 'classical' that have appeared in the literature several times, and some of them new concoctions designed to illustrate key ideas or general applications. It is not possible in this short space to develop the high points to great depth, but what is presented should give a basic understanding of the main ideas.

The chapter begins with an explanation of Bayesian methods and continues with a discussion of some of the key concepts. Next, Bayes' Theorem is introduced and two short examples provided to reinforce the main concepts and illustrate the techniques. This is followed by an in-depth discussion of Bayesian networks, the basis on which causal models are built. Then a simple Bayesian network for one of the earlier examples is built and discussed to demonstrate the technique. The chapter concludes with a summary and references for further reading.

12.2 WHAT ARE BAYESIAN METHODS?

Bayesian decision theory and statistical decision theory in general are concerned with making decisions using statistics that provide information about some of the uncertainties under consideration. A model of the problem domain is built, and the uncertainty is dealt with using statistical methods. Bayesian networks (Pearl 1988) are a graphical representation that can be used to compute a set of Bayesian statistics that have a defined interrelationship. (One might think of it as a non-linear multi-factor model.) Causal models are a specific modelling methodology using Bayesian networks to represent problem domains and were described in a previous chapter. Here the focus is on the method that the model uses to deal with the uncertainties. The statistics are gained from taking a sample of data arising from a statistical experiment. For example, a drug company might use a trial experiment to estimate the effectiveness of a drug. Given a sample of 100 patients to which the drug is administered, and 20 of whom were helped by the drug, one might infer that the drug had an effectiveness (θ) of 20%. This estimate is an example of classical inferential statistics. However, in decision theory we are concerned with the outcomes of the decision (the loss or utility function) and will normally combine the sample statistical results with other relevant data to come up with the best decision. One of the benefits of Bayesian decision theory is that it allows explicit inclusion of other decision-relevant data in addition to the statistical sample information in a simple fashion. An advantage of Bayesian networks is that they explicitly define relationships between factors in the model and can quickly update them when additional information becomes available.

12.3   KEY CONCEPTS

One of the basic ideas of Bayesian statistics is the emphasis placed on the sample. The classical illustration goes back to Jakob Bernoulli (1713). The text (in translation) of Bernoulli's problem is given below, but the emphasis on the sample can be illustrated by the following. Suppose I have a mixture of red and white balls in a container. You must guess the ratio of red to white. With no other knowledge you might guess 1:1. Then I draw a sample of 10 balls, replacing each after it is drawn and record the colour of the ball. There are 6 red and 4 white in the sample. What is your guess for the ratio given this new information from the sample? You might guess 3:2, or you could argue that the sample is small, so the ratio is somewhere between 1:1 (your original guess) and 3:2 (the sample ratio). Suppose then I draw a sample of 100 balls, again replacing them each time. There are 65 red and 35 white in this sample. Your guess may now be a relatively confident one of 3:2 for the ratio, arguing the sample is 'close enough' to this ratio. But after the next sample of 1000 drawn where the numbers are 651 and 349, you might be inclined to guess 65:35 as the ratio. In each case you are weighting the sample information according to the size of the sample and revising your guess based on the sample. This is in contrast to a 'classical' approach that would have you accepting or rejecting your original guess (1:1) based on the probability that the sample drawn had come from the population with 1:1 ratio of red and white balls in the container. Bayesian statistics deals with the probability of a hypothesis, given the same prior information.

Decision-makers also use information in addition to the sample statistics. One kind of additional information is referred to as prior information because it is information known before the sample experiment is conducted. For example, if there are other similar drugs from competitors that have been trial-tested and revealed a 40% effectiveness, then the company will use this information in addition to the sample information from its own trial experiment. Based on this prior information and the sample results, the company may suspect that the trial needs to be repeated before it abandons the drug.

The importance of prior information in decision-making under uncertainty was illustrated nicely by Savage (1954). He considered the following three experiments:

1. A lady, who adds milk to her tea, claims to be able to tell whether the milk or the tea was poured in first. In 10 trials, she correctly determines which was poured first.
2. A music expert claims to be able to distinguish Haydn scores from Mozart scores. In 10 hearings of the music, he correctly identifies the composer.
3. A drunk says he can predict the outcome of a flip of a fair coin. The coin is flipped 10 times, and he is correct on all 10 calls.

In all trials the statistic θ is the probability of the person answering correctly. Classical statistical inference would assume the null hypothesis that the person is guessing as $\theta = 0.5$ for each trial assuming the person is guessing. This hypothesis would be rejected with a significance level of 2^{-10} in all three cases giving strong evidence that the predictions are based on valid claims.

As rational decision-makers, we review each of the cases in turn. In the first case we are not sure what to think, as the lady may have some abilities that we are not aware of. In the second case we accept that the expert can differentiate the two composers as we find the possibility reasonable. The third case is probably a lucky streak or a fraud and we do not assign any mystical powers to the drunk. Clearly, prior information has entered into our decision-making process in all three cases. Bayesian statistics formally incorporates prior information.

By incorporating the utility function to represent the outcome of decisions and prior information known before the sample is taken, models using Bayesian decision theory provide a more intuitively appealing tool for decision-making under uncertainty. Since they are based on probability theory, they provide coherent results for the statistics generated. General loss models can be incorporated explicitly, and there are several techniques for generating prior information important for the analysis. When using a graphical representation, Bayesian networks represent complex models in a graphical form that are easy to understand and can be strongly linked to business processes and associated domain expertise.

In this section, Bayesian statistics are described in general along with their use as the underlying calculus in Bayesian networks and causal models. Some background information on Bayesian statistics is presented followed by a simple detailed example to illustrate the techniques. Next a more complex example in financial audit is described. Finally, the application of a Bayesian network is presented.

12.4 BAYES' THEOREM

In 1763 Thomas Bayes' paper on inverse probability in the binomial distribution was published posthumously in *Philosophical Transactions of the Royal Society*. His formula for estimating the binomial parameter from observations is now called Bayes' Theorem. Laplace (1814) stated the theorem in general form. Jakob Bernoulli first described the problem when he wrote in *Ars Conjectandi* (1713) (English translation in Press 1989):

> To illustrate this by an example, I suppose that without your knowledge there are concealed in an urn 3000 white pebbles and 2000 black pebbles, and in trying to determine the numbers of these pebbles you take out one pebble after another (each time replacing the pebble you have drawn before choosing the next, in order not to decrease the number of pebbles in the urn), and that you observe how often a white and how often a black pebble is withdrawn. The question is, can you do this so often that it becomes ten times, one hundred times, one thousand times, etc., more probable (that is, it be morally certain) that the number of whites and blacks chosen are in the same 3:2 ratio as the pebbles in the urn, rather than in any other different ratio?

The general version of the answer to this problem is still referred to as Bayes' Theorem and is illustrated by the following example.

12.4.1 Burglar Alarm

Consider the burglar alarm example that was presented earlier in Chapter 8. Assume a burglar alarm is recently installed in your home and the following information is given about a situation relating to the alarm. The probability of a burglary at any particular house in the neighbourhood is 0.0001 (there is one burglary expected every 10 000 days). The alarm unit is generally reliable and effective, but still a clever burglar can disable or circumvent it 5% of the time. Because it uses infrared detectors and magnetic switches, the alarm can be falsely triggered about 1% of the time. Your neighbour calls you to tell you that your alarm is sounding. What is the probability that a burglary is taking place? The answer is given by Bayes' Theorem and can be found as follows.

Let $\Pr(B)$ be the probability of a burglary, and $\Pr(A)$ the probability of the alarm sounding. $\Pr(\overline{B})$ denotes the probability of no burglary. Also, let $\Pr(B|A)$ be the probability of B given that A has occurred, in other words the probability of a burglary given that the alarm has sounded. Bayes' Theorem can be expressed as follows:

$$\Pr(B|A) = \frac{\Pr(A|B)\,\Pr(B)}{\Pr(A)}$$

For the burglary example this would be

$$\Pr(B|A) = \frac{\Pr(A|B)\Pr(B)}{\Pr(A|B)\Pr(B) + \Pr(A|\bar{B})\Pr(\bar{B})}$$

$$\Pr(\text{Burglary}|\text{Alarm}) = \frac{0.95 * 0.0001}{0.95 * 0.0001 + 0.01 * 0.9999}$$

or about 0.0094, hardly cause for an immediate panic response (unless the potential loss is substantial). The formula uses the conditional probabilities of A given all possible values of B and the prior probability of these value of B. The key feature is that it converts between the probability of A conditioned on B to the probability of B conditioned on A.

Figure 12.1 (known as a probability tree) illustrates the situation in the burglar alarm example.

Given a very large sample of 100 000 days (about 274 years), we can describe the burglar alarm situation as follows. Out of the sample, we will expect 0.0001 * 100 000 or 100 burglaries (and the balance of the days there will be no burglaries). Given there is a burglary, we expect 0.95 * 100 or 95 of them to be detected, and the other five to go undetected. Using classical probabilities, we are interested in the probability of a burglary given an alarm. This is found by dividing the number of cases where there is an alarm and a burglary by the total number of cases where there is an alarm, or

$$\Pr(B|A) = \frac{\Pr(A, B)}{\Pr(A, B) + \Pr(A\bar{B})}$$

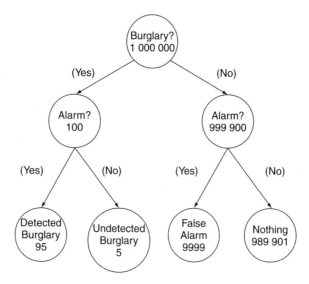

Figure 12.1   Probability tree for burglar alarm situation

which in the example gives:

$$Pr(B|A) = \frac{95}{95 + 9999}$$

or about 0.0094. (Approximately the same as the calculated figure of 0.09 based on the sample size of 100 000 days. Decreasing the sample size would give a less accurate figure.)

The general formula for the discrete version of Bayes' Theorem is given below:

$$Pr(\theta|x_1 \ldots x_n) = \frac{\left(\prod_i Pr(x_i|\theta)\right) Pr(\theta)}{\sum_\Theta \left(\prod_i Pr(x_i|\theta)\right) Pr(\theta)}$$

where the values of a set of observable independent random vector variables X whose values are denoted by $(X_1 \ldots X_n)$ and their conditioned variable Θ has values denoted by θ (which is assumed to be unobservable). The formula provides the probability of a specific value of a statistic given an observed data set. $Pr(\theta)$ is the prior probability of θ. $Pr(\theta|X)$ is the posterior probability of θ. A financial audit example will further illustrate the techniques.

12.4.2 Financial Audit

Assume that a regular daily audit is made of a set of financial transactions. In the past, 80% of the daily audits have no errors, 15% have one and 5% have two (or more) errors. Today's audit is of 100 transactions, and we assume that there will be zero, one, or two (or more) errors. Five transactions are checked, and one error is actually found. What is the probability that the day's transactions have two errors? The answer is about 39% and is found using Bayes' Theorem as follows. Let θ be the error rate for the day. $Pr(\theta)$ denotes the prior probability of finding θ error rate for the day. Our sample contained one error, and $f(X = 1|\theta)$ will denote the probability of getting one error given that the sample error rate is θ. The calculation of $f(X = 1|\theta)$ uses the binomial formula as follows:

$$f(X = r|\theta = p) = \binom{n}{r} p^r (1 - p)^{n-r}$$

where p is the proportion of errors, X is the number of errors found, and n is the sample size. We now have the information given in Table 12.1. From here we can calculate the Bayesian probability for 2% errors as follows:

$Pr(\theta = 0.02|X = 1)$

$$= \frac{Pr(\theta = 0.02)f(X = 1|\theta = 0.02)}{\dfrac{Pr(\theta = 0.02)}{f(X = 1|\theta = 0.02)} + \dfrac{Pr(\theta = 0.01)}{f(X = 1|\theta = 0.01)} + \dfrac{Pr(\theta = 0.00)}{f(X = 1|\theta = 0.0)}}$$

which results in an answer of about 39% (as given earlier).

Table 12.1 Table of values for the financial audit example

	$\theta = 0.00$	$\theta = 0.01$	$\theta = 0.02$
$\Pr(\theta)$	0.80	0.15	0.05
$f(X = 1\|\theta)$	0	0.0480	0.0922

12.4.3 Bayes Formula in Recursive Form

The Bayesian approach has another interesting and useful property that can be seen by looking at the general form of the equation. The equation can be factored so that each incremental observation can be used to update the estimate of θ. Thus, $\Pr(\theta|x_1 \ldots x_n)$ can be expressed in terms of $\Pr(\theta|x_1 \ldots x_{n-1})$ as follows:

$$\Pr(\theta|x_1 \ldots x_n) = \Pr(\theta|x_1 \ldots x_{n-1})$$
$$\times \frac{\Pr(x_n|\theta)}{\Pr(x_n|\theta)\Pr(\theta|x_1 \ldots x_{n-1}) + \Pr(x_n|\bar{\theta})\Pr(\bar{\theta}|x_1 \ldots x_{n-1})}$$

Then letting the prior be denoted by $\Pr(\theta|x_1 \ldots x_{n-1})$ as g(X), we have:

$$\Pr(\theta|x_1 \ldots x_n) = g(X)\frac{\Pr(x_n|\theta)}{\Pr(x_n|\theta)g(X) + \Pr(x_n|\bar{\theta})(1 - g(X))}$$

This equation provides a means of incrementally calculating the probability using Bayes' formula and finds many uses in continuous inspection regimes. Consider the case of the errors in financial transactions given earlier. Assume the 39% figure is not satisfactory, and we would like to decide to either complete a total audit or accept the transactions for the day using the following criteria:

1. Probability of two errors <30%, then accept the audit
2. Probability of two errors >75%, then perform a total audit.

Using the Bayesian approach we simply continue to look at transactions until one or the other of our criteria are met. The 39% figure we have is not decidable based on the criteria, so additional transactions must be examined for error. How many additional error-free transactions would be needed in order to accept the transactions (e.g. have a 30% or less probability of two errors)? The answer is 40 additional error-free transactions and can be found by performing an incremental calculation using Bayes' formula for increasing sample sizes.

12.5 BAYESIAN NETWORKS

A Bayesian network represents a joint probability distribution with a set of dependencies (qualitative part) and a set of local conditional probability distributions (quantitative part) (Castillo *et al.* 1997). From the foregoing it should be clear that conditional probabilities are both useful and important for Bayesian statistics. However, the traditional method of calculating conditional probabilities is cumbersome and inefficient for large numbers of variables. Consider, for example, the problem of encoding an arbitrary joint distribution $\Pr(x)$ for n binomial variables. To store the values explicitly would require 2^n numbers, an impossible task for most systems. Then computing the conditional probability using

$$\Pr\left(x_i|x_j\right) = \frac{\Pr\left(x_i, x_j\right)}{\Pr\left(x_j\right)}$$

would require summation over a large number of values for each probability and then dividing. Instead, a Bayesian network uses dependency information for the n variables to simplify the representation and calculations. These notions of dependency are also familiar to decision-makers and can be elicited with a higher level of confidence. The resulting model using Bayesian networks greatly increases the clarity and the efficiency of the calculations.

In 1988 Pearl gave an axiomatic basis for probabilistic dependencies in which he uses a probability graph known as a Bayesian network. This graph encodes a joint probability distribution for a set of variables by defining the possible states of the variables discretely and using conditional probability tables to relate the dependent variables. The structure of the graph showing dependency (preserving the temporal ordering of the causal relations) and the conditional probability tables are enough to describe the complete joint probability distribution (Pearl 1988). He also included a method of updating the probabilities in the graph using a Bayesian propagation scheme that allows the updates to be done efficiently (instead of exponential time in the number of variables). We now illustrate some of the basic ideas through examples.

12.5.1 Simple Bayesian Network

Consider a simple Bayesian network constructed for the enhanced burglar alarm problem following Shafer and Pearl (1990), beginning with the simple network of the problem as stated previously. Here the alarm is conditioned on a burglary and a telephone call from a friendly neighbour that the alarm has sounded. The problem structure is represented as shown in Figure 12.2 with a node for each of the variables: Burglary, Alarm, and Telephone Call. At each node the conditional probability table is provided that specifies the probability of the node, conditioned on the various values of its parent nodes (i.e. nodes with arrows to it). Burglary has no dependencies and thus will have prior probabilities only. Alarm will depend on burglary, and telephone call on alarm. Figure 12.3 shows the probability tables associated with the Bayesian network.

The marginal distributions for the variables can now be computed, and these are shown in a belief bar diagram (Figure 12.4). Each bar is a percentage probability

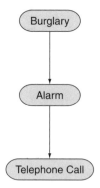

Figure 12.2   Bayesian network for burglar alarm problem showing structure

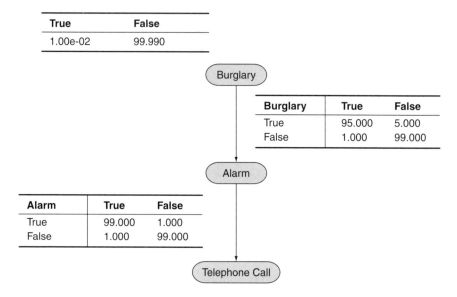

Figure 12.3   Conditional probability tables for burglar alarm network (expressed as percentages)

for the value of the variable shown. The previous problem of the probability of a burglary given the alarm has sounded can be calculated as shown in Figure 12.4.

The question of what is the probability of a burglary, given no additional information is given here as 0.01% or 0.0001. Given that an alarm sounds, we set the finding for Alarm = True, and the Bayesian network updates to reflect the probabilities, given an alarm. These figures are shown in Figure 12.5. As can be seen, the probability of a burglar has now been updated to 0.94% (or 0.0094) as was the case when the figure was calculated from the Bayes formula.

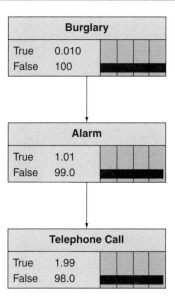

Figure 12.4 Belief bar diagram showing marginal distribution for burglar alarm network

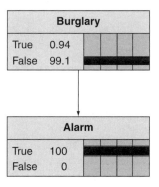

Figure 12.5 Causal model for burglary given Alarm = True

Expanding Figure 12.5 to include the possibility of an earthquake (earthquakes are known to set off burglar alarms), and the probability of a radio announcement that an earthquake has taken place, the Bayesian network is shown in Figure 12.6.

Now you ask for the expected value given a telephone call from the neighbour, and find the probability of a burglary has increased from 0.01% to 0.47% (a burglary is 47 times more likely given that you received a telephone call (see Figure 12.7). Continuing the scenario, Figure 12.8 shows the effect of a radio announcement. Given that there was a radio announcement of an earthquake

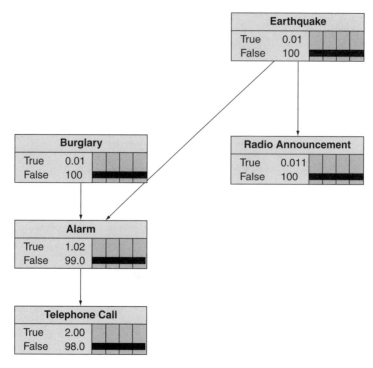

Figure 12.6   Burglar alarm network expanded to include earthquake as a cause

occurring, the probability of a burglary drops to 0.013%. This is still higher than originally, but our suspicions are all but allayed.

This implementation, although simple, demonstrates some of the interesting aspects of Bayesian networks:

1. The understanding imparted by the structure of the graphical model is clear (e.g. earthquakes and burglaries are not related).
2. The effect of an earthquake as an alternative cause for the alarm 'explains away' the possible burglary.
3. The model can be built incrementally as new information is gathered and additional causes identified.
4. The probabilities of a pragmatic problem are greatly reduced from the 2^n required for a classical model.

Structuring the network to represent the problem accurately and using existing data on variables to generate priors and conditional probabilities are discussed at length in Chapters 8 and 9.

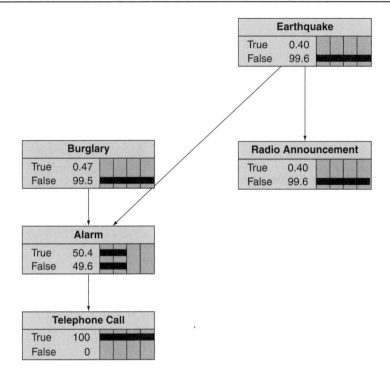

Figure 12.7 Probability of burglar alarm given a telephone call (0.47%)

12.6 SUMMARY

Bayesian decision theory provides a solid foundation for business decision support and the challenge of making decisions under uncertainty. This chapter provided a brief introduction to Bayesian decision theory, which is important to operational risk analysis because it addresses the problem of how to make decisions under uncertainty, and important to operational risk measurement because Bayesian networks form the basis for causal models. Key concepts were defined and the use of Bayesian networks as a tool for decision support was discussed along with examples provided to reinforce the main concepts and illustrate the techniques. Bayesian methods are characterised by their emphasis on the sample data, use of explicit prior probabilities, and use of utilities for outcomes. Bayesian networks have several advantages that make them the preferred tool for Bayesian decision support systems. They explicitly incorporate loss functions and prior information, use a graphical representation, are compact, and make many interesting problems computationally tractable. They lend themselves to stepwise refinement because they can be built and trained incrementally as new information becomes available.

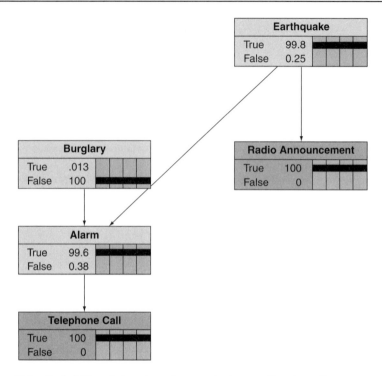

Figure 12.8   Probability of a burglary given a telephone call and a radio announcement (0.013%)

The challenge of using Bayesian networks is to create a structure that is meaningful from information supplied by domain experts. Some recent research work (Heckerman 1995) that has been directed at 'learning' Bayesian networks may help in this area.

12.7   FURTHER READING

The original work on Bayesian networks is Pearl (1988). Other references are available, including Castillo (1997), which is a nice description of graphical methods in general, and Cowell *et al.* (1997). Press (1989) is a good introduction to Bayesian statistics, and Berger (1980) is a solid reference for Bayesian decision theory.

SECTION V
APPENDICES

Glossary

Assignable Loss: Loss that can be explained by a risk factor for a process.

Assurance: Belief that an estimate is true or that an expectation will be realised.

Bayesian: Of or related to the branch of statistics using the basic ideas of inverse probability and inductive inference stemming from the work of Thomas Bayes.

Bayesian Network: A graphical representation used for modelling and calculating uncertainty.

Blunder: An error that is larger than a specified confidence limit (e.g. 99.9% or three standard deviations for a normal distribution).

Business Model: A representation of the key elements of a business activity.

Business Unit: A unit in a firm that produces a profit and loss (P&L) statement.

Causal Factor: A factor whose value impacts a performance measure such as earnings. A change in the causal factor will cause a change in the performance (e.g. earnings).

Causal Models: Models based on causal factors. Causal models use the relation between the factor and earnings to estimate values for earnings from values for the factors.

Causality: Relations between events and actions that support intervention.

Compliance Risk: Error in the procedure used to process the transaction (wrong procedure). A definition associated with the accounting categorisation of loss.

Control: Systems and procedures that enable the firm to realise its objectives and goals.

Control Breakdowns: Failure of a control to be effective in limiting loss although it covers the event.

Control Self-assessment: An approach for risk management in which a questionnaire or series of workshops is used to identify important risks to the firm by asking the responsible parties within the firm to subjectively assess various parts of the organisation and its characteristics.

Controllable Loss: A loss caused by a risk factor that management has decided can be addressed.

Corporate Governance: The creation of an operating environment that provides the required assurance for the goals of the firm.

Correlation: A standardised measure of the covariance between variables.

Coverage Factor: Multiple of standard deviation used to determine the confidence level (e.g. assuming a normal distribution).

Delta: Methodology for calculating uncertainty that uses error propagation techniques.

Delta–EVT: Methodology for calculating operational risk that combines the Delta method for operating loss with extreme value theory (EVT) for blunders and other rare events.

Direct Measurement: A measurement that is performed by counting or comparing with a physical standard.

Earnings: A financial measure of profitability for the firm. Typical measures are net profit, profit before tax, return on equity, return on net assets, and shareholder value added.

Effect: The result of an intervention.

Empirical Data Distribution: A distribution of data values.

Error: The uncertainty in a measurement.

Error Propagation: The technique for calculating the uncertainty of measurements.

Errors and Omissions: Deviations from standards, procedures, or planned activities.

Excess Loss Distribution: The distribution of losses above a threshold u calculated using the EVT method (e.g. unassignable loss).

Excess Value at Risk: The cumulative value of the unexpected losses at a specific confidence level (e.g. 95%) and for a specific period (e.g. one year).

Expected Loss: A loss from a business unit below a given threshold. This loss is part of the operating loss distribution. (Note: This is not expected value, a statistical term.)

Expected Value: The value of a random variable that is most likely to occur.

Extreme Value: A value much larger (or smaller) than the expected value.

Extreme Value Theory (EVT): A statistical technique for dealing with large and small values of data.

Framework (for measurement): A framework creates the needed environment for managing operational risk in a systematic way by providing a set of assumptions, definitions, and a methodology.

Frequency (of loss): The number of losses occurring in a period.

Generalised Pareto Distribution (GPD): A parametric distribution class belonging to the extreme value theory.

Indirect Measurement: A measurement that is calculated from other values (usually direct measurements).

Intervention: An action taken in order to affect performance (the effect).

ISO: International Standards Organisation.

Likert Scale: An ordinal scale used extensively in surveys.

Loss: A negative change in earnings.

Loss Categorisation: An approach for risk management in which operational losses are entered into a database along with an explanation of the loss and an attribution to a category of losses. A data model for losses is needed to begin a loss database (e.g. BBA 2000), detailed analysis is required to ensure the categories can be used for risk measurement, and ideally all losses fit into one and only one category and can be aggregated.

Loss Models: Models based on loss data. Loss models normally separate the frequency and severity of loss events and analyse each statistically.

Maximum Operating Loss: The value of operating loss from the operating loss distribution at a specific confidence level (e.g. 95%) (also maximum expected loss).

Maximum Excess Loss: The value of an operating loss from the excess loss distribution at a specific confidence level (e.g. 95%) (also maximum unexpected loss).

Measure: A numerical value that corresponds to a physical property.

Methodology: A systematic approach.

Operating Loss Distribution: The distribution of losses estimated for a value-adding process using the Delta method (e.g. assignable loss).

Operational Risk: A measure of the uncertainty in business performance due to business activities.

Overall Loss Distribution: The combination of operating loss and excess loss distributions using a compatible threshold.

Partition: A conditioning variable used to calculate conditional expected value. Sometimes referred to as the weighting factor for a weighted average.

Peaks Over Threshold (POT): A methodology for estimating excess values over a threshold (originally developed for the physical sciences and later applied to insurance).

Performance: Measure of business activity that contributes to the goals of the firm.

Performance Analysis: An approach for risk management in which the performance measures of the businesses are used to develop associated risk measures. Examples of this approach include those based on the Value Chain (Porter 1985) and the Balanced Scorecard (Kaplan and Norton 1996).

Performance Driver: A causal factor that creates a change in earnings for a change in the factor.

Poisson: Distribution (also a process) that reflects a discrete number of realised occurrences of an event with a low probability.

Precision: The amount of systematic uncertainty (or systematic error) in a measurement due to the measurement method.

Process Analysis: An approach for risk management in which the operational processes of the firm are analysed at a task level in order to determine the possible risk of errors in the procedures, their execution, and in the associated controls for the process. Detailed diagrams of process tasks and controls are then created and used to compile a list of key control points and related risks in the process.

Random Error (Type B): The amount of uncertainty in a measurement that cannot be assigned to the measurement method.

Rare Event: An event that occurs infrequently, or with a frequency that is low compared with a specific level (e.g. once per 10 years).

Reconciliation Risk: Error in the account entry (wrong account). A definition associated with the accounting categorisation of loss.

Relative Error: The uncertainty expressed as a percentage of the measured amount.

Reliability: A measure of the random error in the expected value for a measurement, usually the standard error of the mean.

Risk: The amount of expected loss or shortfall to target. The probability of an adverse result times the shortfall to expectation.

Risk Factor: A causal factor that creates a change in earnings for a change in the factor and has random uncertainty associated with it.

Risk Model: A representation of the key elements of risk.

Scenario: A set of specific values for a model.

Sensitivity: The amount of change in an effect for a unit change in a causal factor.

Severity (of loss): The amount of loss (usually for a single loss event).

Systematic Error (Type A): Uncertainty in a measurement that can be assigned to the measurement method (precision).

Threshold: The value of loss in the loss distribution that separates expected losses (those that are less than the threshold) and excess losses (those that are greater than the threshold).

Timeliness Risk: Delay in processing the information (wrong time). A definition associated with the accounting categorisation of loss.

Trained Causal Model: A causal model that has had its conditional probabilities calculated (e.g. using frequencies from actual data values).

Unassignable Loss: Loss that cannot be explained by a risk factor.

Uncontrollable Loss: Either an unassignable loss or an assignable loss that management has decided will not be addressed.

Unexpected Loss: A loss above a given threshold. This loss is part of the excess loss distribution.

Valuation Risk: Error in the amount of the transaction (wrong amount). A definition associated with the accounting categorisation of loss.

Value at Risk (VaR): The cumulative value of the expected losses at a specific confidence level (e.g. 95%) and for a specific period (e.g. one year).

Value-adding Function: The mathematical relationship between the value added in a business activity and a set of performance factors for the activity.

Value-adding Process: Building block by which a firm creates a product valuable to its customers.

Volatility: A measure of random fluctuations over a period.

Bibliography

Alexander, C., ed. (1996). *The Handbook of Risk Management and Analysis.* Chichester: Wiley.

Altman, E., Marco, G. and Varetto, F. (1994). Corporate distress diagnosis: Comparisons using linear discriminate analysis and neural networks (the Italian experience), *Journal of Banking and Finance,* **18**, 505–529.

Amram, M. and Kulatilaka, N. (1999). *Real Options: Managing Strategic Investment in an Uncertain World.* Boston, MA: Harvard Business School *Asia Week,* 27 September 1996. Press.

AS/NZS 4360 (1999). Joint Standards Australia/Standards New Zealand Committe OB/7.

Avenhaus, R. (1977). *Material Accountability: Theory Verification, and Applications.* New York: Wiley.

Bank for International Settlements (1998a). *Framework for the Evaluation of Internal Control Systems* (January 1998). Basle: BIS.

Bank for International Settlements (1998b). *Operational Risk Management* (September 1998). Basle: BIS.

Bank for International Settlements (1999). *A New Capital Adequacy Framework* (January 1999). Basle: BIS.

Barnett, V. and T. Lewis (1995). *Outliers in Statistical Data,* 3rd edn. Chichester: Wiley.

Berger, J. (1985). *Statistical Decision Theory and Bayesian Analysis,* 2nd edn. New York: Springer-Verlag.

Bernouilli, J. (1713). *Ars Conjectandi.* German translation by Deutch, H. (1999). *Wahrscheinlichkeitsrechnung.* Frankfurt: Frankfurt am Main.

British Banker's Association (BBA) (2000). *Draft BBA Standard Operational Risk Loss Categorization Format.* http://www.bba.org.uk

Cacciabue, P. C. and I. A. Papazoglou, eds. (1996). *Probabilistic Safety Assessment and Management ESREL'96—PSAM-III* (Crete, Greece), Vols. 1–3. London: Springer-Verlag.

Caouette, J. B., E. I. Altman and P. Narayanan (1998). *Managing Credit Risk: The Next Great Financial Challenge.* New York: Wiley.

Castillo, E. (1988). *Extreme Value Theory in Engineering.* San Diego: Academic Press, Inc.

Castillo, E., J. Gutierez and A. Hadi (1997). *Expert Systems and Probabilistic Network Models*. New York: Springer-Verlag.

Champy, J. and M. Hammer (1995). *Re-engineering the Corporation*. New York: Nicholas Brealey.

Chernoff, H. and L. Moses (1959). *Elementary Decision Theory*. New York: Wiley.

CICA (Canadian Institute of Chartered Accounts) (1995). *Guidance on Control*. Toronto: CICA.

CMRA and Meridien Research (2000). *Dependence on Risk Model Must be Mitigated to Avoid Increased Losses*. Newton, MA: Meridien Research, CMRA.

Committee of Sponsoring Organizations (COSO) of the Treadway Commission (1992). *Internal Control–Integrated Framework*. Jersey City: American Institute of Certified Public Accountants.

Cowell, R., D. A. Lauritzen and D. Spiegelhalter (1999). *Probabilistic Networks and Expert Systems*. New York: Springer-Verlag.

Cruz, M., R. Coleman and G. Salkin (1998). Modeling and measuring operational risk, *The Journal of Risk*, **1**(1), 63–72.

DeMoivre, A. (1756). *Doctrine of Chances*. Reprinted 1967, Chelsea Publishing.

Deutsch, H-P. and R. Eller (1999). *Derivatives and Internal Models: Modern Risk Management*. London: Macmillan.

Dewatripont, M. and J. Tirole (1993). *The Prudential Regulation of Banks*. London: MIT Press.

Drucker, P. F. (1967). *The Effective Executive*. New York: Harper & Row.

Efron, B. and R. Tibshirani (1993). *An Introduction to the Bootstrap*. New York: Chapman & Hall.

Electronic Telegraph, 17 April 1997.

Elton, E. J. and M. J. Gruber (1991). *Modern Portfolio Theory and Investment Analysis*, 4th edn. New York: Wiley.

Embrechts, P., C. Klüppelberg and M. Thomas (1997). *Applications of Mathematics: Stochastic Modelling and Applied Probability*. Heidelberg: Springer-Verlag.

Embrechts, P., C. Klüppelberg and T. Mikosch (1991). *Modelling Extremal Events*. Berlin: Springer-Verlag.

European Union (1999). *A Review of Regulatory Capital Requirements for EU Credit Institutions and Investment Firms*. Consultation Document (November 1999).

Fay, S. (1996). *The Collapse of Barings*. London: W.W. Norton.

Fisher, R. and L. Tippet (1928). Limiting forms of the frequency distribution of the largest or smallest member of a sample, *Proceedings of the Cambridge Philosophical Society*, **24**, 180–190.

Gapper, J. and N. Denton (1996). *All that Glitters: The Fall of Barings*. Harmondsworth: Penguin.

Gilks, W. R., S. Richardson and D.J. Spiegelhalter (1996). *Markov Chain Monte Carlo in Practice*. New York: Chapman & Hall.

Gumbel, E. J. (1958). *Statistics of Extremes*. New York: Columbia University Press.

Heckerman, D. (1995). *A Tutorial on Learning With Bayesian Networks*. http://www.research.microsoft.com/pub/tr/tr-95-06.ps, Redmond, WA: Microsoft.

Howard, W. and W. Byers (1997). The valuation of options, *Financial Services Review*, Bank of England, **Autumn**.

Huff, H. (1991). *How to Lie With Statistics*. New York: Penguin.

ICAEW (The Institute of Chartered Accountants in England and Wales) (1999). *No Surprises: The Case for Better Risk Reporting*. London: ICAEW.

ISO Guide (1993). *Guide to the Expression of Uncertainty in Measurement*, ISO/TAG 4/WG 3. Geneva: International Standards Organisation.

Jaffa, S. (1997). *Great Financial Scandals*. London: Robson Books.

Jeffreys, H. (1960). *Theory of Probability*, 3rd edn. Oxford: Oxford University Press.

Jensen, F. (1996). *An Introduction to Bayesian Networks*. New York: Springer-Verlag.

Johnson, N., S. Katz and N. Balakrishman (1994). *Continuous Univariate Distributions*, Vols. 1 and 2. New York: Wiley.

Jorion, P. (1995). *Big Bets Gone Bad*. San Diego: Academic Press.

Jorion, P. (1997). *Value at Risk: The New Benchmark for Controlling Market Risk*. Chicago: Irwin.

Kaplan, R. S. and D.P. Norton (1996). *The Balanced Scorecard*. Boston, MA: Harvard Business School Press.

Kharouf, J. (1996). *Futures*, **August**. Financial Communications Co.

King, J. L. (1996). Advanced treaty verification techniques: providing assurance on unknown activities. *Proceedings of PSAM III, Probability and Safety Assessment Management Conference*, Crete, Greece.

Klugman, P., H. Panjer and G. Wilmott (1998). *Loss Models: From Data to Decisions*. New York: Wiley.

Knight, J. A. (1997). *Value Based Management: Developing a Systematic Approach to Creating Shareholder Value*. New York: McGraw-Hill.

KonTraG (1998). *Gesetz zur Kontrolle und Transparenz im Unternehmensbereich*. Deutsche Bundestag.

Laplace, M. (1814). *A Philosophical Essay on Probabilities*. Reprinted 1951, Dover Publications.

Markowitz, H. (1959). *Portfolio Selection: Efficient Diversification of Investments*. New York: Wiley.

Markowitz, H. (1976). Investment for the long run: new evidence of an old rule, *The Journal of Finance*, **31**.

McNeil, A. (1998). On extremes and crashes, Risk, **January**. London: Risk Publications.

McNeil, A. and T. Saladin (1997). The peaks over thresholds method for estimating high quantiles of loss distributions, *XXVIIth International ASTIN Colloqium*, pp. 23–43.

Moody's (2000). *Historical Default Rates of Corporate Bond Issues, 1920–1999*. New York: Moody's Investors Service, Global Credit Research.

NatWest Group Web Page. `http://www.natwestgroup.com/pr_nwenq.html`.

Neumann, P. (1995). *Computer Related Risks*. New York: ACM Press.

New York Times, Friday 27 June 1997.

Olve, N., J. Roy and M. Wetter (1999). *Performance Drivers: A Practical Guide to Using the Balanced Scorecard*. New York: Wiley.

Pearl, J. (1988). *Probabilistic Reasoning in Intelligent Systems: Networks of Plausible Inference*, revised second printing. San Mateo, CA: Morgan Kaufmann.

Pearl, J. (2000). *Causality: Models, Reasoning, and Inference*. Cambridge: Cambridge University Press.

Pearson, K., A. Lee and L. Bramley-Moore (1899). Genetic (reproductive) selection: Inheritance of fertility in man, *Philosophical Transactions of the Royal Society*, **73**, 534–539.

Perrow, C. (1999). *Normal Accidents*. Princeton, NJ: Princeton University Press.

Pickands, J. (1975). Statistical inference using extreme order statistics, *Annals of Statistics*, **3**, 119–131.

Popper, K. (1959). *The Logic of Scientific Discovery*. New York: Basic Books.

Porter, M. E. (1985). *Competitive Advantage: Creating and Sustaining Superior Performance*. New York: The Free Press.

Press, S. J. (1989). *Bayesian Statistics*. New York: Wiley.

Rappaport, A. (1998). *Creating Shareholder Value*. New York: The Free Press.

Reiss, R. D. (1987). Estimating the tail index of the claim size distribution, *Blaetter der DGVM*, **18**, 21–25.

Ross, S. (1997). *Introduction to Probability Models*. San Diego: Academic Press.

Savage, L. J. (1954). *The Foundations of Statistics*. London: Constable & Co., reprinted 1972, Dover Publications.

Schum, D. (1994). *The Evidential Foundation of Probabilistic Reasoning*. New York: Wiley.

Shafer, G. (1996). *The Art of Causal Conjecture*. Cambridge, MA: MIT Press.

Shafer, G. and J. Pearl, eds. (1990). *Readings in Uncertainty*. San Mateo, CA: Morgan Kaufman.

Shewhart, W. A. (1931). *Economic Control of Quality of Manufactured Product*. New York: D. Von Nostrand Company, Inc.

Simpson, E. H. (1951). The interpretation of interaction in contingency tables, *Journal of the Royal Statistical Society, Series B*.

Smith, R. L. (1987). Estimating tails of probability distributions, *Annals of Statistics*, **15**, 1174–1207.

Sobel, D. (1996). *Longitude*. London: Fourth Estate Ltd.

Standard & Poor's (1995). *Bank Ratings Criteria*. New York: S&P.

Taylor, J. (1982). *An Introduction to Error Analysis*. Sausalito, CA: University Science.

The Group of Thirty (1993). *Derivatives: Practices and Principles*. Washington, D. C.: The Group of Thirty.

Tukey, J. (1960). A survey of sampling from contaminated distributions. In Olkin, I., ed., *Contributions to Probability and Statistics*. Stanford, CA: University Press.

Tukey, J. (1977). *Exploratory Data Analysis*. Reading, MA: Addison-Wesley.

Tversky, A. and D. Kahneman (1990). Judgment under uncertainty: heuristics and biases. In Shafer, G. and J. Pearl, eds., *Readings in Uncertainty*. San Mateo, CA: Morgan Kaufman.

Two-Ten Communications, 4 April 1996).

Wall Street Journal, Monday 25 November 1985.

Weiss, D. M. (1993). *After the Trade is Made: Processing Securities Transactions*, 2nd edn. New York: Institute of Finance.

Weiss, R. and M. Thomas (1997). *Statistical Analysis of Extreme Values*. Basel: Birkhauser.

Wilson, T. (1996). Calculating risk capital. In Alexander, C., ed., *Handbook of Risk Management and Analysis*. Chichester: Wiley.

Index

A New Capital Adequacy Framework (BIS), 38
accounting categorisation, 22
accuracy of measurements, 205
activity, 114
advanced uses of causal models, 172
American National Standard for Expressing Uncertainty
—U.S. Guide to the Expression of Uncertainty in Measurement, 193
analytical approach to a trained causal model, 161
assessing possible intervention (in causal models), 152
assignable loss, 57, 58
  definition, 243
associations (relative to causality), 137
assurance, 8
  definition, 243
attribution of loss, 21
Australian AS 4360, 42
automobile journey, 4

balance sheet(Genoa Bank), 124
Balanced Scorecard, 7, 53
Bank of New York, 29
Bank for International Settlements
  A New Capital Adequacy Framework, 38
  Framework for the Evaluation of Internal Control Systems, 36
  Operational Risk Management, 38
banking supervision, 36
Banque Paribas, 30
Barings, 26
basic steps (in causal models for operational risk), 166

Bayes (Thomas), 227
Bayes' theorem, 233
  discrete version, 234
  financial audit, 233
  recursive form, 231
Bayesian methods, 19, 227–240
  decision theory, 228, 230
Bayesian networks, 141
  and causal models, 142
  definition, 243
  dependencies, 142
  intervention, 141
  random variables, 142
  reversibility, 235
  simple, 142
  updating, 234
benchmark loss model, 98
benchmarks in measurement, 206
benefits of managing operational risk, 65
Bernoulli's problem, 229
blunders, 14, 19, 196
  definition, 243
borrowing risk, 117
British Bankers Association (BBA)
  loss categorization scheme, 50
Burglar alarm and Bayes' theorem, 231
burglar alarm example (causal model), 139
business model, 58, 123
  definition, 243
  Genoa Bank, 115
  processes, 115
  risk factors, 58, 113
business unit, 57, 114
  definition, 243

Cadbury Committee, 41
CAMEL, 35

Canadian Institute of Chartered
  Accountants (CICA), 40
carrying cost (cost of carry), 88
causal, 137
causal factor, 57
  definition, 243
causal modelling
  analytical approach, 228
  and Bayesian networks, 139
  burglar alarm example, 141
  concepts, 161
  empirical approach, 237
  for Burglar alarm, 184
  for compliance, 137
  for consistency, 185, 161
  trained, 163
  using a trained model, 13, 57
causal models
  advanced uses of, 172
  advantages of, 151
  advantages of using for operational risk,
    160
  and Bayesian networks, 141
  and simulation, 154
  assessing possible intervention, 152
  definition, 139, 243
  example, 167, 168, 171
  for compliance and consistency, 181
  for efficiency and effectiveness, 173
  for operational risk, 160, 165, 166
  for settlement risk, 151
  implementation of, 156
  loss data and EVT, 172
  performance of, 154
  practical issues, 156
  scenario and simulation, 154
causal relations, 142
  sprinkler example, 142
causality, 13, 137
  definition, 138, 243
causation, 13
cause-and-effect, 138
chi-squared test, 104, 109
CICA, 35
COCO, 40
collateral valuation error, 91
combining uncertainty measures, 78
compliance, 118
  risk, 22, 68, 118, 243
conditional independence, 145
conditional probability tables, 236
control breakdowns, 19, 57

  definition, 243
  self-assessment, 9, 49, 243
control (operational), 8, 9
controllable
  loss, 57, 244
  risk, 13
corporate governance, 8, 9, 40
  definition, 244
correlation, 138, 198
  definition, 244
COSO, 9, 35, 40
covariance matrix and error propagation,
  201
coverage factor, 64, 197
  definition, 244
credibility of measurements, 206
credit
  default error (Genoa Bank), 129
  exposure (Genoa Bank), 128
  scoring error (Genoa Bank), 129
  scoring model for loan origination, 177
cumulative distributions for Delta and
  EVT, 82

default rates, 91
  Genoa Bank, 129
delivery activity, 120
Delta method, 61, 82
  advantages, 74
  definition, 244
  earnings as a function of causal factors,
    83
  examples, 76, 124
  Genoa Bank, 124
  implementation steps, 84
  investment process example, 74
  key concepts, 89
  lending process example, 69
  operating loss distribution, 75
  risk factors, 92
  service process example, 132
  summary calculations, 61, 73
Delta-EVT™, 116
  business models, 113
  definition, 244
  example (Genoa Bank), 122–31
  introduction, 16–18, 47
  loss models, 120
  measures (risk), 122
  methodology, 61–7
  risk models, 115–9
  summary (Genoa Bank), 132–5

dependencies in Bayesian networks, 142
Deutsche Morgan Grenfell, 27
direct measurement, 196
  definition, 244

earnings, 8, 57, 116
  definition, 244
  function, 68, 78, 92, 116, 118, 119
effect, 151
  definition, 244
empirical
  approach to a trained causal model, 161
  data distribution, 161
  definition, 244
error, 192
  definition, 192, 244
  for a factor, 79
  for a function, 79
  in a variance estimate, 202
  model, 194
  relative, 195
error propagation, 189–207
  covariance matrix, 201
  definition, 244
  error in a variance estimate, 202
  example, 203
  example of defining what to measure, 191
  example of measuring a door, 191
  example of precision in, 191
  example of randomness in, 191
  expected value, 200
  guide to maintaining quality assurance in, 193
  importance of environment (context), 191
  law, 75, 199
errors, 57
  and omissions, 79, 244
  combining, 196
  random (Type B), 195
  representation of, 195
  sources of, 196
  systematic (Type A), 76
estimating lambda for the Poisson distribution, 104
European Union
  A Review of Regulatory Capital Requirements for EU Credit Institutions and Investment Firms, 39
EVT, 209–225
  applied to internal losses, 81

as it relates to Delta method, 210
basic concepts, 82
calculation of excess loss distribution, 172
causal models, 97
definition, 244
distribution classes, 212
exceedances, 106
Frechet, 210
Genoa Bank, 132
GPD fit, 102
implementation steps, 105
loss model example, 101
loss models, 211
maximum, 61
maximum loss, 211
method, 132, 213
S&P 500 analysis, 70
example of loss events, 100
exceedances in EVT, 210
excess function for GPD, 216
excess loss, 64, 215
  definition, 244
  distribution, 134
  Genoa Bank, 109
  value at risk, 64, 70, 80
excess value at risk, 64, 122
  definition, 244
expected loss, 66
  definition, 244
expected value, 200
  and error propagation, 200
  definition, 244
extreme value, 13, 211
  theory (*See* EVT)

factors
  coverage, 197, 244
  risk, (*See* risk factor)
financial audit and Bayes' theorem, 233
formula
  for Error Propagation, 199
  for GPD distribution, 103
  for Poisson distribution, 103
framework (for measuring operational risk), 12, 17, 47–71
  assumptions, 54
  criteria, 48, 64
  definition, 244
  diagram, 59
  introduction, 47
  implementation steps, 66

Framework for the Evaluation of Internal Control Systems (BIS), 36
Frechet formula, 212
frequency (of loss), 97, 100, 103
    definition, 244

general guidelines (for causal models applied to operational risk), 165
generalised extreme value (*See* GEV)
generalised Pareto distribution (*See* GPD)
    definition, 244
Genoa Bank
    balance sheet, 124
    business model, 123
    credit default error, 129
    credit exposure, 128
    credit scoring error, 129
    default rates, 129
    Delta method, 124
    Delta method summary calculations, 132
    EVT method, 132
    example using causal models, 167
    excess loss, 134
    GPD fit, 134
    in-depth example, 122
    income statement, 124
    investment process, 125, 168
    lending process, 128, 168
    losses over threshold, 133
    nostro breaks, 127
    operational risk measures, 133
    operational risk measures summary, 135
    POT, 133
    recovery error, 130
    service process, 130–1, 171
    settlement error, 127
    threshold, 132
    traded products, 126
    valuation error, 126
    volume volatility, 131
genuine cause, 145
GEV, 211
    definition, 244
Governance (*See* corporate governance)
GPD, 103
    distribution formula, 216
    definition, 244
    excess function, 134
    fit, 102, 224
    fitting, 217
    threshold sensitivity, 97

Group of Thirty study, 35
Guidance on Control, 40

high frequency low impact loss, 12
historical loss model, 98
    example, 99
human factors categorization, 22

ICAEW (International Chartered Accountants of England and Wales), 35
implementation of causal models, 165
    for operational risk, 156
income statement (Genoa Bank), 124
independence of measurements, 206
indirect measurement, 197
    definition, 245
Internal Control—Integrated Framework (COSO), 40
internal losses
    and EVT, 222
    and POT, 223
intervention, 10
    definition, 245
    in Bayesian networks, 142
investment process, 84
    example, 125
    Genoa Bank, 116
ISO Guide (International Standards Organisation), 83, 192

Jardine Fleming, 27

KonTraG, 35, 41

large losses (table of), 105
law of error propagation, 199
lending process, 89
    example, 128
    Genoa Bank, 117
likelihood function, 102
Likert scale, 49
    definition, 245
loss, 57
    assignable, 57, 58
    definition, 245
    excess, 64, 215
    frequency, 97, 100, 103
    low frequency high impact, 12
    high frequency low impact, 12
    historical, 21–34
    maximum excess, 64, 122

maximum expected (*See* maximum operating loss)
maximum operating, 64, 122
maximum unexpected (*See* maximum excess loss)
operating, 64
unassignable, 57, 58
uncontrollable, 57
unexpected, 8, 65
very large, 24, 60
loss categorization, 21
accounting, 22
definition, 245
human factors, 22
value-based, 23, 50
loss data (for causal models), 172
loss distribution (excess), 215
loss model, 107, 121
database fields, 108
definition, 245
frequency, 57, 97, 120
table of losses, 10
losses
other, 31
over threshold (Genoa Bank), 133
time-dependent, 220
low frequency high impact loss, 12

maximum
excess loss, 64, 122, 244
expected loss (*See* maximum operating loss)
likelihood for thresholds, 219
loss and EVT, 211
operating loss, 64, 122, 244
unexpected loss (*See* maximum excess loss)
mean excess function, 216
measure, 10
definition, 245
of uncertainty for operational risk, 75
measurement, 206
benchmark, 206
credibility, 196
direct, 198
error, 12, 194
framework, 204 (*See also* framework)
identifying outliers, 206
independence, 197
indirect, 12, 61
methodology, 61, 204
mixture model, 206

relevance, 205
reliability and accuracy, 206
sensitivity, 10
methodology, 12, 57
definition, 245
Delta, 73–95
EVT, 97–110
model error, 77
modelling, 13
Delta-EVT™ models, 113, 136
causal models, 137–157
causal models for operational risk, 159–188
Monte Carlo simulation, 107
with Poisson frequency and GPD severity, 97, 99, 229

National Institute of Standards and Testing (NIST), 192
National Westminster, 28
New Capital Adequacy Framework (BIS), 38
NIST (*See* National Institute of Standards and Testing)
nostro breaks (Genoa Bank), 127

operating loss, 64
distribution, 64, 80, 245
operational control, 8
operational risk
benefits of management, 8
definition, 24, 245
failures, 38
management, 10, 63, 65
measures, 7, 63, 133, 135
Operational Risk Management (BIS), 38
origination activity, 118
other losses, 31
overall loss distribution, 64

parametric distributions, 99
partition, 76
definition, 245
partitioning, 83
peaks over threshold (*See* POT)
performance, 8, 58
analysis, 52, 245
definition, 245
driver, 57, 246
Poisson, 104, 109
chi-squared test, 220

Poisson (*continued*)
  definition, 246
  distribution, 103
  distribution formula, 104
  estimating lambda, 107
  fitting, 97
POT, 215
  definition, 245
  determining threshold, 223
  for internal losses, 133
  Genoa Bank, 101
potential cause, 145
practical issues in using causal models,
  156
precision, 191, 196
  definition, 246
predictive models, 13
prior information, 230
process analysis, 50
  definition, 246
  in a business model, 115
  models, 181
profit error volatility, 197
propagation of uncertainty, 199

random errors (Type B), 196
  definition, 246
random variables (in Bayesian networks),
  141
rare event, 12, 55
  definition, 246
reconciliation risk, 68, 118
  definition, 246
recovery error (Genoa Bank), 130
recovery rates (Genoa Bank), 130
regulation, 35–43
  banking supervision, 36–39
  corporate governance, 40–43
relative error, 77, 195
  definition, 246
relevance of measurements, 206
reliability of measurements, 205
  definition, 246
repayment activity, 118
reversibility (in Bayesian networks), 142
*Review of Regulatory Capital
  Requirements for EU Credit Institutions
  and Investment Firms Consultation
  Document*, 39
risk, 7
  compliance, 68, 118
  credit, 3

  definition, 246
  market, 3
  measures, 122
  models, 115, 117, 118, 246
  operational, 24 (*See also* operational
    risk)
  reconciliation, 68, 118
  timeliness, 68, 118
  valuation, 68, 118
risk factor, 115, 116, 118, 119
  definition, 246
  in a business model, 57, 68, 76, 114

S&P 500 analysis using EVT, 213
sales activity, 120
Savings and Loan Disaster, 35
scenarios, 154
  and simulation with causal models, 98
  definition, 246
  loss model, 70, 121
sensitivities of measurement, 78, 206
  definition, 246
service process, 131
  calculations, 92
  example, 130
  Genoa Bank, 119
settlement
  activity, 117
  error (Genoa Bank), 127
  model for trading transactions, 173
  risk, 117
severity
  definition, 246
  loss distribution, 103
shareholder value, 3
Simpson's Paradox, 146
  Berkeley admissions example, 147
  causal model for Berkeley admissions,
    146
simulated loss, 99
simulation using causal models, 154
sprinkler example (causal relations), 142
spurious association, 144, 145
standard error, 75, 79
subjective loss model, 98
Sumitomo Bank, 25
systematic errors (Type A), 196
  definition, 246

threshold, 62, 79
  calculating, 80
  concept, 215

definition, 246
for POT, 132
Genoa Bank, 219
maximum likelihood for, 217
sensitivity, 61, 63, 69
time-dependent losses, 220
timeliness, 118
risk, 22, 68, 118, 247
trade process (causal model for
compliance in), 184
trading activity, 117
trained causal model (getting), 161
definition, 247
using, 163
transaction models, 177
credit scoring, 173
settlement, 173
Treadway, 40
Turnbull Report (*See* UK Combined Code)
Type A errors (*See* systematic errors)
Type B errors (*See* random errors)

UK Combined Code (Turnbull Report), 41
unassignable loss, 57, 58
definition, 247
uncertainty
formula for combining, 75
propagation of, 199
uncontrollable
loss, 57, 247
risk, 14

unexpected loss (*See also* excess loss)
definition, 247
updating Bayesian networks, 142

valuation, 126
error, 22, 68
risk, 68, 86, 118, 247
value at risk, 109
definition, 247
excess loss, 64, 94, 122
operating loss, 64, 80
Value Based Management, 7
value chain, 53
value-adding
function, 56, 247
process, 57, 67, 114, 247
value-based categorization, 23
VaR (*See* value at risk)
very large loss, 24
volatility, 93
definition, 247
earnings, 1, 7, 8, 11
measure, 8
volume, 79
volume, 85
calculations, 131
volatility, 84

Watchlist (causal model for consistency),
185